PARABLES FOR PREACHERS

Parables for Preachers
The Gospel of Matthew
YEAR A

Barbara E. Reid, O.P.

THE LITURGICAL PRESS
Collegeville, Minnesota

www.litpress.org

Year A: 0-8146-2550-9
Year B: 0-8146-2551-7
Year C: 0-8146-2552-5

1	2	3	4	5	6	7	8

Library of Congress Cataloging-in-Publication Data

Reid, Barbara E.
     Parables for preachers / Barbara E. Reid.
         p.   c.m.
     Includes bibliographical references.
     Contents: — [2] Year B. The Gospel of Mark.
     ISBN 0-8146-2551-7 (v. 2 : alk. paper)
     1. Jesus Christ—Parables—Homiletical use.   2. Bible. N.T. Mark—Criticism, interpretation, etc.   3. Bible. N.T. Mark—Homiletical use.   4. Lectionary preaching—Catholic Church.
     BT375.2.R45   1999
     226.8'06—dc21   99-28090
                                                                              CIP

In gratitude to those preachers,
especially my Dominican sisters,
whose telling of the gospel story
has fed and converted me.

Contents

Matthean Parables in the Lectionary

Matthean parables are assigned for the gospel reading on thirteen Sundays of Year A. All are repeated in the weekday Lectionary as well. Four parables of Matthew that do not appear in the Sunday Lectionary are assigned for weekday reading.

SUNDAY AND WEEKDAY LECTIONARIES:

The following Matthean parables appear in both the Sunday and weekday Lectionaries:

Matt 5:13-16	Fifth Sunday of Ordinary Time
	Tuesday of the Tenth Week of Ordinary Time
Matt 7:21-27	Ninth Sunday of Ordinary Time
	Thursday of the First Week of Advent (7:21, 24-27)
	Thursday of the Twelfth Week of Ordinary Time (7:21-29)
Matt 13:1-23	Fifteenth Sunday of Ordinary Time
	Wednesday of the Sixteenth Week of Ordinary Time (13:1-9)
	Thursday of the Sixteenth Week of Ordinary Time (13:10-17)
	Friday of the Sixteenth Week of Ordinary Time (13:18-23)
Matt 13:24-43	Sixteenth Sunday of Ordinary Time
	Saturday of the Sixteenth Week of Ordinary Time (13:24-30)

Matt 25:31-46   Thirty-Fourth Sunday of Ordinary Time;
Feast of Christ the King

Monday of the First Week of Lent

WEEKDAY LECTIONARY:

The following Matthean parables appear only in the weekday Lectionary:

Matt 11:16-19   Friday of the Second Week of Advent

Matt 15:1-2, 10-14   Tuesday of the Eighteenth Week of Ordinary Time (second option)

Matt 18:12-14   Tuesday of the Second Week of Advent

Tuesday of the Nineteenth Week of Ordinary Time

Matt 24:42-51   Thursday of the Twenty-First Week of Ordinary Time

Abbreviations

GNS	Good News Studies Series
HTR	*Harvard Theological Review*
ICC	International Critical Commentary
Int	*Interpretation*
JBL	*Journal of Biblical Literature*
JR	*Journal of Religion*
JSJ	*Journal for the Study of Judaism*
JSNT	*Journal for the Study of the New Testament*
JSNTSup	JSNT Supplement Series
JSOT	*Journal for the Study of the Old Testament*
JTS	*Journal of Theological Studies*
LTP	*Laval théologique et philosophique*
LumVie	*Lumière et Vie*
LumVit	*Lumen Vitae*
LXX	Septuagint
	(Greek Translation of the Hebrew OT)
MillStud	*Milltown Studies*
NAB	*New American Bible*
NJB	*New Jerusalem Bible*
NJBC	*New Jerome Biblical Commentary*
	(Ed. R. E. Brown *et al.*)
NTM	New Testament Message
NovT	*Novum Testamentum*
NRSV	*New Revised Standard Version*
NT	New Testament
NTS	*New Testament Studies*
OBT	Overtures to Biblical Theology
OT	Old Testament
RB	*Revue Biblique*
RevExp	*Review & Expositor*
RevQ	*Revue de Qumran*
RSR	*Religious Studies Review*
SacPag	Sacra Pagina

SBEC	Studies in the Bible and Early Christianity Series
SBL	Society of Biblical Literature
SBLDS	Society of Biblical Literature Dissertation Series
SBLMS	Society of Biblical Literature Monograph Series
ScEs	*Science et Esprit*
SJT	*Scottish Journal of Theology*
SNTSMS	Society for New Testament Studies Monograph Series
Str-B	[H. Strack and] P. Billerbeck, *Kommentar zum Neuen Testament*
TBT	*The Bible Today*
TS	*Theological Studies*
TToday	*Theology Today*
USQR	*Union Seminary Quarterly Review*
WBC	Westminster Bible Companion
WUNT	Wissenschaftliche Untersuchungen zum Neuen Testament
ZNW	*Zeitschrift für die neutestamentliche Wissenschaft*

Introduction

A disciple once complained,
*   "You tell us stories,*
*   but you never reveal their meaning to us."*
Said the master,
*   "How would you like it if someone*
*   offered you fruit and masticated it*
*   before giving it to you?"*[1]

In the Synoptic Gospels, Jesus rarely explains his parables.[2] They are meant to be wrestled with by each generation of hearers who allow themselves to be disturbed and challenged by Jesus' subversive stories. Yet Sunday after Sunday the preacher is asked to open up the meaning of parables to their congregations. How can a preacher avoid offering premasticated fruit? How can the one who opens up the Scriptures do so in a way that enhances the savory offerings therein without ruining the power of the story? How can a preacher offer fresh fare when the same parable appears time after time in the Lectionary?

---

[1] Anthony de Mello, *The Song of the Bird* (Garden City, N.Y.: Doubleday, 1984) 1.

[2] The exceptions in the Gospel of Matthew are the seed parable, explained at 13:18-23 (// Mark 4:13-20 // Luke 8:11-15), the parable of the weeds and the wheat interpreted at 13:36-43, and the explanation of defilement from within at Matt 15:15-20 (// Mark 7:17-23). Most scholars believe these to be creations of the early Church and not from the lips of Jesus. In line with Matthew's emphasis on the ethics of discipleship, two parables unique to him have moralizing interpretations in their conclusions (18:35; 21:31-32). See chaps. 9 and 11.

The first aim of this book is to aid preachers by bringing together current biblical research on the parables, in the hope that it will open up new vistas of meaning for them and will spark their own creativity. Second, the book offers an understanding of how parables communicate, and invites the preacher to try out parabolic techniques of preaching. The Synoptic Gospels show Jesus preaching primarily by means of parables, spoken and lived. A greater understanding of the dynamics and meaning of Jesus' parables in their original context can aid preachers today in creating the same effect in modern believers in a new context. This book is intended not only for preachers, but for all who are interested in a deeper understanding of the parables, particularly teachers, catechists, liturgy planners, and members of groups for homily preparation, Bible study, or faith sharing.

PARABLES IN THE LECTIONARY

The term "parable" covers a wide range of figurative speech: similitudes, extended metaphors, symbolic expressions, exemplary and true-to-life stories. Included in this volume are all passages except one[3] in which the term *parabolē* ("parable") occurs in the Gospel of Matthew.[4] Also included are similes with variations of the phrase *homoios estin*, "[such] is like . . ." (7:24, 26; 11:16; 13:24, 31, 33, 44, 45, 47, 52; 18:23; 20:1; 22:2; 25:1) and *houtōs*, "in the same way" (5:16; 13:40, 49; 18:14, 35; 20:16) or *hōsper*, "just as" (25:14, 32). Included as well are the parables about Saying and Doing (21:28-32), and about Faithful Servants (24:42-51),[5] though Matthew does not explic-

---

[3] The parable of the fig tree in Matt 24:32-33 is omitted from the Lectionary. The Markan version (13:28-32) is the gospel for the Thirty-third Sunday of Ordinary Time. The Lukan account (21:29-33) is used on Friday of the Thirty-fourth Week of Ordinary Time.

[4] The term *parabolē* occurs sixteen times in the Gospel of Matthew (13:3, 10, 13, 18, 24, 31, 33, 34, 35, 36, 53; 15:15; 21:33, 45; 22:1; 24:32), twelve times in Mark, eighteen times in Luke, and twice in Hebrews. For the other Synoptic Gospels see Barbara E. Reid, *Parables for Preachers. Year B* (Collegeville: The Liturgical Press, 1999) and *Parables for Preachers. Year C* (Collegeville: The Liturgical Press, 2000).

[5] Luke dubs his version (Luke 12:41) a parable.

itly call these parables. There are other sayings and stories that could well be considered parabolic not included in this study. In one sense, the whole gospel can be regarded as a parable. As John R. Donahue puts it, the parables "offer a Gospel in miniature and at the same time give shape, direction, and meaning to the Gospels in which they are found. To study the parables of the Gospels is to study the gospel in parable."[6]

Parables are noticeably absent from the Gospel of John. The fourth evangelist never uses the term *parabolē,* nor does he preserve any of Jesus' stories in the same parabolic form as do the Synoptic writers. Nonetheless symbolic speech abounds in the Fourth Gospel. The closest thing to a parable is found in chapter 10, where Jesus speaks of himself as the Good Shepherd and the gate for the sheep. And in John 10:6 Jesus' disciples have the same difficulty in understanding this "figure of speech" *(paroimia)* as they do with the parables in Mark 4:10-12 and pars. The term *paroimia* occurs two more times in the Gospel of John (16:25, 29), where Jesus assures the disciples that a time will come when he will no longer speak in "figures" but plainly. This comes on the heels of the comparison of the disciples' anguish at Jesus' departure with that of a woman in labor. As she forgets her pain after her child is born, so will the disciples' grief turn into joy (16:21-24).

In chapter 1 we explore the dynamics of Jesus' parables. Understanding how a parable "works" is the first step. In chapter 2 is a sketch of contemporary trends in biblical interpretation of the parables. Next is an overview of the Gospel of Matthew, its author, historical context, and major theological themes. The remaining chapters examine each of the parables of the Gospel of Matthew in the order in which they appear in the Lectionary for Year A. We will first treat the parables that appear in the Sunday Lectionary, followed by those that appear only in the weekday Lectionary. The concluding chapter and bibliography point toward further areas of study.

---

[6] John R. Donahue, *The Gospel in Parable* (Philadelphia: Fortress, 1988) ix.

CHAPTER ONE

Preaching Parabolically

TO PREACH AS JESUS DID[1]

Jesus was not the first to preach in parables. There is a long tradition of such storytelling in the ancient world, not only by religious figures, but by rhetoricians, politicians, prophets, and philosophers as well. In the Hebrew Scriptures there are several examples of parables. In 2 Samuel 12:1-12, for example, the prophet Nathan tells King David a parable about a rich man who took a poor man's lone ewe lamb and made it into a meal for a visitor. The song of the vineyard in Isaiah 5:1-7 and the sayings about plowing and threshing in Isaiah 28:23-29 present agricultural metaphors not unlike those used by Jesus in his parables. The Jewish rabbis also spoke in parables.[2]

One result of parabolic preaching is that the storyteller allows the listener to back away from a sensitive topic and enter into a make-believe (but true-to-life) situation, where one can see more clearly what is right. Nathan successfully brought David to repentance for taking Uriah's wife when the king

---

[1] An earlier version of this chapter, entitled "Preaching Justice Parabolically," appeared in *Emmanuel* 102/6 (1996) 342–47.

[2] On rabbinic connections with Jesus' parables see Philip L. Culbertson, *A Word Fitly Spoken* (Albany: State University of New York Press, 1995); Brad H. Young, *Jesus and His Jewish Parables. Rediscovering the Roots of Jesus' Teaching* (New York: Paulist Press, 1989); *The Parables. Jewish Tradition and Christian Interpretation* (Peabody: Hendrickson, 1998).

5

angrily pronounced sentence on the rich man of the parable. In the Synoptic Gospels we see Jesus using the same technique, for example, when addressing the chief priests and Pharisees in Matthew 21:28-46. After addressing to them the parable of the two sons and that of the wicked tenants, Matthew comments that when they heard his parables "they knew that he was speaking about them" (21:45). Contemporary preachers can become more skilled in using the same dynamics of storytelling as did Jesus, and thus engage their listeners more effectively with the gospel message.

ENCOUNTER WITH THE HOLY

Before attempting to emulate Jesus' way of preaching, a preacher must know Jesus and his message first-hand. An effective preacher speaks from his or her personal and ongoing encounter with Christ in study, in prayer, in other people, and in all creation. Just as Jesus' constant communion with God[3] shaped his preaching, so must this be the foundation for the contemporary preacher. It is evident when a person speaks of the Holy, whether they speak from their own experience or merely pass on what they have heard or studied. Intimate experience of the Divine in prayer is what energizes, sustains, and transforms the preacher. The inability to bring about deeply unitive experiences of prayer by one's own efforts keeps the preacher aware that these are gifts. So too is the ministry of preaching. It is God's word that a preacher speaks.

It is the joy of having experienced oneself as the object of God's love and delight that impels the contemplative preacher to share this message. There is the ever-present danger that the other demands of ministry erode the minister's time for prayer. Another pitfall is to let a striving for prayerfulness at all times

---

[3] In the Gospel of Matthew Jesus is portrayed as praying alone on a mountain after the feeding of the five thousand (14:23), and in the Garden of Gethsemane (26:36-46). In numerous episodes he teaches his disciples about prayer (5:44; 6:5-13; 18:19; 21:22; 24:20). People bring their children to him and request that he lay hands and pray over them (19:13). He is intent on the Temple being a house of prayer (21:13).

take the place of specific time set aside for contemplative prayer. One who allows this to happen runs the risk of preaching a hollow word.

THE FAMILIAR RADICALLY TWISTED

In his parables, Jesus always began with the familiar. The images and situations he painted in his stories were from the fabric of daily life of his audience. He told how God is encountered in sowing and reaping (Matt 13:1-9), in weeding and harvesting (Matt 13:24-30), in baking bread (Matt 13:33), in searching for what is lost (Matt 18:12-14). In this way he would capture people's attention and draw them along with him to the end of the story. In the same manner, an effective preacher today transforms the gospel images and situations into ones that relate to the everyday world of those gathered. For example, the majority of the assembly will quickly tune out when the homily begins, "When I was in the seminary . . ." Or if the gospel presumes rural, pre-industrial experiences when the gathered community is composed of urban professionals, the homilist will need to recontextualize the message for the contemporary situation.

In Jesus' parables no sphere of life is outside God's realm: the political, social, economic, ecclesial, and theological are all intertwined, as in the parables of the workers in the vineyard (Matt 20:1-16), the wicked tenants (Matt 21:33-43), the great banquet (Matt 22:1-14), and the talents (25:14-30). Jesus' preaching brought a vision of all life as locus for the sacred; nothing is outside the realm of the holy. Likewise, a preacher today will help the assembly to see that holiness is not found by separating oneself from "the world," but is encountered in all reality. He or she will lead people to see God in the midst of the contradictions and the chaos, in the crucifying and dying, not only in the peacefulness and the rising to new life.

Jesus' parables do not stay on the level of the familiar. Always there is a catch. They were not pleasant stories that entertained or that confirmed the status quo. They were startling and confusing, usually having an unexpected twist that left the hearers pondering what the story meant and what it demanded.

As John Dominic Crossan puts it, "You can usually recognize a parable because your immediate reaction will be self-contradictory: 'I don't know what you mean by that story but I'm certain I don't like it.'"[4]

Jesus' parables are invitations to see the realm of God as God sees it and to act as Jesus acted. Such a vision demands profound changes in the way the hearer thinks about God and the realm of God, both as it can be in the here and now and in its future fullness. By shattering the structures of our accepted world parables remove our defenses and make us vulnerable to God.[5] Preachers should be suspicious of interpretations that reinforce life as it is.[6] The gospel is always about change. An effective preacher studies the text so as to understand what it originally meant and then tries to repeat that unsettling dynamic in their own preaching.

THE RIDDLE OF INTERPRETATION

What catches up the hearer is that Jesus' parables are usually open-ended; Jesus rarely interpreted these stories for his disciples.[7] For example, at the end of the story of the prodigal son (Luke 15:11-32), does the elder brother go in to the party after the father pleads with him? Or does he remain outside, angry and resentful? There lies the challenge. Jesus does not give the answer, but leaves it up to the hearer to determine the rest of the story. Over the ages each community of Christians has had to work out their responses to the challenges of Jesus' teaching; this task is no less incumbent upon believers today. Just as Jesus did not give the interpretation of his parables, neither do effective preachers provide pat answers.

---

[4] John Dominic Crossan, *The Dark Interval: Towards a Theology of Story* (Niles, Ill.: Argus Communications, 1975) 56.

[5] Ibid., 122.

[6] This is the function of myth rather than parable. See Crossan, *The Dark Interval*, 47–62.

[7] There are more exceptions to this in the Gospel of Matthew (see above, p. 1. n. 2).

Because they are told in figurative language, the parables are capable of conveying distinct messages to different people in diverse circumstances.[8] For instance, to a person in need of forgiveness, the parable in Luke 15:11-32 is the story of a lost son or daughter, who is invited to let himself or herself be found by God and be lavished with love that cannot be earned. For a person in authority, the same story may serve as a call to emulate the character of the father who searches out ones who have embarked on a destructive path and runs to meet them and bring them back, at great personal cost. For persons who try always to be faithful to following God's ways, the story invites them to let go of joyless resentment and slavish attitudes in their service of God. The point of the story depends on one's point of entry and the character with whom one identifies. A preacher cannot be content with one stock interpretation, but must continually plumb the depths of the text for other possible meanings. On each occasion she or he must discern which of the many possible messages is the word that now needs be spoken.

One of the features of Matthew's parables, however, is that interpretive layers have dulled the open-endedness of the interpretation. In Matthew's Gospel Jesus is portrayed as teacher *par excellence*. As a result, Matthew tends to finish off the parables with an ethical admonition. He has in many instances tacked on a conclusion that teaches the moral of the story. With redaction criticism it is possible to come closer to the original form of these parables which, in all likelihood, did not have such a neat finish.

STANCE WITH THE MARGINAL

The preacher always tells the story slant, inviting the hearers to take a particular position in the narrative. When a parable offers a variety of interpretive positions, a question that a preacher will want to keep in mind is from what stance

---

[8] See Mary Ann Tolbert, *Perspectives on the Parables. An Approach to Multiple Interpretations* (Philadelphia: Fortress, 1979).

does the parable offer good news to those who are poor? In the parable of the workers in the vineyard (Matt 20:1-16), for example, the parable has a different meaning if heard from the perspective of the overlooked unemployed who stand all day in the marketplace than if one hears it from the comfortable security of laboring all the day with an assured wage in view. The Gospels consistently portray Jesus as taking a stance with the marginal. Accordingly, his parables invite contemporary listeners into that stance as well.[9]

Jesus' parables proclaim that God is not neutral. Rather, God takes the part of those who are poorest and most oppressed.[10] In a congregation where poverty is the prevailing reality, the parables offer comfort and hope. In gatherings of Christians who are comfortable financially and socially, however, one of the most crucial tasks of the preacher is to take up the perspective of those who are marginalized and invite the congregation to do the same. The point is not to make people who are well-to-do feel guilty, but rather to move them to see from the perspective of those most disadvantaged and to ask, what would love require of me? If one is not poor, then Christian discipleship demands solidarity with the poor, service to the needs of the least, and readiness to suffer persecution that follows from these actions.

A COMMUNAL ENDEAVOR

One of the more difficult aspects of preaching, especially in contemporary American culture, is to present gospel living as a communal endeavor, not a pursuit of individual salva-

---

[9] A focus on Jesus and the marginalized has not been prominent in Matthean studies; much more attention has been given to this dimension in the Gospel of Luke. See Amy-Jill Levine, *The Social and Ethnic Dimensions of Matthean Salvation History* (SBEC 14; Lewiston: Mellen, 1988) and Warren Carter, *Matthew and the Margins* (Maryknoll: Orbis, 2000).

[10] See, e.g., Clodovis Boff and Jorge Pixley (*The Bible, the Church, and the Poor* [Theology and Liberation Series; Maryknoll, N.Y.: Orbis, 1989]) who demonstrate how in every section of the Bible, God's concern is always for the poor.

tion.[11] From its inception, the people of God is a community bound together by the covenant. But there is a further twist in the vision of community that Jesus' parables present. In the story of The Great Feast (Matt 22:1-14), for example, the people of God encompasses all—particularly the most despised and outcast. Or, consider Jesus' parable of the workers in the vineyard (Matt 20:1-16) for an entirely unsettling vision of a just community. The configuration is not that of each one pulling his or her own weight with appropriate compensation. Rather, the believing community is one in which each member has the means by which to subsist for the day, no matter what his or her contribution to the group.

BREVITY

The parables of Jesus are short and to the point. Some are only one line long. Like the Argentinian poet Jorge Luis Borges who laughed at those who wanted "to go on for five hundred pages developing an idea whose perfect oral expression is possible in a few minutes,"[12] Jesus knew the art of pithy expression. The brevity of the parables makes them easy to remember and enhances their ability to communicate forcefully. Likewise, when a preacher can convey his or her message briefly, there is a better chance that the word will be remembered and its transforming potential will be more fully released.

A LIVED PARABLE

The ultimate aim of preaching is that the word be acted upon. The desired effect is that people's hearts be moved to praise of God that finds further expression in transformative action. Such a word gives hope and courage to those oppressed.

---

[11] See further Edward J. Van Merrienboer, "Preaching the Social Gospel" in *In the Company of Preachers*, ed. R. Siegfried and E. Ruane (Collegeville: The Liturgical Press, 1993) 176–90.

[12] John Dominic Crossan (*Cliffs of Fall. Paradox and Polyvalence in the Parables of Jesus* [New York: Seabury, 1980] 3) relays this quote from the Prologue of Jorge Luis Borges, *Ficciones* (New York: Grove, 1962).

It declares that injustice is not God's desire and emboldens impoverished communities to act together for change. For those who are privileged, the preached word moves them not only to love and to stand with the wronged, but to act in solidarity with them to dismantle unjust structures.

The power of Jesus' preaching came from his very life being a parable.[13] His paradoxical choice of death to bring life, of self-emptying to bring fullness for all, of humiliation and suffering to bring dignity and joy to the oppressed, proclaimed a radically different way to God. It was a life that issued an invitation to conversion and left people struggling to understand its meaning and demands. Effective preachers give such a parabolic witness in our day. No preaching takes root unless the life of the preacher is a living witness.[14] This witness, like the parables, prompts all whose lives are touched by the preacher to ask, "What does this mean?" "What am I to do?" "What does this ask of me?" If the life of a preacher does not present a paradox, then the power of the gospel he or she preaches is weakened.

Effective preachers are aware that they preach what their own lives proclaim imperfectly. The word takes root, though, when the preacher visibly joins in the struggle with the gathered community, together seeking to conform their lives ever more to that of Christ. Together they seek contemplative intimacy with God, engage in serious study of the word, both in the biblical text, and in their lived reality.

Such a preacher must be willing to be consumed by a passion for the gospel and its all-encompassing demands, willing even to risk rejection and opposition. The prophet Jeremiah, who tried to hold in the word, says it became "like fire burning in my heart" (Jer 20:9) and he could not resist speaking it forth.

---

[13] See Crossan, *The Dark Interval*, 123–28 on "The Parabler Becomes Parable" and John R. Donahue, "Jesus as the Parable of God in the Gospel of Mark," *Int* 32 (1978) 369–86.

[14] Pope Paul VI underscored this in his address to members of the *Consilium de Laicis* on October 2, 1974, when he said, "Modern man [*sic*] listens more willingly to witnesses than to teachers, and if he [*sic*] does listen to teachers, it is because they are witnesses" (*Evangelii Nuntiandi*, §21, p. 41).

With such passion for the gospel, a preacher becomes a sign of hope, not a prophet of doom. In parabolically proclaiming the vision of Jesus, it is not naive optimism that the preacher declares, nor a depressing guilt trip, but a word that galvanizes the community to conversion of heart and transformative action that is undergirded by profound love for all God's people.[15]

[15] For an excellent treatment of practical ways of preaching parables that preserve their story dynamics and their metaphorical power see chap. 3 of David Buttrick, *Speaking Parables* (Louisville: Westminster John Knox, 2000).

CHAPTER TWO

Interpreting Parables

SPOILING THE PUNCH LINE

To have to interpret a parable is like having to explain a joke when someone misses the punch line. Yet, because of our familiarity with the parables, our lack of understanding of their rhetoric and of how Jesus' first audience would have reacted to his stories, we can miss the punch line of a parable. A critical step in the preparation for preaching a parable is serious biblical study that attempts to retrieve, as far as possible, what the story meant in its original telling. The preacher then attempts to re-effect such a dynamic in the contemporary context. Preaching that simply explains the original meaning to the assembly is instructional, but does not achieve its purpose.

DIFFICULTIES IN UNDERSTANDING THE PARABLES

In the Gospels, the disciples question Jesus about the parables because they do not understand (Matt 13:10-17 and pars.). The parables are far from simple stories that make Jesus' teaching easy to grasp. Although Jesus used familiar imagery, the stories remained enigmatic and confusing.[1] They are no less challenging to contemporary interpreters. Three factors

---

[1] Andrew Parker (*Painfully Clear. The Parables of Jesus* [Biblical Seminar 37; Sheffield: Sheffield Academic Press, 1996]) argues that Jesus' parables were not meant to be enigmatic. They were painfully clear and confrontational.

contribute to our difficulty in understanding: the nature of the parables, the nature of the Gospels, and the nature of our sources of knowledge about the ancient world.

THE NATURE OF THE PARABLES

Parables, by their very nature, are puzzling. They are figurative speech, symbolic language, with more than one level of meaning.[2] The term "parable" (*parabolē* in Greek; *māshāl* in Hebrew) has a wide range of meanings. It can refer to a proverb, such as "physician, cure yourself" (Luke 4:23). A wisdom saying or a riddle, such as, "It is not what enters one's mouth that defiles that person; but what comes out of the mouth is what defiles one" (Matt 15:11) is dubbed a parable (Matt 15:15). A similitude, or a slightly developed comparison can be called a parable, as the lesson *(parabolē)* of the fig tree (Matt 24:32-35). The author of Hebrews twice uses the term in the sense of "symbol" (Heb 9:9; 11:19).

Gospel commentators often divide the parables of Jesus into three categories: similitude, parable, and exemplary story.[3] Similitudes are concise narratives that make a comparison between an aspect of God's realm and a typical or recurrent event in real life (e.g., seed growing in Mark 4:26-29; or baking bread, Matt 13:33). Parables are usually longer and more detailed. They tell a story about a one-time fictitious, but true-to-life event, such as that of a householder whose enemies sow weeds in his wheat field (Matt 13:4-30) or of a king who forgives a servant when settling accounts (Matt 18:21-35). An exemplary story (e.g., the Good Samaritan in Luke 10:29-37) presents a specific example that illustrates a general principle. It differs from a similitude and a parable in that its comparison is between two things that are similar, not dissimilar.

Whichever form a parable takes, it is not an entertaining story that confirms the status quo. Its purpose is to persuade

---

[2] See John Dominic Crossan, *Cliffs of Fall. Paradox and Polyvalence in the Parables of Jesus* (New York: Seabury, 1980) 1–24 on Paradox and Metaphor; and pp. 65–104 on Polyvalence and Play.

[3] E.g., M. Boucher, *The Parables* (NTM 7; Wilmington: Glazier, 1981) 19–23.

the hearer to adopt a particular view of God and of life in God's realm. Their aim is to convert the hearer. They turn the world upside down by challenging presumptions, reversing expectations, and proposing a different view of life with God. Their open endings make it necessary for the hearers of every age to grapple with their implications.

THE NATURE OF THE GOSPELS

Another difficulty in knowing Jesus' originally intended meaning of a parable has to do with the nature of the Gospels in which the parables are found. In the first place, the Gospels are written documents, whereas the parables were originally communicated orally. The shift from oral communication to written affects meaning. In addition, the literary context in which a gospel parable is placed may give it a different sense than it had in its original spoken context.

Moreover, the Gospels do not record the exact words of Jesus. The gospel parables are two stages removed from the stories told by the earthly Jesus. Jesus' parables were preached by his followers, and underwent modifications in the retelling. As they took written form, some thirty to fifty years after Jesus' death, the parables were reshaped by each evangelist to meet the needs of his particular community of faith. The intent of the gospel writers was not to preserve as accurately as possible the exact words of Jesus; rather they, like modern preachers, reinterpreted Jesus' stories for their new contexts. As a result, we find various versions of the same parable in different Gospels. Similar parables are placed in different settings, directed to different audiences, with resultant different meanings.

Analysis of the history of the traditions also reveals that often in the retelling of Jesus' parables moralizing and/or allegorizing tendencies were introduced. Whereas his original stories began as paradoxical challenges, they were many times tamed into illustrations of moral actions. This is especially true of the Gospel of Matthew. It is necessary to sift through the layers of the tradition so as to uncover as best we can, the originally upsetting contrasts Jesus' stories presented.

THE NATURE OF OUR SOURCES OF KNOWLEDGE ABOUT THE ANCIENT WORLD

A further difficulty in knowing what Jesus intended to say and how his first audiences understood the parables is that our sources of knowledge about the ancient world are partial and incomplete. New discoveries from archaeology and of previously unknown manuscripts continue to enlighten us about the world of Jesus. Similarly, new methods of biblical interpretation bring to light fresh possibilities of meaning. Knowledge of the historical, social, economic, political, religious, and cultural world of Palestine and the Hellenistic world of the first century allows us to draw probable conclusions about a parable's original meaning, but the business of interpretation never rests on certitude.

METHODS OF PARABLE INTERPRETATION[4]

Allegorical Interpretation

The earliest approach to parable interpretation, the allegorical method,[5] is found in the Gospels themselves. This approach treats parables as allegories, that is, a series of metaphors in which each detail of the story is given a symbolic meaning. The first biblical example concerns the parable of the sower and the seed (Matt 13:1-9 and pars.). The allegorical explanation in Matthew 13:18-23 and pars. is that the seed is the word and the different types of soil represent the various ways that people hear and respond to the word. The seed that falls on the path represents those whose hearing is quickly derailed by Satan; those on rocky ground have no root and quickly fall away when tribulation comes; for those sown among thorns the word is choked off by worldly anxiety; those on rich soil

---

[4] See David B. Gowler, *What Are They Saying about the Parables?* (New York: Paulist, 2000) for a good summary of the various directions in recent parable interpretation and their major proponents.

[5] See Carolyn Osiek, "Literal Meaning and Allegory," *TBT* 29/5 (1991) 261–66; Barbara E. Reid, "Once Upon a Time . . . Parable and Allegory in the Gospels," *TBT* 29/5 (1991) 267–72.

hear and accept the word and bear abundant fruit. A similar allegorical interpretation of the parable of the weeds and the wheat (Matt 13:24-30) is found in Matthew 13:36-43.[6] Most scholars recognize these as interpretations of the early faith communities, and not from Jesus himself.

The allegorical approach was the preferred method of patristic and medieval biblical scholars. From Origen (second century C.E.) until the rise of modern biblical criticism, this method held sway. A good example is the interpretation of the parable of the Good Samaritan (Luke 10:29-37) used by Augustine and others: the traveler is Adam, representing humankind. He descends from Jerusalem, the lost paradise, to Jericho, that is, the world. The robbers are evil spirits that deprive him of virtue and immortality. That he is left half dead means that he is alive insofar as he can know God, but dead in that he is in the power of sin. The priest and Levite are the law and the prophets of Israel, unable to help. The Samaritan is Christ, outsider to the theological claims of Israel. His animal is the body of Christ, on which are borne the sins of humanity. The inn is the Church, where oil and wine, the sacraments, heal the traveler's wounds. The inn-keeper, representing the apostles, is authorized to continue caring for the wounded man until the return of the Samaritan, that is, until the second coming of Christ.[7]

One Main Point

At the end of the nineteenth century the German biblical scholar Adolph Jülicher[8] revolutionized the study of parables by arguing that a parable has only one main point. With the dawn of historical critical methods, Jülicher further insisted that the point must be sought in the historical context of the teaching of Jesus.

---

[6] Another pre-critical approach is proof-texting, which was used to interpret this parable in medieval times as justification for the burning of heretics.

[7] See, e.g., Irenaeus, *Adversus haereses* III.17,3.

[8] Adolph Jülicher, *Die Gleichnisreden Jesu* (2 vols.; Tübingen: Mohr [Siebeck] 1888, 1899).

Since that time there has been much debate over whether there was any allegorical dimension at all to the original parables of Jesus. Some scholars contend that all allegorical elements are the later interpretations by the evangelists or the early Christian communities from whom they received the parables. Other exegetes do not so rigidly distinguish between parable and allegory. They argue that the gospel parables are allegorical in nature if one understands allegory not as a series of metaphors, but as an extended metaphor in narrative form.

More Or Less Allegorical

One difference from earlier allegorical interpretation is that critics today do not try to find symbolism behind as many details. In addition, they attempt to find meanings that would be intelligible in Jesus' day. One solution is to think of parables on a sliding scale of more or less allegorical.[9]

There is a further difficulty with Jülicher's insistence that there is *one* main point in a parable. With many interpretations possible, how can we know which is *the* main point originally intended? It may be that each main character (human or not) in a parable may reveal an important point.[10] For example, in the sower parable (Matt 13:1-9 and pars.) if the sower is the focus, the point is God's lavish generosity (through Jesus' preaching, teaching, and healing) in sowing the word on all kinds of soil, good and bad alike. If the focus is the seed, the message is that the word is effective. Despite early failure or unremarkable initial results, it will eventually bear fruit in abundance. If the soil is the focal point, as in the interpretation in Matthew 13:18-23, then the emphasis is for believers to make sure to be fertile soil, cultivating themselves to be receptive and nurturing to the word. Finally, if the harvest is highlighted, then the point is that the reign of God far exceeds all

---

[9] Craig Blomberg, "Interpreting the Parables: Where Are We and Where Do We Go from Here?" *CBQ* 53 (1991) 50–78; *Interpreting the Parables* (Downers Grove, Ill.: InterVarsity Press, 1990) 29–69; and Klyne Snodgrass, *The Parable of the Wicked Tenants* (Tübingen: Mohr [Siebeck] 1983) 13–26.

[10] Blomberg, *Interpreting*, 21, advances that most parables make three main points.

expectation. The explosiveness and grand scale of the yield, "thirty, sixty, and a hundredfold," is beyond anything a typical farmer experienced.

The task of the preacher is to discern *which* of the many possible points is the main one that the assembly needs to hear at this place and time. A significant contribution by Jülicher for preachers is the insight that a parable communicates best when it is told with one main point, or punch line, not as a series of metaphors.

Historical Criticism: Getting to the Original Story

A very significant advance in parable interpretation came with the rise of historical critical methodology.[11] With the use of form and redaction criticism, in particular, historical critics investigate the kinds of alterations made in the transmission of the parables and attempt to recover the most primitive form.[12] One of the most influential scholars in this century that employed this method in parables research was Joachim Jeremias.[13] He identified ten principles of transformation by which the early Church adapted Jesus' parables to their own situation: (1) translation from Aramaic to Greek; (2) shift from a Palestinian to a Hellenistic environment; (3) embellishment of details; (4) remodeling along the lines of Old Testament and folk-story themes; (5) change of audience from interested crowds or opponents to disciples; (6) shift from a warning to the multitude about the gravity of the eschatological crisis to a hortatory use to direct the conduct of Christians; (7) metaphors assume greater christological and ecclesial significance; (8) allegorization of details; (9) tendency toward collection and conflation; (10) placement in a secondary setting. Recognizing these tendencies in

[11] See Edgar Krentz, *The Historical-Critical Method* (Guides to Biblical Scholarship; Philadelphia: Fortress, 1975).

[12] See Helmut Koester, "Recovering the Original Meaning of Matthew's Parables," *Bible Review* 9/3 (1993) 11, 52.

[13] Joachim Jeremias, *The Parables of Jesus* (8th ed.; New York: Scribner's, 1972). Similarly, Rudolf Bultmann, *History of the Synoptic Tradition* (rev. ed.; New York: Harper & Row, 1968); A. T. Cadoux, *The Parables of Jesus* (London: James Clarke, 1931).

the transmission of the tradition, and using his vast knowledge of first-century Palestine, Jeremias worked to uncover the original words and settings of the parables of Jesus.

Another significant contribution was made by C. H. Dodd,[14] who argued that the parables be understood against the context of Jesus' eschatological proclamation. For him, all the parables convey the message that the kingdom of God is inaugurated and realized in Jesus. Scholars today question that a single lens, such as realized eschatology, is adequate to unfold all the rich dimensions of the parables.

Historical methods are still extremely valuable to try to determine what was the original form of Jesus' parables and in what historical context they were spoken. This is one important step in a preacher's preparation. But the task of the preacher goes beyond simply recounting what the story meant in Jesus' day.

Social Science Approach

Closely related to historical critical methods is the recently developed science of social study of the New Testament.[15] This area of study engages biblical scholars, experts in social science, classicists, and ancient historians, who collaborate to reconstruct not only the history, but also the economic, social, and political life of Greek and Roman civilizations of the first centuries before and after Christ. They use art, contemporary literature, inscriptions, coins, and archaeological finds to gain knowledge of the institutions, social dynamics, and horizons of consciousness of people who lived at the time of Jesus.[16]

---

[14] Charles D. Dodd, *The Parables of the Kingdom* (London: Collins, 1961; first published by James Nisbet and Co., 1935).

[15] See Carolyn Osiek, *What Are They Saying about the Social Setting of the New Testament?* (2d ed. New York: Paulist, 1992); Bruce J. Malina and Richard L. Rohrbaugh, *Social-Science Commentary on the Synoptic Gospels* (Minneapolis: Fortress, 1992); John J. Pilch, *The Cultural World of Jesus. Sunday by Sunday, Cycle A* (Collegeville: The Liturgical Press, 1995).

[16] One of the first to use this method with parable interpretation was Kenneth E. Bailey, *Poet and Peasant* and *Through Peasant Eyes* (combined ed.; Grand Rapids: Eerdmans, 1984). See also Douglas Oakman, *Jesus and the Economic Question of His Day* (SBEC 8. Lewiston/Queenston: Edwin Mellen, 1986).

An example is Richard Rohrbaugh's reading of the parable of the talents/pounds (Matt 25:14-20 // Luke 19:11-27).[17] Reading from the point of view of a peasant of a first-century Mediterranean agrarian society rather than with the assumptions of a capitalist from the West, the parable results as a warning to those who mistreat the poor, not to those who lack adventurous industry.

One caution about this method is that it is a modern construction, not devised specifically for biblical study. A question remains of how well it can be applied to ancient texts and societies. Nonetheless, this approach opens up fresh meanings and can offer satisfactory solutions for details that other methods leave as inexplicable. It can also advance new possibilities for action in the contemporary world that would lead to genuine social change.

Literary Approaches

Another turning point in parable study came in the 1960s with the work of Amos Wilder and Robert Funk, who moved into methods of literary interpretation.[18] They explore the aesthetics of the language in the parables, their poetry, imagery, and symbolism. They analyze how metaphor moves from a literary figure to a theological and hermeneutical category, providing a key to a new understanding of the parables.

A related direction of literary study is narrative criticism.[19] This approach analyzes the plot, character development, point

[17] Richard L. Rohrbaugh, "A Peasant Reading of the Parable of the Talents/Pounds: A Text of Terror?" *BTB* 23 (1993) 32–39.

[18] Robert Funk, *Language, Hermeneutic, and Word of God* (New York: Harper & Row, 1966); *Parables and Presence* (Philadelphia: Fortress, 1982); Amos Wilder, *The Language of the Gospel* (New York.: Harper & Row, 1964); *Jesus' Parables and the War of Myths* (Philadelphia: Fortress, 1982). John Dominic Crossan (*In Parables: The Challenge of the Historical Jesus* [New York: Harper & Row, 1973; *The Dark Interval* [Sonoma: Polebridge, 1988]) bridges two methods when he begins with tradition-critical considerations and then moves to a literary metaphorical approach. See also Mary Ann Tolbert, *Perspectives on the Parables* (Philadelphia: Fortress, 1979); Bernard Brandon Scott, *Hear Then the Parable. A Commentary on the Parables of Jesus* (Minneapolis: Fortress, 1989).

[19] E.g., Dan O. Via, *The Parables: Their Literary and Existential Dimension* (Philadelphia: Fortress, 1967). See also Mark A. Powell, *What is Narrative*

of view, and dramatic movement of the story apart from its historical context. Narrative criticism also attends to the response evoked by the text in the reader.

Rhetorical criticism has also become an important tool for analyzing parables as persuasive speech. This method studies how the type of argument, its arrangement, and its style of presentation bring about the desired effect.[20]

Finally, semiotic or structuralist methods[21] have been applied to the parables, although most people find them too complicated and diffuse to be of help. The aim is to uncover the deep structures of meaning through analysis of the synchronic structure. Grids delineating the subject, object, sender, recipient, helper, and opponent are employed to this end.

Literary methods deal with the finished form of the text as we have it, not the process through which it has come. They recognize that meaning is constructed in the interaction between text and reader, quite apart from the original intention of the author. They can be very useful in showing the ongoing function of the parable in any context to invite participation in Jesus' understanding of God and the divine realm.

Liberation Approaches

A new approach to biblical interpretation was born in Latin America some three decades ago.[22] Its underlying principle

---

Criticism? (Guides to Biblical Scholarship; Philadelphia: Fortress, 1990). The recent work of Warren Carter and John Paul Heil, *Matthew's Parables* (CBQMS 30; Washington, D.C.: CBA, 1998) uses an audience-oriented approach.

[20] See Elisabeth Schüssler Fiorenza, *Rhetoric and Ethic. The Politics of Biblical Studies* (Minneapolis: Fortress, 1999).

[21] See Daniel Patte, *What Is Structural Exegesis?* (Guides to Biblical Scholarship; Philadelphia: Fortress, 1976). See Dan O. Via, "Parable and Example Story: A Literary-Structuralist Approach," *Semeia* 1 (1974) 105–33 for an example of this method as applied to the parable of the Good Samaritan.

[22] See Christopher Rowland and Mark Corner, *Liberating Exegesis. The Challenge of Liberation Theology to Biblical Studies* (Louisville: Westminster/John Knox, 1989); Clodovis Boff and Jorge Pixley, *The Bible, the Church, and the Poor* (Theology and Liberation Series; Maryknoll: Orbis, 1989); Carlos Mesters, *Defenseless Flower. A New Reading of the Bible* (Maryknoll: Orbis, 1989).

is that reflection on experience precedes theoretical analysis. And it is the experience of people who are poor and oppressed that is the starting point. The second step is critical analysis of the social and political causes of oppression. In the process a correlation is sought between the present situation and biblical stories of deliverance and liberation. The final move is to strategize and act for liberation. This method relies on the faithful reflection of ordinary people of faith, not solely or even primarily on that of biblical scholars. It is a communal endeavor that seeks to embody God's word of justice and hope in this world, here and now.

With regard to parable interpretation, this method challenges approaches that would claim to discover universal messages in Jesus' stories, applied and reapplied from one generation to the next and from one social context to another. It asks questions like: "What if the parables of Jesus were neither theological nor moral stories but political and economic ones? What if the concern of the parables was not the reign of God but the reigning systems of oppression that dominated Palestine in the time of Jesus? What if the parables are exposing exploitation rather than revealing justification?"[23]

A drawback to this approach is that some find that the kind of study required of social and political structures as well as biblical and ecclesial tradition is too much to ask of simple believers. For some there is more solace in an approach that provides sure doctrines, simple morality, literal, authoritative interpretations of the Bible, and an assurance of future reward for enduring present oppression and suffering.

An advantage to this method is that it can be used in tandem with historical, social science, and literary methods, while providing the lens through which to view the text. It is an invaluable tool for engaging Jesus' stories in a new context in a way that can challenge the unjust structures in our day and bring Good News to those oppressed. The danger, of course, is

---

[23] William R. Herzog II, *Parables as Subversive Speech. Jesus as Pedagogue of the Oppressed* (Louisville: Westminster/John Knox, 1994) 7. See also Warren Carter, *Matthew and the Margins* (Maryknoll: Orbis, 2000).

that one who would preach this way risks rejection and persecution as did the first proclaimer of the parables.

CONCLUSION

No one method provides the definitive key. Each contributes significantly to our understanding of what the parables meant, how they convey their meaning, and what they can mean for us today. It is important for a preacher to know what method a biblical commentator is using, so as to understand what results it will yield. Likewise, preachers themselves should consciously choose the hermeneutical model by which they construct their preaching.[24]

The next chapter gives an overview of the Gospel of Matthew. Subsequent chapters deal with the parables in the order in which they appear in the Lectionary. Attention will be given to how the use of differing interpretive methods results in different meanings. The focus is biblical interpretation, only one of the many tasks of the preacher. It remains for the preacher to discern which approach conveys the needed message for the particular assembly gathered in a specific place and time.

[24] See Raymond Bailey, ed., *Hermeneutics for Preaching. Approaches to Contemporary Interpretations of Scripture* (Nashville: Broadman, 1992); Mary Margaret Pazdan, "Hermeneutics and Proclaiming the Sunday Readings," *In the Company of Preachers* (Collegeville: The Liturgical Press, 1993) 26–37.

CHAPTER THREE

Overview of the Gospel of Matthew

RETRIEVING THE CONTEXT

In his book *The Gates of the Forest* Elie Wiesel tells the story of "When the great Rabbi Israel Baal Shem-Tov saw misfortune threatening the Jews it was his custom to go into a certain part of the forest to meditate. There he would light a fire, say a special prayer, and the miracle would be accomplished and the misfortune averted."

"Later, when his disciple, the celebrated Magid of Mezritch, had occasion, for the same reason, to intercede with heaven, he would go to the same place in the forest and say: 'Master of the Universe, listen! I do not know how to light the fire, but I am still able to say the prayer.' And again the miracle would be accomplished."

"Still later, Rabbi Moshe-Leib of Sassov, in order to save his people once more, would go into the forest and say: 'I do not know how to light the fire, I do not know the prayer, but I know the place and this must be sufficient.' It was sufficient and the miracle was accomplished."

"Then it fell to Rabbi Israel of Rizhyn to overcome misfortune. Sitting in his armchair, his head in his hands, he spoke to God: 'I am unable to light the fire and I do not know the prayer; I cannot even find the place in the forest. All I can do is to tell the story, and this must be sufficient.' And it was sufficient."[1]

---

[1] Elie Wiesel, *The Gates of the Forest* (tr. Frances Frenaye; New York: Holt, Rinehart and Winston, 1966) i–iii.

Wiesel's account illustrates the power of stories, even when the details of their original context are lost. This is the situation we face when trying to retrieve the original settings and meanings of Jesus' parables. The form in which they have come to us is now three stages removed from their first telling. Like Rabbi Israel of Rizhyn, all we have is the story. To understand the meaning of a parable, it would most helpful if we could retrieve the contexts in which it was shaped and reshaped. To that end, we will sketch briefly the setting and situation of Matthew's community as best can be determined from our current "armchairs."

MATTHEW THE TAX COLLECTOR?

Like many ancient authors, the evangelist nowhere identifies himself. The apostle Matthew may be responsible for an earlier stage of the gospel tradition, or he may have been a missionary to the area where this gospel was composed. But most scholars agree that he was not the author of the gospel. One reason is that the composer copied extensively from the Gospel of Mark. If the evangelist had been an eyewitness apostle why would he not tell the story in his own words? Moreover, one wonders how a tax collector, marginalized by observant Jews, came to have the kind of religious and literary education to be able to produce this gospel. In addition, the theological concerns of the gospel are those of second generation Christians. Still, for the sake of brevity, we will continue to refer to the author as "Matthew."

Almost all scholars believe that the evangelist was a Jewish Christian, writing for a community that was predominantly Jewish Christian. The author's knowledge of the First Testament and his preoccupation with things Jewish, particularly the role of the Law, are indications that he was a Jew. A few scholars[2] hold that Matthew was a Gentile because he

---

[2] E.g., In *The Vision of Matthew* (N.Y.: Paulist, 1979) John P. Meier argues that Matthew was a Gentile (pp. 17–25). In *Matthew* (NTM 3; Wilmington: Glazier, 1980) he allows that the author was "a learned Christian, perhaps a Jew, perhaps a Gentile Semite" (p. xi).

seems unfamiliar with the distinctions between the Pharisees and the Sadducees (e.g., Matt 16:5-12; 22:23). He also appears to have misunderstood the Hebrew parallelism in Zechariah 9:9, thinking that the prophet is speaking of two beasts (Matt 21:1-9). Finally, the anti-Jewish polemic, especially in chapter 23, may point to a Gentile author.

These, however, are not sure indicators of the evangelist's non-Jewish identity. By the time of this gospel's writing, the Sadducees were no longer a force with which to be reckoned. Matthew has simply used a generic phrase "Pharisees and Sadducees" for the religious leaders. His misinterpretation of Zechariah 9:9 does not undo the evidence of the evangelist's thorough knowledge of the Hebrew Scriptures, seen in his frequent biblical citations and allusions. Finally, the denunciations of the Jews can be explained as a Jewish Christian's attempt to define his community in relation to Jews of other strands of Judaism.[3]

SETTING

Although we do not know the precise locale for the Matthean community,[4] there are clues in the text that reveal something of its situation. Allusions to the destruction of the Jerusalem Temple (Matt 21:41-42; 22:7; 24:1-2) indicate that Matthew is writing after 70 C.E. The numerous references to cities[5] and to gold and silver[6] point to a prosperous urban environment. It is not known, however, to what extent these

---

[3] See Hayim Goren Perelmuter, *Siblings. Rabbinic Judaism and Early Christianity at Their Beginnings* (New York: Paulist, 1989) for various strands of Judaism and how they related to one another.

[4] As Donald Senior observes, "We do not know the size or complexity of the church to which Matthew's gospel was first directed. It may have consisted of several small household communities in a circumscribed local area" (*What Are They Saying about Matthew?* Rev. ed. [New York/Mahwah: Paulist, 1996] 107 n.1).

[5] The word *polis*, "city," occurs twenty-six times in Matthew, as compared with four times in Mark.

[6] This phrase occurs twenty-eight times in Matthew, whereas it appears only once in Mark and four times in Luke.

terms reflect the actual world of the Matthean community. One can know about gold and silver without having it oneself. It is probable that, like other Christian communities, Matthew's was a cross-section of women and men of diverse social and civic status, ethnic identities, and levels of wealth. Generally, the extreme top echelons of elite and the very poor were absent.[7]

The relationship of this Christian community to their Jewish counterparts is one of the most puzzling questions in Matthean studies.[8] The tensions are evident in the gospel: there are references to "their synagogues" (4:23; 9:35; 10:17; 12:9; 13:54), "your synagogues" (23:34), "their scribes" (7:29), and "the Jews to the present (day)" (28:15). There are references to Jewish persecution of Jesus' followers (10:17; 23:34), and bitter denunciation of the scribes and Pharisees (chap. 23). Throughout the gospel there are stories of exemplary faith of those who are not Jews: the Magi (2:1-12); a Roman centurion (8:5-13); a Canaanite woman (15:21-28); a Roman soldier (27:54). That Jesus' message is for Gentiles is seen clearly in the final commission

---

[7] Warren Carter, *Matthew and the Margins* (Maryknoll: Orbis, 2000) 25–26. Carter (pp. 27–30) also observes that the number of Christians in Matthew's community was small. Different means of calculating the number yield anywhere from nineteen to one hundred fifty to a thousand; in any case, a small percentage of the total population.

[8] For a summary of research on this question see Graham Stanton, "The Origin and Purpose of Matthew's Gospel: Matthean Scholarship from 1945 to 1980," *Aufstieg und Niedergang der Römischen Welt*, ed. H. Temporini and W. Haase; II (Principat), 25.3; (Berlin/New York: Water de Gruyter, 1985) 1910–21. More recently see Amy-Jill Levine, *The Social and Ethnic Dimensions of Matthean Salvation History* (SBEC 14; Lewiston/Queenstown/Lampeter: Mellen, 1988); J. Andrew Overman, *Matthew's Gospel and Formative Judaism: The Social World of the Matthean Community* (Minneapolis: Fortress, 1990); Anthony J. Saldarini, *Matthew's Christian-Jewish Community* (CSHJ; Chicago: University of Chicago Press, 1994); Donald A. Hagner, "The *Sitz im Leben* of the Gospel of Matthew," *Treasures New and Old. Recent Contributions to Matthean Studies* (ed. David R. Bauer and Mark Allan Powell; SBL Symposium Series 1; Atlanta: Scholars Press, 1996) 27–68; Donald Senior, "Between Two Worlds: Gentile and Jewish Christians in Matthew's Gospel," *CBQ* 61/1 (1999) 1–23; Douglas R. A. Hare, "How Jewish Is the Gospel of Matthew?" *CBQ* 62/2 (2000) 264–77.

(28:19),[9] and more subtly in the inclusion of Ruth and Rahab in Jesus' genealogy (1:5); the saying "in his name the Gentiles will hope" (12:21); and in the parables of the tenants (21:33-43) and the marriage feast (22:1-10).

Yet at the same time Matthew stresses a specific outreach to Israel. Only in Matthew does Jesus tell his disciples to go only to "the lost sheep of the house of Israel" (10:6; similarly 15:24). And Matthew's Gospel, overall, is strongly Jewish in tone with its emphasis on righteousness, the abiding validity of the Law, and fulfillment of Scriptures.[10]

These tensions in the gospel show that it is designed to offer for Matthew's Jewish Christians an account of Jesus' life and mission that enables them to relate to the two loyalties that pull them. On the one hand they are Jews, who are trying to define themselves in relation to other Jews who have not accepted Jesus. The latter would see them as disloyal to the Mosaic covenant, having joined a group who would seem to them pagans. On the other hand they are Christians, trying to relate to a community in which the majority is now Gentile, for whom the continued adherence of Jewish Christians to Jewish law and customs would prove problematic. Matthew's Gospel tries to defend and define Jewish Christianity on the one hand and unity with Gentile Christians on the other. It validates their continuity with the past promises to Israel while at the same time justifies their new allegiance to the person of Christ and his mission.

Most scholars date this gospel to approximately 85 C.E. Allusions to the destruction of the Jerusalem Temple (Matt 21:41-42; 22:7; 24:1-2) indicate that Matthew is writing after 70

---

[9] Recently D. C. Sim (*The Gospel o Matthew and Christian Judaism: The History and Social Setting of the Matthean Community* [Studies of the New Testament and Its World; Edinburgh: T. & T. Clark, 1998]) advanced the hypothesis that Matthew 28:19 should be read as a justification of the mission of Matthew's community solely to Jews while other Christian groups take responsibility for the Gentile mission, the legitimacy of which they approved, although they themselves directed their missionary efforts only at Jews. This has not received wide acceptance. See the critique by Senior, "Between Two Worlds," 8–12.

[10] See below, pp. 39–41, on the theme of the Law in Matthew.

C.E. This dating also allows time for circulation of the Gospel of Mark, composed around 68–70 C.E., one of Matthew's sources. It is also in the mid-80s that the Council of Jamnia instituted the *Birkat hammînîm,* the "blessing" of heretics. A version of it was found among the manuscripts of the Cairo Geniza.[11] It reads, "For the renegades let there be no hope, and may the arrogant kingdom soon be rooted out in our days, and the Nazarenes and the *mînîm* (heretics) perish as in a moment and be blotted out from the book of life and with the righteous may they not be inscribed. Blessed are thou, O Lord, who humblest the arrogant."[12] This "benediction" gave solemn liturgical expression to the increasing separation between Jews of the synagogue and followers of Jesus.[13] It brings to a head the growing hostility that finally ends in complete separation.

As for the locale of the Matthean community, the oldest guess and still most often suggested place is Antioch of Syria.[14] It was the third largest city of the empire, with a sizable Jewish population. It was an important center of emerging Christianity as well.[15] That Antioch witnessed struggles among Jewish Christians over observance of the Law is attested by Galatians 2:11-13, where Paul describes his clash with Peter. Tensions over observance of the Law by Gentile converts would also have surfaced in Antioch (see Acts 11:19-26). Of course these

---

[11] A geniza is a storage place for sacred manuscripts that have outlived their usefulness; Jewish practice forbids their destruction. Between 1890 and 1898 important ancient manuscripts were discovered in a geniza in Old Cairo.

[12] This translation is from J. Jocz, *The Jewish People and Jesus Christ* (London: SPCK, 1949) 53.

[13] See Hagner, "*Sitz im Leben,*" 40–42, for references and further discussion on the effect of Jamnia on Jewish-Christian relations. Hare, "How Jewish?" 267–69 cautions that there is no evidence to support the notion that expulsion of Christians from the synagogues was general policy in all Palestine and the Diaspora or even that it was connected with the *Birkat Hammînîm.*

[14] See Raymond E. Brown and John P. Meier, *Antioch and Rome: New Testament Cradles of Catholic Christianity* (New York/Ramsey: Paulist, 1983).

[15] Paul made Antioch one of his missionary bases (Acts 13:1-3). And, according to Acts 11:26, it was there that the followers of Jesus were first called "Christians."

characteristics pertain to many cities of the first century. Other suggestions for locale include: Caesarea Maritima, Sepphoris, Alexandria, Edessa, Tyre, and Sidon.

COMPOSITION

Our earliest patristic source of information is Eusebius, who quotes Papias of Hierapolis (ca. 125 C.E.) as saying, "Matthew compiled the Sayings *(logia)* in the Hebrew language, and everyone translated them as well as he could" (*HE* 3.39.16). Irenaeus and Origen, in turn, took Eusebius's statement to mean that Matthew composed his gospel in Hebrew or Aramaic. However, there is no firm evidence that Papias was in a position to know the facts of Matthew's method of composition. His statement, moreover, is full of ambiguities and there is no indisputable evidence from the Greek text of the gospel that it was translated from a Hebrew or Aramaic original.

Most modern scholars believe Matthew used the Markan tradition, a sayings source called "Q," and oral and written traditions unique to him, dubbed the "M" source.[16] The evangelist's own words are thought to capture well his method of composition: "every scribe who has been instructed in the kingdom of heaven is like the head of a household who brings from his storeroom both the new and the old" (13:52).

---

[16] This modified Two-Source Theory is still the most widely accepted to explain the relationships between the Synoptic Gospels. A minority of modern scholars have followed the lead of William R. Farmer (*The Synoptic Problem: A Critical Analysis* [Dillsboro: Western North Carolina Press, 1976]) in reviving the Greisbach hypothesis from the last century. They hold that Matthew was the first gospel written, which Luke expanded, and Mark condensed both. See also B. C. Butler, *The Originality of St. Matthew: A Critique of the Two-Document Hypothesis* (Cambridge: Cambridge University, 1951). Alternatively, W. F. Albright and C. S. Mann (*Matthew*. AB26; Garden City: Doubleday, 1971) question whether there is any literary relationship among these three Gospels. They suggest that their similarities come from a common dependence on a very early Aramaic or Hebrew gospel. Michael Goulder (*Midrash and Lection in Matthew*. London: SPCK, 1974) proposes Matthean dependence on Mark but dispenses with Q.

Matthew both faithfully transmits and creatively shapes the tradition.

With regard to his revisions of the Markan tradition, Matthew often streamlines Mark and converts narration into dialogue. He retains some 600 of Mark's 660 verses, following Mark more closely from chapter 13 onward than in the first twelve chapters. He supplements Mark's story with infancy narratives, resurrection appearance stories, and large blocks of Jesus' teaching. Matthew makes adaptations for his predominantly Jewish Christian community, omitting explanations of Jewish customs (e.g., Matt 15:2; cf. Mark 7:3-4), emphasizing more explicitly how Jesus fulfills the Scriptures (e.g., Matt 3:15; 8:17), and giving more attention to the question of the Law and its observance (e.g., Matt 5:17-48).

Matthean parables are generally more dramatic than those of Mark. They are marked by grand scale, apocalyptic imagery, stark contrasts, and reversals. They have more allegorical elements than those of Mark or Luke. Matthew's parables particularly stress the ethics of discipleship in light of the eschatological crisis.[17]

STRUCTURE

A number of scholars see in Matthew's Gospel a tightly woven plan of five central blocks of narrative and discourse, framed by the infancy narratives and the passion-resurrection account. The delineation of John P. Meier illustrates this approach:[18]

---

[17] Donahue, *Gospel in Parable*, 63–64.

[18] John P. Meier, *Matthew* (NTM 3; Wilmington: Glazier, 1980) vii–viii; similarly, W. D. Davies and Dale C. Allison Jr., *The Gospel According to Saint Matthew* (3 vols.; ICC; Edinburgh: T. & T. Clark, 1988, 1991, 1997) 1.58–72. Benjamin W. Bacon was the first scholar to propose such a fivefold structure in *Studies in Matthew* (London: Constable, 1930). Warren Carter (*Matthew and the Margins* [Maryknoll: Orbis, 2000]) also sees five major teaching sections (chaps. 5–7; 10; 13; 18; 24–25) but delineates six major narrative blocks: (1) 1:1–4:16 God Commissions Jesus; (2) 4:17–11:1 Jesus Manifests God's Empire and Commission in Words and Actions; (3) 11:2–16:20 Responses to Jesus' Ministry; (4) 16:21–20:34 Jesus will be Crucified and Raised; (5) 21:1–27:66 Jesus in Jerusalem: Conflict and Death; (6) 28:1-20 God Raises Jesus.

I. Infancy Narratives: 1:1-2:23

II. Five Books of Narratives and Discourses[19]

    1. The Son Begins to Proclaim the Kingdom

        A. Narrative: Beginnings of the Ministry: 3:1–4:25

        B. Discourse: The Sermon on the Mount: 5:1–7:29

    2. The Mission of Jesus and His Disciples in Galilee

        A. Narrative: The Cycle of Nine Miracle Stories: 8:1–9:38

        B. Discourse: The Mission, Past and Future: 10:1–11:1

    3. Jesus Meets Opposition from Israel

        A. Narrative: Jesus Disputes with Israel: 11:2–12:50

        B. Discourse: Parables: 13:1-53

    4. The Messiah Forms the Church and Prophesies His Passion

        A. Narrative: The Itinerant Jesus Prepares for the Church by His Deeds: 13:54–17:27

        B. Discourse: Church Life and Order: 18:1-35

    5. The Messiah and the Church on the Way to the Passion

        A. Narrative: Jesus Leads His Disciples to the Cross as He Confounds His Enemies: 19:1–23:29

        B. Discourse: The Last Judgment: 24:1–25:46

III. Climax: Passion, Death, and Resurrection: 26:1–28:20

One critique of this structure is that it relegates the Infancy and Passion Narratives to a marginal position, when, in fact, they are central to Matthew's story. In addition, the motif of Jesus as the "New Moses" is present in the gospel, but whether it is the central theme that moves the evangelist to delineate five books in imitation of the Pentateuch, is questionable.[20]

Some scholars see a chiastic pattern to Matthew's Gospel, also divided into sermons and narratives, with chapter 13 as the hinge. The outline of Peter Ellis is one such:[21]

---

[19] These are each marked by the concluding formula: "When Jesus finished these words" (7:28; 11:1; 13:53; 19:1; 26:1).

[20] See further D. Allison, *The New Moses: A Matthean Typology* (Minneapolis: Fortress, 1993), who concludes that this is one of many themes in Matthew, and not the most important.

[21] Peter F. Ellis, *Matthew: His Mind and His Message* (Collegeville: The Liturgical Press, 1974).

a   Narratives   chaps. 1–4
  b   Sermons   chaps. 5–7
    c   Narratives   chaps. 8–9
      d   Sermons   chap. 10
        e   Narratives   chaps. 11–12
          f   Sermon   chap. 13
        e'   Narratives   chaps. 14–17
      d'   Sermons   chap. 18
    c'   Narratives   chaps. 19–22
  b'   Sermons   chaps. 23–25
a'   Narratives   chaps. 26–28

In this configuration, Matthew 13:35 is seen as the hinge piece of the narrative. Prior to this turning point Jesus addresses all Jews; afterward he devotes his attention solely to those who have already become his disciples.

Not all scholars see Matthew's structure in such neat patterns. One wonders whether a structure that a contemporary commentator sees as perfectly symmetrical and balanced was consciously so designed by the evangelist. Another approach is to regard Matthew more a storyteller whose structure is determined by his retelling of Mark's story. The gospel's construction has more seams and turns than the above outlines allow. One such example is that of Donald Senior:[22]

  I.   1:1–4:11   Origin of Jesus
  II.   4:12–10:42   Galilean ministry of teaching (chaps. 5–7) and healing (chaps. 8–9) as a model for disciples' ministry (chap. 10)
  III.   11:1–16:12   Varying responses to Jesus (rejection by Jewish opponents, faith of disciples)
  IV.   16:13–20:34   Jesus and his disciples on the Way to Jerusalem
  V.   21:1–28:15   Jerusalem; Jesus' final days of teaching in the temple
  VI.   28:16-20   Finale: back to Galilee; disciples sent to the whole world; Jesus' abiding presence

---

[22] Donald Senior (*What Are They Saying about Matthew?* [Rev. ed.; New York/Mahwah: Paulist, 1996] 34–37) proposes this outline and evaluates several others.

In this outline Matthew's plan is seen as much less systematic, yet it delineates well the major movements and theological motifs of the gospel. It takes into account the fluid nature of narrative in a way that the more rigid structures do not.

THEOLOGICAL THEMES

Christology

Prominent in Matthew's Gospel is the portrait of Jesus as Son of God and Son of David. "Son of God" punctuates crucial moments in the story: Jesus' baptism (3:17); his temptation (4:3, 6); Peter's profession of faith (16:16); the transfiguration (17:5); the trial and crucifixion (26:63; 27:40, 43, 54).[23] That Jesus is unique Son of God is no secret in Matthew as it is in Mark. Ten times[24] the title "Son of David" highlights the paradox that Jesus is the Jewish Messiah[25] though rejected by most Israelites. Another important ascription is "Son of Humanity."[26]

Wisdom motifs also underlie Matthew's presentation of Jesus.[27] While some see the Matthean Jesus as Wisdom incarnate (11:2-19, 25-30; 23:37-39),[28] others find a Wisdom influence, but not a Wisdom christology.[29] A special emphasis of

---

[23] Also 8:29; 14:33.

[24] Matt 1:1, 20 [in 1:20 it refers to Joseph]; 9:27; 12:23; 15:22; 20:30, 31; 21:9, 15; 22:42. Three of these instances have parallels in Mark (10:47, 48; 12:35) and in Luke (18:38, 39; 20:41).

[25] *Christos,* "Messiah," occurs 16 times in Matthew; in Mark 8 times; in Luke 12 times.

[26] This occurs 31 times in Matthew; 14 times in Mark; 26 times in Luke. See Excursus below, pp. 101–02.

[27] See below, chap. 17.

[28] E.g., M. Jack Suggs, *Wisdom, Christology, and Law in Matthew's Gospel* (Cambridge: Harvard University, 1970); Felix Christ, *Jesus Sophia: Die Sophia-Christologie bei den Synoptikern* (ATANT 57; Zürich: Zwingli, 1970); Fred W. Burnett, *The Testament of Jesus-Sophia: a Redactional-Critical Study of the Eschatological Discourse in Matthew* (Washington D.C.: University Press of America, 1981); Celia Deutsch, *Hidden Wisdom and the Easy Yoke: Wisdom, Torah and Discipleship in Matthew 11:25-30* (Sheffield: JSOT, 1987).

[29] E.g., Frances Taylor Gench, *Wisdom in the Christology of Matthew* (Lanham/New York/Oxford: University Press of America, 1997). Russell Pageant ("The Wisdom Passages in Matthew's Story," *Treasures New and Old,* 197–232)

Matthew is on Jesus as authoritative Teacher (7:29). The Matthean Jesus uses this title of himself (23:8; 26:18) and is cast in the role of the New Moses. That Jesus is Emmanuel, "God-with-us" frames the whole gospel (1:23; 28:20).

Discipleship[30]

Disciples of Jesus in the Gospel of Matthew are those who follow Jesus and hear his word and obey it (7:21-27; 13:9, 23; 21:6; 26:19). Matthew portrays the disciples as having greater understanding than does Mark (Matt 13:51; 14:33; cf. Mark 6:52; Matt 16:12; cf. Mark 8:21), though they are still fallible (13:10, 36; 26:69-75). Peter has a more prominent role in Matthew. It is in this gospel that Jesus declares him "rock" upon which the Church is built (16:18-19).

Women disciples are evident, though there appear to be two streams of tradition in tension.[31] The one has a strong patriarchal perspective in which only male disciples are called (4:18-22; 9:9-13, 16-22), listed as apostles, and entrusted with the mission (28:16). Men play the main roles and do the speaking in the narratives.

The other strand of tradition preserves stories of women who play a significant role. In Jesus' genealogy four women are noted: Tamar (1:3), Rahab (1:5), Ruth (1:5), and Solomon's mother (1:6).[32] Though Matthew's story of Jesus' birth and the events

---

uses reader-response analysis to reach the conclusion that Matthew employs the story of Wisdom not to elaborate on the identity of Jesus but to interpret the plot of the story of Jesus: the pattern of Wisdom's rejection and withdrawal is repeated in the rejection and death of Jesus.

[30] For a narrative study of the topic see Richard A. Edwards, *Matthew's Narrative Portrait of Disciples* (Harrisburg: Trinity Press International, 1997).

[31] Elaine M. Wainwright, *Towards a Feminist Critical Reading of the Gospel According to Matthew* (BZNW 60; Berlin/New York: de Gruyter, 1991); "The Gospel of Matthew," in *Searching the Scriptures* (vol. 2; New York: Crossroad, 1994) 635–77; *Shall We Look for Another? A Feminist Rereading of the Matthean Jesus* (Maryknoll: Orbis, 1998).

[32] See Amy-Jill Levine, *The Social and Ethnic Dimensions of Matthean Salvation History* (SBEC 14; Lewiston/Queenston/Lampeter: Mellen, 1988) 89–106.

leading to it center on Joseph, Mary nonetheless plays a crucial role (1:18-25). The healing of Simon's mother-in-law (8:14-15) preserves the traces of a call story that has been refashioned into a healing story. The Canaanite woman (15:21-28) plays a critical part in expanding Jesus' understanding of his mission. A woman prophetically anoints Jesus before his passion (26:6-13). Pilate's wife insists on Jesus' innocence (27:19). Women disciples witness the crucifixion (27:55-56) and burial (27:61) after the men have betrayed, denied, and deserted Jesus. Mary Magdalene and another Mary are the first to see the risen Christ and to be commissioned with the Good News (28:1-10).

These two currents reflect a struggle in Matthew's community over a more inclusive vision of Christian discipleship and mission. Not only were there questions concerning the admission of Gentiles and their observance of the Law, but tensions over the roles of women as well.

Church

Matthew is the only evangelist to use the word *ekklēsia*, "church" (16:18; 18:17).[33] His narrative first centers on the gathering of disciples into what will become the church. In chapter 18 are found explicit directions for how to live as a reconciled community of believers. There is, however, no detailed blueprint for church order or selection of leaders. In fact, in 18:15-20 there is stress on decision-making and action by the whole community.

The Role of the Law

The question of Jesus' relationship to the Law arises again and again in this gospel. The term *dikaiosynē*, "righteousness" or "right relation," and related words appear more often in Matthew than in any other gospel.[34] The Matthean Jesus has

---

[33] The word is found mostly in the Pauline letters, where it appears sixty-two times, in Acts of the Apostles (twenty-three times), and in the book of Revelation (twenty times).

[34] *Dikaiosynē*, "righteousness," occurs 7 times in Matthew (3:15; 5:6, 10, 20; 6:1, 33; 21:32); not at all in Mark; once in Luke (1:75); and twice in John (16:8,10). The adjective *dikaios*, "upright" or "righteous," occurs 16 times in Matthew (1:19; 5:45; 9:13; 10:41; 13:17, 43, 49; 20:4; 23:28, 29, 35; 25:37, 46; 27:4,

come to fulfill, not abolish, the Law (5:17-19). He denounces lawlessness[35] (7:23; 13:41; 24:12) and advocates observance of the tiniest detail of the Law (5:18). But there are also texts in which Jesus seems to abrogate the Law (5:31-42) or to bend its interpretation (12:1-8).

Matthew's complex portrait of Jesus' attitude toward the Law is tied to the complicated situation of his community and to the christology of the First Gospel. Like the Jewish Christians, Jesus does not repudiate the Mosaic Law. He is not the teacher of a new Law; rather, he is the authentic interpreter of the Law. Controversies ensue when his interpretations differ from those of other Jewish leaders (e.g., 5:21-42; 12:9-14). Jesus both affirms God's age-old fidelity as manifest in the Law and newly interprets it with his person and message.

It is still a much debated question whether this community was situated inside or outside the synagogue. Do the conflicts between Jesus and the Jewish religious leaders reflect an intrafamily conflict?[36] Or are the Matthean Jewish Christians now separate from Jews of the synagogue?[37] Whichever side one takes, it is clear that this group is seeking to define its own

---

19, 24); twice in Mark (2:17; 6:20); 11 times in Luke (1:6, 17; 2:25; 5:32; 12:56; 14:14; 15:7; 18:9; 20:20; 23:47, 50); and three times in John (5:30; 7:24; 17:25). The verb *dikaioō*, "to make righteous," occurs twice in Matthew (11:19; 12:37); five times in Luke (7:29, 35; 10:29; 16:15; 18:14); and not at all in Mark or John.

[35] The Greek word *anomia* literally means "without law." It is often translated "evildoers."

[36] See, e.g., Reinhart Hummel, *Die Auseinandersetzung zwischen Kirche und Judentum im Matthäusevangelium* (München: Kaiser Verlag, 1963); J. Andrew Overman, *Matthew's Gospel and Formative Judaism: The Social World of the Matthean Community* (Minneapolis: Augsburg Fortress, 1990); Anthony Saldarini, *Matthew's Christian-Jewish Community* (Chicago: University of Chicago, 1994); Graham Stanton, *A Gospel for a New People: Studies in Matthew* (Edinburgh: T. & T. Clark, 1992).

[37] E.g., W. D. Davies and D. C. Allison, *The Gospel According to Saint Matthew* (Vol. 1; ICC. Edinburgh: T. & T. Clark, 1988); Douglas Hare, *The Theme of Jewish Persecution of Christians in the Gospel According to St. Matthew* (SNTSMS 6; Cambridge: Cambridge University, 1967); Georg Strecker, *Der Weg der Gerechtigkeit: Untersuchung zur Theologie des Mattäus* (Rev. ed.; Göttingen: Vandenhoeck & Ruprecht, 1966).

identity and situate itself vis-à-vis the Jewish tradition. A message of continuity with discontinuity pervades.

Kingdom of Heaven

The phrase *basileia tou ouranou*, "kingdom of heaven," occurs thirty-two times in Matthew and is unique to this gospel. In Matthew 19:23-24 it is used interchangeably with *basileia tou theou*, "kingdom of God," the phrase preferred by Mark and Luke. Matthew's substitution of "heaven" for "God" is most likely a circumlocution designed to avoid pronouncing the divine name.

It is difficult to find an adequate phrase in English to convey the meaning of *basileia tou ouranou*. Translating it as "kingdom of heaven" is problematic, first, because it conveys the notion of a locale with fixed boundaries. It has long been recognized that God's *basileia* signifies divine "kingly rule" or "reign," not "kingdom" in a territorial sense. A further problem with Matthew's phrase is that the "kingdom of heaven" would seem to be found only in the beyond, in the transcendent sphere, at some future time. Although the Matthean Jesus does teach his disciples to pray for (6:10) and seek (6:33) the final coming of God's *basileia* (see also 16:27-28), he also proclaims that it is drawing near (3:2; 4:17), and has already come (12:28).

A further difficulty with the translation "kingdom of heaven" is that it presents an image of God as king, conveying a male, monarchical model of God's rule. For communities of believers whose experience of governance is democratic, and who have become conscious of the limitations and dangers of having solely male images of God, "kingdom" is an inadequate term.[38] Finally, in a first-century Palestinian context the term *basileia* would first call to mind the Roman imperial system of domination and exploitation. Jesus' annunciation of the *basileia* of God/heaven offered an alternative vision to that of

---

[38] For further critique of the monarchical model of God as king and for explorations of other models see Sallie McFague, *Models of God* (Philadelphia: Fortress, 1987) esp. 63–69. See further Gail Ramshaw, *God Beyond Gender* (Minneapolis: Fortress, 1995) esp. 59–74.

the empire of Rome. The *basileia* that Jesus announced was one in which there was no more victimization or domination. This *basileia* was already present incipiently in Jesus' healing and liberative practices, the inclusive table sharing of his followers, and their domination-free relationships. The political threat that such a subversive *basileia* vision presented to the Roman imperial system is clear from the crucifixion of Jesus.[39]

Recognizing that no phrase adequately captures all that *basileia tou ouranou/theou* signifies, alternative translations of *basileia* have been suggested: "kin-dom," "rule," "reign," "realm," "empire," "domain," and "commonweal." With adequate explanation, some leave it untranslated, as *basileia*.

It is important that whatever translation one adopts, it convey the sense of God's saving power over all creation, already inaugurated in a new way with the incarnation and ministry of Jesus. It is continued in the faithful ministry of the believing community, but not yet fully manifest. It is not a fixed place located in the beyond. Nor is it coterminous with the Church. It is authoritative power and empowerment by God-with-us.[40]

PURPOSE

Various theories have been offered for Matthew's purpose in constructing the gospel as he did. The evangelist's motives may have included any or all of the following: to instruct and exhort members of his community; to provide a handbook for church leaders to assist them in preaching, teaching, worship, mission, and addressing polemic;[41] to provide liturgical reading and sermon material. In various ways, all see Matthew as retelling the story of Jesus in such a way that the Good News was addressed to his community's changed and changing situation, bringing them new vision and hope. This is the same task that is entrusted to preachers of the gospel today.

---

[39] Elisabeth Schüssler Fiorenza, *Jesus: Miriam's Child, Sophia's Prophet* (New York: Continuum, 1994) 92–93.

[40] See David Buttrick, *Speaking Parables* (Louisville: Westminster John Knox, 2000) 22–38, on preaching the kingdom of God.

[41] Benedict T. Viviano, "Matthew," *NJBC*, 631.

Use in the Early Church and Pastoral Use Today

From the beginning Matthew has been the gospel most used by the Church in its worship. Contrary to most modern scholars,[42] the early patristic writers believed that Matthew was the first gospel to be written. Moreover, its claim to apostolic authority and its catechetical usefulness gave it primacy of place. Consequently, the Gospel of Matthew has traditionally been the one most commented upon[43] and preached.

The First Gospel still speaks in powerful ways to contemporary Christians, especially with its rich spirituality, its unique emphasis on Jesus' promise to be with us always "until the end of the age" (28:20), its emphasis on ethics, its pastoral procedures for reconciliation and formation of community, and its ability to bridge the difficult path of both keeping what is essential from tradition and of navigating new waters.[44] A prime pastoral concern to which preachers should give most careful attention is the impact that use of Matthew's Gospel has on Jewish–Christian relations. Statements in the gospel narratives that reflect the historical tensions of an emerging Jewish Christian community struggling to understand and define itself in relation to Jews who did not follow Jesus need to be clearly explained as such so that they not be used to fuel anti-Judaism in contemporary contexts. Rather, the Gospel of Matthew can serve Christians and Jews in our

[42] Most biblical scholars think that the Gospel of Mark was composed before Matthew, either just before or just after the destruction of the Temple in 70 C.E. Mark served as a source for both Matthew and Luke. A minority of scholars, most notably William Farmer (*The Synoptic Problem: A Critical Analysis* [New York: Macmillan, 1964]), has revived the hypothesis of Greisbach, arguing that Mark conflated Matthew and Luke.

[43] The first known commentary on Matthew is that of Origen (ca. 185–254 C.E.).

[44] See Daniel J. Harrington, "Matthew's Gospel: Pastoral Problems and Possibilities," in *The Gospel of Matthew in Current Study* (David E. Aune, ed. Grand Rapids: Eerdmans, 2001) 62–73; Mark Allan Powell, *God With Us: A Pastoral Theology of Matthew's Gospel* (Minneapolis: Fortress, 1995); Ronald D. Witherup, *Matthew. God With Us* (Spiritual Commentaries; New York: New City Press, 2000); Leslie J. Hoppe, *A Retreat With Matthew* (Cincinnati: St. Anthony Messenger Press, 2000).

ongoing dialogues toward mutual understanding, respect, and acceptance.[45]

With this understanding of the evangelist and his concerns, we turn now to the Matthean parables in the order in which they appear in the Lectionary.

---

[45] See Harrington, "Pastoral Problems," 62–73; Anthony J. Saldarini, "Reading Matthew Without Anti-Semitism," in *The Gospel of Matthew in Current Study* (David E. Aune, ed. Grand Rapids: Eerdmans, 2001) 166–84.

CHAPTER FOUR

Salt and Light
(Matt 5:13-16)

Fifth Sunday of Ordinary Time

Tuesday of the Tenth Week of Ordinary Time

Jesus said to his disciples:
"You are the salt of the earth.
But if salt loses its taste, with what can it be seasoned?
It is no longer good for anything
but to be thrown out and trampled underfoot.

You are the light of the world.
A city set on a mountain cannot be hidden.
Nor do they light a lamp and then put it under
a bushel basket;
it is set on a lampstand,
where it gives light to all in the house.
Just so, your light must shine before others,
that they may see your good deeds
and glorify your heavenly Father."

SALT AND LIGHT

Only last week I heard said of a man, "he's really the salt of the earth." Everyone in the conversation knew what the metaphor meant. We understood that this man was a solid citizen. He could never be anything but reliable and trustworthy. This common understanding may, however, hinder rather than help interpret Matthew 5:13.

Two metaphors are juxtaposed in this gospel pericope: followers of Jesus are salt and light. In its literary context in the Gospel of Matthew, this passage follows on the heels of the Beatitudes and precedes the discussion of Jesus' relation to the Law. It is part of the Sermon on the Mount, and is addressed by Jesus to his disciples.

TRANSMISSION OF THE TRADITION

From the parallel passages in Mark and Luke, it is clear that the sayings originally circulated independently. In Mark and Luke the sayings appear separately, in different forms and contexts from Matthew, and with divergent meanings. In Mark the metaphor of the lamp is part of the parables chapter (4:21); the salt saying appears at Mark 9:49-50.[1] Luke preserves two versions of the lamp metaphor: Luke 8:16 from the Markan tradition; and Luke 11:33 from Q. The salt saying is found in Luke 14:34-35.[2] There are also similar parabolic sayings about light in the Coptic *Gospel of Thomas* and the Oxyrhynchus papyri.[3]

---

[1] Mark 4:21-25 is the Gospel reading for Thursday of the Third Week of Ordinary Time. Mark 9:49-50 is part of the larger pericope (9:41-50) assigned for Thursday of the Seventh Week of Ordinary Time.

[2] Luke 8:16-18 appears in the Lectionary on Monday of the Twenty-Fifth Week of Ordinary Time. Luke links the lamp saying in 11:33 with the metaphor of the eye as the lamp of the body (Luke 11:34-36). These latter verses are parallel to Matt 6:22-23. Neither Luke 14:34-35 nor Luke 11:33-36 appears in the Lectionary. Matt 6:22-23 is assigned for Friday of the Eleventh Week of Ordinary Time.

[3] The Oxyrhynchus papyri are documents recovered from the site of an Egyptian city by this name that flourished in the Middle Roman period. It is located about 125 miles south of Cairo and was excavated in several seasons beginning in 1897. The documents are written in Greek, on papyrus and parchment, and date from the first to the ninth centuries, C.E. The contents range from official documents to personal letters to fragments of biblical texts. Three fragments of the *Gospel of Thomas* were found among the Oxyrhynchus papyri in 1898 and 1903. The apocryphal *Gospel of Thomas* is an anthology of 114 sayings attributed to Jesus. Unlike the canonical Gospels, it is not a narrative. The prologue identifies Didymus Judas Thomas as the recorder of the sayings. This figure was revered as an apostle and twin brother of Jesus in Syria, the most likely place of composition for *Gos. Thom.* The complete *Gos.*

It is important to keep in mind that each version varies in meaning. We focus here on the particular message conveyed by Matthew. It is notable that Matthew begins each saying, "*You* are . . ." As the first word of the sentence, "you" is emphatic. The metaphors bespeak an aspect of discipleship already inherent in Jesus' followers, not something they are to strive to become.[4]

SALT OF THE EARTH

What meaning would this metaphor convey to Jesus' audience? And to Matthew's? Unlike our society that is very conscious of the danger of too much salt consumption, such was not the case in the time of Jesus. Salt was a critical necessity, as attested by Sirach 39:26: "Chief of all needs for human life are water and fire, iron and salt." One important use for salt was to season and preserve food. Job asks, "Can a thing insipid be eaten without salt?" (6:6).

Salt was important for liturgical functions and is listed among the provisions necessary for the temple (Ezra 6:9). It was prescribed as a necessary part of cereal offerings (Lev 2:13) and burnt offerings (Ezek 43:24). The instructions for blending incense included the addition of salt so as to keep the fragrant

---

Thom. exists only in a Coptic translation from the Greek, that dates to the fourth century. This text was found among the Nag Hammadi library in 1945. The three Greek fragments found at Oxyrhynchus date to approximately the mid-second century. It is possible that an Aramaic version existed as early as the first century, but as yet there is no sure evidence for this. A number of parables and sayings in *Gos. Thom.* are parallel to those found in the Synoptic Gospels. They are an important source for investigation of the transmission of the tradition. Scholars are divided over whether *Gos. Thom.* is a mid-to-late second century harmony, dependent on the canonical Gospels, or whether it represents an earlier, independent tradition. For a modern English translation with introduction and notes see Marvin Meyer, *The Gospel of Thomas. The Hidden Sayings of Jesus* (San Francisco: Harper, 1992).

[4] By contrast, in Mark 9:49-50 and Luke 14:34-35 salt represents a quality of discipleship. Mark's saying, "everyone will be salted with fire" (9:49), equates salt with persecution, and its ability to purify. The unique conclusion in Mark 9:50, "Keep salt in yourselves and you will have peace with one another," uses salt as a metaphor for the spirit of charity that preserves community.

powder "pure and sacred" (Exod 30:35). Elisha purified a spring with salt (2 Kgs 2:19-22). The practice of rubbing new-borns with salt (Ezek 16:4) was either for medicinal or religious reasons, or possibly both. Older Catholics may remember when placing salt on the infant's tongue was part of the baptismal ritual, as a symbol of incorruptibility.

Covenants were ratified with salt (Num 18:19; 2 Chr 13:5). Because of the preservative nature of salt, a covenant sealed with salt was one that was meant to last forever. To "eat salt" with another signifies a bond of friendship and loyalty (Ezra 4:14; Acts 1:4). To season one's speech with salt (Col 4:6) is to speak with graciousness and wisdom.

Salts of various kinds are necessary for the fecundity of the soil, but soil that is "nothing but sulphur and salt" is a desert wasteland (Deut 29:22; Ps 107:34; Job 39:6; Jer 17:6; Zeph 2:9). Conquerors scattered salt on cities they had destroyed as a symbolic reinforcement of its destruction (Judg 9:45).[5]

In sum, the uses of salt in the ancient world included: seasoning, preservation, purification, and judgment.[6] In saying to his disciples, "You are the salt of the earth" Jesus could have meant that they perform any and all of these functions: that they draw out the liveliness and savor of God's love in the world; they are a sign of God's eternal fidelity; they bring to judgment all that is opposed to God's *basileia*.[7]

LOSING ITS TASTE

It is the second half of the saying that has posed the most interpretive difficulties: "But if salt loses its taste, with what can it be seasoned?" One approach is to look to possible situations in which salt can lose its taste. Some commentators pro-

---

[5] Polybius and Livy also mention such a practice by the Romans. The Assyrian king Tiglath-Pilesar I tells of doing this to the city of Hunusa. See Theodore Gaster, *Myth, Legend and Custom in the Old Testament* (New York: Harper and Row, 1969) 428–30 for more examples.

[6] See Lawrence B. Porter, "Salt of the Earth," *Homiletic and Pastoral Review* 95 (July 1995) 51–58.

[7] See above, pp. 41–42 on "kingdom of heaven."

pose that Jesus had in mind salt crusts that form at the edges
of the Dead Sea. This salt is not chemically pure, but mixed
with other minerals and plant residues. When the salt is dis-
solved by moisture the impurities left behind would be useless
refuse.[8] But this image is the reverse of the process envisioned
in Matthew 5:13. The gospel speaks not of salt being purified
of foreign elements, but just the opposite.

Others suggest that salt only loses its taste when dis-
solved. Is this saying a warning, then, to disciples not to let
their ardor or the gospel message become diluted? Is it an admonition against half-hearted discipleship?[9] How such a thing
might happen is not specified in Matthew 5:13. In its wider literary context, this saying immediately follows Jesus' words of
blessing for disciples who bear insult and persecution for his
sake (Matt 5:11-12). In this light, the salt saying may be encouragement to flagging disciples whose "saltiness" is dissi-
pating under the rigors of persecution. The theme of witness
in the face of persecution appears also in Matthew 10:18; 24:14;
28:18-20.[10]

What sort of persecution might Matthean Christians be
enduring? It was probably not the dramatic, "throw them to
the lions" kind of persecution. More common would have been
economic harassment as a minority group, conflicts with Jews
of the synagogue, and the like. In the context of their theological clashes, Matthew's emphatic "*you* are the salt" reinforces to
members of his community that it is they, not their counterparts in the synagogue, who are truly the wise teachers.[11] Another kind of "persecution" arose from struggles over the degree
of accommodation to the surrounding Hellenistic culture that

---

[8] Joachim Jeremias, *The Parables of Jesus*. 2d rev. ed. (New York: Scribners, 1972) 169.

[9] John R. Donahue, *The Gospel in Parable* (Minneapolis: Fortress, 1988) 121.

[10] Eduard Schweizer (*The Good News According to Matthew* [Atlanta: John Knox, 1975] 101, 103) finds in the saying a contrast between what is small and insignificant, and its great effect. Only a pinch of salt is needed to season the whole world. However, this contrast is clearer in other parables, such as that of the Mustard Seed, and is not the primary focus in the salt metaphor.

[11] W. Nauck, "Salt as a Metaphor in Instructions for Discipleship," *Studia Theologica* 6 (1952) 177.

was possible for Christians without compromising the gospel. The question of strife that comes from countercultural Christian praxis is no less real for modern disciples.

Another line of interpretation notes that where salt was a precious commodity and highly taxed, as Josephus attests (*Ant.* 8.2.3), it may have been diluted, e.g., mixed with gypsum, so that the seller maximized the profit fraudulently.[12] In such a case, it would be the poor who would be purchasing salt that had little "saltiness."[13] The saying, then, could be a warning to disciples not to let their witness become corrupted or diluted by participating in unjust practices against the poor.

As for being cast out and trampled underfoot, some envision a situation similar to the practice of Arab bakers who cover the floor of their ovens with slabs of salt. The salt acts as a catalyst for the fuel, usually dried camel dung. Over time the catalytic effect of the salt wears out and the salt is cast into the street and trampled underfoot.[14]

BECOMING FOOLISH

Each of these explanations above works with images from possible situations in which salt can lose its "saltiness." Another approach is to look to alternative translations of verse 13b. The verb *mōrainō*, translated in the *NAB* as "loses its taste," literally means, "to become foolish" (as at Sir 23:14 [LXX]; 1 Cor 1:20; Rom 1:22). This is the verb used in both Matthew 5:13 and Luke 14:34. Mark 9:49 uses a different expression, *analon genētai,* literally, "becomes unsalty." These variations may provide a clue to Jesus' original words. It may be that the Aramaic original was *taphel*, which, like the Hebrew root *tpl*, has a double meaning: (1) to be "unsalty"; (2) to talk foolishly. In this case, Mark would have preserved the original meaning, while Mat-

---

[12] So Robert H. Gundry, *Matthew. A Commentary on His Literary and Theological Art* (Grand Rapids: Eerdmans, 1992) 75.

[13] A. H. McNeile, *The Gospel According to St. Matthew* (London: Macmillan, 1952) 55.

[14] Jeremias (*Parables*, 168) notes, however, that if the saying refers to salt as food, this explanation is not adequate.

thew and Luke anticipated the equation of "saltlessness" and "foolishness," a notion that is found in rabbinic literature.[15]

Following on this insight, Jeremias proposes that the next phrase, *en tini halisthēsetai*, be translated not, "How shall it (the salt) regain its salinity?" (so Mark 9:50), but rather, "with what shall (food) be salted." Luke's wording in 14:34, *en tini artuthēsetai*, "with what can it be seasoned," supports this. In Colossians 4:6 the verb *artuō* is coupled with "salt" in the metaphor, "speech seasoned with salt." The force of the saying in Matthew 5:13, then, is that the disciples are salt; if they lose their saltiness, with what will the earth (humankind)[16] be salted? The implied answer is: nothing. There is no "salt-substitute."

This manner of approaching the metaphoric saying, then, regards "salt losing its taste" not as a real possibility, but an utterly ridiculous proposal. Just as salt cannot lose its taste, neither can disciples lose their ability to season, preserve, purify, and judge. Such would be a complete contradiction in terms. Disciples cannot cease to be who they are, just as salt can never stop being salt.

In support of this interpretation is a similar rabbinic saying of Joshua ben Hananya (ca. 80–120 C.E.). He was asked by philosophers in the Atheneum at Rome, "If salt becomes savorless, with what can it be salted?" He replied, "With an after-birth of a mule." They ask further, "Has the mule an after-birth?" to which the rabbi responds, "Can salt become savorless?" (*b. Bek.* 8b).[17] This exchange illustrates that it is just as

---

[15] In Rabbinic literature salt is a metaphor for wisdom. For references see Nauck, "Salt as a Metaphor," 164–78. The rabbis also likened the Torah to salt (*b. Sop.* 15:8).

[16] The word "earth," *gē*, is used in six different senses in Matthew. It connotes: (1) soil, as in the parable of the sower (Matt 13:5, 8, 23); (2) the ground, as when Jesus orders the crowd to sit down on the ground in Matt 15:35 (see also Matt 10:29; 25:18, 25; 27:51); (3) the land, as opposed to sea, in Matt 14:24, 34; (4) the land of a region, in a territorial sense, e.g., "land of Judah" in Matt 2:6 (similarly, Matt 2:20, 21; 4:15; 9:26, 31; 10:15; 11:24; 27:45); (5) earth in contrast to, or paired with, heaven in Matt 5:18, 35; 6:10, 19; 11:25; 16:19 [2x]; 18:18 [2x]; 18:19; 23:9; 24:30, 35; 28:18; (6) the inhabited globe and its inhabitants, as in Matt 9:6; 10:34; 12:42; 17:25; 18:19; 23:35. This last sense is the most likely for Matt 5:13.

[17] See Nauck, "Salt as a Metaphor," 174–75.

impossible for salt to become insipid as it is for a mule to give birth. Both Jesus' saying and that of Rabbi Joshua ben Hananya may reflect a common ancient proverb.

WARNING

The saying in Matthew 5:13 concludes with a sober warning. Should such an unthinkable thing happen as salt losing its saltiness, the consequences are dire. The salt is "no longer good for anything" since it does not do what it is supposed to do. Instead of exercising its function of judging, it will itself be judged and condemned. The expression *(ek)ballō exō*, "to be thrown out," is used by Matthew, not only in 5:13, but in several other passages to speak of judgment and condemnation. Unsalty salt cast out and trampled joins the metaphors of trees that do not bear good fruit being cut down and thrown into the fire (3:10; 7:19), eyes that cause one to sin being plucked out and thrown away (5:29), weeds thrown into the fiery furnace (13:39-42), refuse tossed from a dragnet (13:48), and wedding guests not properly attired cast into the darkness outside (22:13).[18]

LIGHT OF THE WORLD

Only Matthew joins the light metaphor to the salt saying. He is also unique in equating the disciples with light. And he alone, among the canonical gospel writers, joins the saying about a city set on a mountain to that of the lamp set on a stand.[19] Matthew is not the first, however, to connect the images of light and a visible city on a mountaintop. The prophet Isaiah offers an eschatological vision of Jerusalem, set upon Mount Zion, as God's mountain, the highest mountain, to which all the nations shall stream (2:2). The passage concludes, "O house of Jacob, come, / let us walk in the light of the LORD!" (2:5).[20]

---

[18] The verbs *ballō*, "to throw," and *ekballō*, "to throw out," are used in a context of judgment in Matt 3:10; 5:26, 29; 7:19; 8:12; 13:42, 48. In Matt 18:8, 9; 22:13; 25:30 the verb is used with the preposition *exō*, "outside," as in Matt 5:13.

[19] In *Gos. Thom.* the two are juxtaposed in sayings §32 and §33.

[20] See also Isa 4:5; 60:1-22.

In the Gospel of Matthew, "mountain" is particularly significant as a place for Jesus' teaching (5:1; 24:3), divine revelation (17:1, 9), and the postresurrection commissioning of the
disciples (28:16).[21] In ancient cultures mountains were thought
to be places of proximity to God. Pagan sanctuaries were customarily built upon hills (Deut 12:2). Many of the Israelites'
encounters with God were on mountaintops.[22] Paradigmatic
was the revelation of God to Moses on Mount Sinai. Matthew's
emphasis on Jesus as teacher and revealer on a mountaintop
underscores his special theme of Jesus as the New Moses. Matthew 5:14 alludes to Jesus' disciples continuing in his footsteps
as authoritative teachers of Israel.

In a context of polemics with their Jewish neighbors, and
competing claims for authoritative interpretation of the Law,
Matthew stresses for his community, "*You* are the light of the
world."[23] Jesus' followers claim to carry forward the covenant of
God with Israel that made them "a light for the nations" (Isa
42:6). There is also a political twist. Cicero (*Cataline* 4.6) described
Rome as a "light to the whole world." Jesus' saying asserts, not
the imperial domination system, but his beatitudinal way of life,
carried forth by his disciples, is the "light of the world."

Just as the city cannot be hidden, a lamp is not lit and then
immediately extinguished (5:15). In a one-room, windowless
Palestinian house, an oil lamp set on a stand could illumine
the whole house. It would be unthinkable to waste precious
fuel by lighting a lamp only to snuff it out right away. Using a
vessel (*modios*, "bushel basket") to put out the light would prevent emission of dangerous sparks.

WITNESS TO THE WORLD

The two images, city set on a mountain, and lamp on a
stand in a house, speak of the all-encompassing nature of the

---

[21] In Matthew *oros*, "mountain," appears 16 times, as compared with 11
times in Mark, 12 times in Luke, and 4 times in John.

[22] Exod 19:20; 34:2, 29; Deut 10:1; 11:29; 1 Sam 7:1; 1 Kgs 18:42; 1 Chr 16:39-40.

[23] From the context of Mark 4:21 and Luke 8:16 the lamp would seem to be
the word revealed to the disciples, which they are to proclaim. This meaning is
clearer in *Gos.Thom.* §33.

disciples' witness. Not only do they shine forth for all *(pasin)* in their own household, i.e., members of the believing community, but for the whole world. Unlike the fourth evangelist, Matthew does not use "world," *kosmos,* to signify all that opposes the gospel.[24] Rather, it is the habitation of humans, where the gospel is proclaimed (Matt 26:13).

The concluding verse (v. 16) equates "light" with good works.[25] What the disciples are, "light" (v. 14), is known by visible good deeds. This stress on the ethics of discipleship is found repeatedly in Matthean parables.[26] The purpose of the good deeds is that they lead to praise of God (v. 16). And so, the metaphors of salt and light now converge to point in one direction. Both salt and light are most effective when they draw attention, not to themselves, but to something beyond themselves. When used in seasoning food, salt works best when it enhances the flavor of the meal and is not even noticed by the one eating. Similarly, a well-placed lamp is one that does not itself stand out, but rather illumines well what is noteworthy in the room.[27] Just so, the effect of the disciples' good works is not to attract attention to themselves, but to point to God, who is to be glorified. If Christians are light, the luminosity is not their own, but reflects God, who is light (Pss 27:1; 26:9; Mic 7:8), and Christ, who is the "great light" seen by those who dwelt in darkness (Matt 4:16; Isa 8:23).

---

[24] In the Gospel of John the *kosmos,* "world," is set dualistically over against the divine realm (e.g., 8:23; 13:1) and is a symbol of opposition to God and God's plan of salvation for humankind (e.g., 9:39; 12:31; 16:11). The remark of W. F. Albright and C. S. Mann (*Matthew* [AB26; Garden City: Doubleday, 1971] 55) that "The function of the disciples as light is to be detached from the world, and yet their very existence is such that they cannot but exercise an influence on that world," would fit a Johannine worldview much better than a Matthean. There is no emphasis on separation of Jesus' followers from the "world" in Matthew.

[25] Similar statements are found elsewhere in the NT: Phil 2:15; Rom 2:19; Acts 13:47; and in rabbinic literature, e.g., "You are the lights of Israel" (*T. Levi* 14:3) and "Let there be light—that is the works of the righteous" (*Gen. Rab.* 2).

[26] See Donahue, *The Gospel in Parable,* 64–65.

[27] I am indebted to Rev. Paul Kollman for this insight from his homily at St. Thomas the Apostle parish in Chicago on February 4, 1996.

The meaning of Matthew 5:14-15 about the city and the lamp are much less ambiguous than the salt saying in verse 13. When these are linked, they present images of unthinkable situations: salt cannot become "unsalty"; a city on a mountain cannot be invisible; a lamp is not immediately extinguished. The disciples, who are salt, likewise, cannot cease to season, preserve, purify, and judge. As light, they cannot be unseen; nor can their witness be snuffed out.

"YOUR HEAVENLY FATHER"

Matthew 5:16 is the first of many references in the First Gospel to God as "your heavenly Father." Only in the Gospel of John is "Father" found on the lips of Jesus more frequently.[28] In Matthew, Jesus speaks to his disciples about "your Father in heaven" ten times;[29] "your Father" eight times;[30] and teaches them to pray to God as "our Father" (6:9). When speaking of his own relationship with God, Jesus refers to "my Father in heaven" nine times;[31] "my Father" seven times;[32] and "the Father" four times.[33] He addresses God, "Father, Lord of heaven and earth" (11:25) and "Father" (11:26). He speaks of the Son of Humanity coming "in the glory of his Father" (16:27) and of the righteous shining like the sun "in the kingdom of their Father" (13:43). The expression "your heavenly Father" is unique to Matthew with the exception of Mark 11:25.

The frequent, almost exclusive, use of the metaphor "Father" for God in Matthew's Gospel presents a serious difficulty for many contemporary believers. Preachers have a crucial role to play in expanding the language and images we use for God. It is important that preachers understand the theological

---

[28] In the Gospel of John Jesus speaks about or addresses God as "Father" one hundred seventeen times; in Matthew forty-two; in Luke seventeen; and in Mark four times.

[29] Matt 5:16, 45, 48; 6:1, 14, 26, 32; 7:11; 18:14; 23:9.

[30] Matt 6:4, 6[2x], 8, 15, 18; 10:20, 29.

[31] Matt 7:21; 10:32, 33; 12:50; 15:13; 16:17; 18:10, 19, 35.

[32] Matt 11:27; 20:23; 25:34; 26:29, 39, 42, 53.

[33] Matt 11:27 (2x); 24:36; 28:19.

and pastoral difficulties that ensue when God is spoken of predominantly or exclusively as "Father."

First, it is important to remember that all language about God is metaphorical. No word or phrase or image ever captures the full reality of God. And the Bible provides a rich variety of metaphors for God. Some are nonhuman images: God as rock (Deut 32:15), a consuming fire (Deut 4:24), a lion carrying off its prey (Hos 5:14), a mother eagle giving her nestlings refuge under her wings (Deut 32:11-12; Ps 91:4). Human metaphors for God are both male and female: shepherd (Psalm 23), warrior (Ps 78:65), king (Ps 5:2), a woman giving birth (Deut 32:18; Isa 42:14), a mother caring for her child (Isa 49:14-16; 66:12-13), a midwife (Ps 22:10-11; Isa 66:9), to name a few.

All these images say something about what God is like, but none adequately expresses the fullness of divinity. God is more than any words can say. Yet *which* of the images we choose to speak about God is immensely important, particularly when it is a human metaphor. Although we assert theologically that God has no gender, human metaphors for God are gendered. The difficulty arises when we speak of God in exclusively or predominantly male images. Because the metaphors work in two directions, when we use only male images for God, then being male is equated with being God-like; being female is not being like God. But the Scriptures clearly state that both male and female are created in the image of God (Gen 1:27).

Because the gospels present Jesus speaking so frequently of God as "Father" and teaching his disciples to do likewise (Matt 6:9-13 // Luke 11:1-4), many Christians believe that this is the term *par excellence* revealed by God through Jesus. Joachim Jeremias[34] was quite influential in reinforcing this idea. He made four assertions: (1) "*ʾAbba*" represents a special use of Jesus that was central to his teaching; (2) "*ʾAbba*" derived from baby talk and expressed a special kind of intimacy with God; (3) Jesus' address of God as "father" was distinct from the practice of other Jews; and (4) from the usage of the early Church.

---

[34] Joachim Jeremias, *The Prayers of Jesus* (Philadelphia: Fortress, 1967) 11–65.

There is still much scholarly debate over Jeremias' conclusions. Newer finds and re-examination of known texts show that the address of God as "Father" was not unique to Jesus. It is found in the Hebrew Scriptures, several Qumran texts, Philo, Josephus, and rabbinic literature.[35] That "father" was an important term for God in the early church is clear not only from the Gospels, but also from Romans 8:15 and Galatians 4:6, where Paul says that the Spirit helps the believer pray, "Abba! Father!"

The three times that the Aramaic word *ʾabbā* appears in the New Testament (Mark 14:36; Rom 8:15; Gal 4:6) it is immediately followed by the Greek translation, *patēr*. All other occurrences of "father" in the New Testament are in Greek. The preservation of the Aramaic word *ʾabbā* in texts of Greek-speaking communities may well be a recollection of Jesus' own use. However, because of the nature of the Gospels,[36] and the fact that Jesus' first followers also spoke Aramaic, it is not possible to prove definitively that the term derived directly from Jesus.[37] The notion that *ʾabbā* originated from baby talk has been disproved on linguistic grounds.[38] As for conveying intimacy, whenever

---

[35] Mary Rose D'Angelo ("*ABBA* and 'Father': Imperial Theology and the Jesus Traditions," *JBL* 111/4 [1992] 611–30) cites the following examples: Sir 23:1,4; Wis 2:16-20; 14:3; 3 Macc 6:3-4, 7-8; Tobit 13:4; 4Q372 1.16; 4Q460; fragment 2 of the *Apocalypse of Ezekiel*; Jos. *Ant.* 2.6.8 §152; Philo, *Op. mund.* 10,21,72-75; *m. Yoma* 8:9; *b. Taʾan.* 25b. Joseph A. Fitzmyer ("*ʾAbbā* and Jesus' Relation to God" in *According to Paul* [New York: Paulist, 1993] 47–63), however, makes the distinction that the citations from the Hebrew Scriptures and Qumran attest forms of the Hebrew *ʾāb*, not the Aramaic *ʾabbā*. Moreover, in these texts God is spoken of as Father of *corporate* or *national* Israel (emphasis added). Finally, the rabbinic references are of a later date than the New Testament texts. He concludes, "there is no evidence in the literature of pre-Christian first-century Palestinian Judaism that *ʾabbā* was used in any sense as a personal address for God by an individual Jew" and for Jesus to do so is something new (p. 55).

[36] There are three stages in the transmission of the Gospels: (1) Jesus' actions and teaching; (2) several decades of oral preaching of Jesus' words and deeds by his followers; (3) the written tradition. The written tradition preserves how Jesus' early followers understood and adapted his message to the needs of their day.

[37] As D'Angelo notes ("*ABBA*," 615), no one attributes the Aramaic expression *maranatha* (Rev 22:20) to Jesus.

[38] James Barr, "*ʾAbbā* and the Familiarity of Jesus' Speech," *Theology* 91 (1988) 173–79; Fitzmyer, "*ʾAbbā* and Jesus' Relation to God," 47–63.

"Father" appears as a title for God in ancient Jewish and Christian literature it always occurs in a context where a petitioner is seeking refuge from affliction or looking for assurance of forgiveness. It is God's *power* and providence as "Father" that is invoked, not intimacy or tenderness. When early Christians, living under Roman imperial rule, invoked God as "Father," they presented a challenge to imperial authority. They were saying, somewhat subversively, that God, not the emperor, who claimed the title *pater patriae,* was the supreme power for them.

Not all the questions about the historical Jesus' use of "Father" for God can be resolved with certitude. Nonetheless, there are several important implications. First, the belief that Jesus had a unique relationship with God does not depend on whether or not he called God "Father," nor on whether he addressed God in a unique way. Nor does it diminish God in any way if we use terms other than "Father." In fact, we say more, not less, about God when we expand our repertoire of divine images and terms of address.

Second, to insist on the exclusive address of God as "Father" because that was the unique term revealed by Jesus falters in several ways. One, it cannot be proven that this way of addressing God was unique to Jesus or central to his teaching.[39] Two, it overlooks other images Jesus used when speaking of God. The parables of the woman mixing bread dough (Matt 13:33 // Luke 13:20-21), the woman searching for the lost coin (Luke 15:8-10), and the widow persistently pursuing justice (Luke 18:1-8)[40] provide examples of female images of God in Jesus' teaching. These words of Jesus are no less revelatory of God than the times he calls God "Father." Three, it is Jesus himself who is the supreme revelation of God, not the metaphor "Father." Four, it is eclectic literalism to single out addressing God as "Father" as the most important part of the gospel to which Christians must literally adhere. When it comes to other words of Jesus, such as "turn the other cheek"

---

[39] "Father" cannot be said to be central to Jesus' teaching about God in the Gospel of Mark, for example, where the term occurs only four times.

[40] See below, pp. 111–12 and B. Reid, *Parables for Preachers. Year C* (Collegeville: The Liturgical Press, 2000) 186–91; 227–36.

(Matt 5:39), "love your enemies" (Matt 5:44), "Go, sell what you have, and give to (the) poor" (Mark 10:21), we allow much more readily for less literal interpretations.

Even if we could determine with certitude that Jesus called God "Father," that would not settle the issue for today. We would still need to grapple with the meaning this image conveys in contemporary Church and society. For the early Jews and Christians invoking God as "Father" called upon divine power and authority in contrast to that claimed by the emperor. That is far from its meaning today. The naming of God as "Father" serves to absolutize a patriarchal world view, transferring male dominance from earth to heaven.[41] In order to challenge systems of domination in our day, as Jesus did, we must invoke God by other names than "Father."

The task of Christians in every age is to discern what it means in a new context to be faithful to the words and deeds of Jesus. Just as Christians of the last century determined that abolition of slavery was being most faithful to the gospel, even though Jesus' teachings presumed the institution of slavery, so today we face the challenge of eliminating sexism and systems of domination, though these are woven into the fabric of the Gospels.

Finally, stressing the loving, intimate, caring aspects of fatherhood is not a satisfactory solution. When it is asserted that "Father" is not meant as dominating or patriarchal, men gain their feminine side, but women gain nothing. The male image of God remains firmly in place, only made more appealing.[42] Benevolent patriarchy is still patriarchy.[43]

One last difficulty regarding the phrase "your heavenly Father" is that speaking of God as "heavenly" keeps the divine at a distance. It emphasizes God as transcendent, removed from the human realm. Repeated or exclusive use of "your heavenly Father" not only reinforces patriarchy, but diminishes the sense of "Emmanuel, which means God is with us." (Matt 1:23).

---

[41] Phyllis Trible, "God the Father," *TToday* 37 (1980) 118.

[42] Elizabeth Johnson, *She Who Is* (New York: Crossroad, 1992) 49.

[43] Ibid., 34.

PREACHING POSSIBILITIES

In the context of the other readings (Isa 58:7-10; Ps 112:4-7, 8a, 9; 1 Cor 2:1-5) for the fifth Sunday of Ordinary Time, it is the theme of light that is most salient. The first reading is an excerpt from a section of Isaiah that exhorts Israel to true fasting. It defines the fasting that God desires as, "Setting free the oppressed, / breaking every yoke; / Sharing your bread with the hungry, / sheltering the oppressed and the homeless; / Clothing the naked when you see them, / and not turning your back on your own" (Isa 58:6-7). The consequence is, "Then your light shall break forth like the dawn" (58:8). For Christians in a post-Epiphany season, the emphasis is not on fasting, but on the light that shines forth.[44] It carries forward the Epiphany theme of Christ our light, a light now manifest in the righteous deeds of Christians.

Whereas the gospel does not specify how it is that Jesus' disciples are light, the first reading gives concrete examples. The text from Isaiah emphasizes not only that light shines forth from those who perform righteous deeds, but also such persons themselves experience light that rises for them in the darkness (58:10). The Responsorial Psalm also affirms that God is light for the upright, who in turn radiate light in darkness.

The preacher might take direction from the meaning of *mōrainō* in the gospel, which links "unsaltiness" and "utter foolishness," to encourage contemporary believers that it is unthinkable that they be anything but what they are called to be as disciples. Just as salt cannot cease to be salty, so they cannot cease to be the sign of God's presence in the world. Like salt, they draw out the liveliness and savor of God's love in the world; they preserve the witness of that enduring love, and they are a sign of judgment to all that is opposed to God's rule. The preacher might speak a word of warning along with this word of encouragement: just as salt does not cease to be salt, its effectiveness can be diluted. So also with disciples. He or she might name some contemporary sources of dissipation in

[44] Reginald Fuller, *Preaching the Lectionary* (Collegeville: The Liturgical Press, 1984) 117–18.

our culture, such as accommodation to acquisitiveness and materialism, or dispersal of energies that could be corralled for prayer and good works.

A homilist might also develop the notion that neither salt nor light call attention to themselves, but are most effective when they are not noticed. Just so, the good that disciples embody and put into practice points not to themselves, but serves to glorify God.

CHAPTER FIVE

Two Builders
(Matt 7:21-27)

Ninth Sunday of Ordinary Time

Thursday of the First Week of Advent (Matt 7:21, 24-27)

Thursday of the Twelfth Week of Ordinary Time
(Matt 7:21-29)

Jesus said to his disciples:
"Not everyone who says to me, 'Lord, Lord,'
will enter the kingdom of heaven,
but only the one who does the will of my Father in heaven.
Many will say to me on that day,
'Lord, Lord, did we not prophesy in your name?
Did we not drive out demons in your name?
Did we not do mighty deeds in your name?'
Then I will declare to them solemnly,
'I never knew you. Depart from me, you evildoers.'
"Everyone who listens to these words of mine and acts on them
will be like a wise man who built his house on rock.
The rain fell, the floods came,
and the winds blew and buffeted the house.
But it did not collapse; it had been set solidly on rock.
And everyone who listens to these words of mine
but does not act on them
will be like a fool who built his house on sand.
The rain fell, the floods came,
and the winds blew and buffeted the house.
And it collapsed and was completely ruined."

LITERARY CONTEXT

The parable of the Two Builders (vv. 24-27) concludes Matthew's Sermon on the Mount. It employs a common parabolic device: the contrast of two opposite characters, which invites the hearer to chose the preferred way. The three verses preceding the parable (vv. 21-23) offer a related, but slightly different, contrast.

THE FINAL JUDGMENT

The first three verses place us at the moment of eschatological crisis. "On that day" in v. 22 is an allusion to the day of final judgment. This phrase appears often in the prophetic literature of the First Testament in reference to the day on which Yahweh would be manifest in power and glory.[1] While Israel expected this to be a glorious day when Yahweh would overturn their enemies, the prophets spoke of it as a day of judgment for Israel (Amos 5:18-20) and a day of wrath with cosmic consequences (Joel 2:1-2, 30-31). The day brings restoration, however, for those who heed the call to repentance (Joel 3:1). In the New Testament "that day" is the day when the Son of Humanity[2] comes with power and glory (Matt 24:30, 36; 24:42; Luke 17:24).

SAYING "LORD, LORD"

The first verses of this gospel pericope (vv. 21-23) contrast saying "Lord, Lord," with doing the will of God.[3] There are several ways in which hearers of the Gospel of Matthew have encountered saying "Lord, Lord." First, there are numerous healing stories in which the person who is suffering, or another who intercedes for them, approaches Jesus and addresses him as "Lord": a leper (8:2); a centurion on behalf of

---

[1] Isaiah, Jeremiah, Ezekiel, Hosea, Joel, Amos, Obadiah, Micah, Zephaniah, Haggai, and Zechariah all prophesy about "that day."

[2] See below, pp. 101–02 on "Son of Humanity."

[3] A similar contrast is set up in the parable of the Two Sons in Matt 21:28-32. See chap. 11.

his servant (8:6, 8); the storm-tossed disciples (8:25); two men who were blind (9:28 and 20:30, 31, 33); Peter, as he ventures onto the water (14:28) and then becomes fearful (14:30); a Canaanite woman pleading for her daughter (15:22, 25, 27); the father of a boy suffering from epilepsy (17:15). In each of these incidents, the supplicant implores Jesus as "Lord," to use his power to alleviate their suffering. In this context the warning in Matthew 7:21 is that one who would enter into God's reign must not only recognize and call upon Jesus' saving power when in need, but must himself or herself be actively engaged in deeds that manifest the will of God.

Alternatively, Matthew may be alluding to a context of worship. From Paul's letters we know that "Jesus is Lord" was a common liturgical acclamation of early Christians (Rom 10:9; 1 Cor 12:3; Phil 2:11). In light of this, Matthew 7:21 asserts that a lasting relationship with Jesus requires much more than simply proclaiming him as "Lord," or regularly participating in liturgical gatherings. Doing God's will must accompany such proclamation.

In the context of final judgment, Matthew's use of "Lord" in 7:21 casts Jesus in the role of eschatological judge, the one who decides definitively who will enter into the divine realm and who will not (as also Matt 25:11, 37, 44).

ADDRESSING JESUS AS "LORD"

The book of Exodus recounts that YHWH was the name revealed by God when Moses insisted on knowing the divine name (Exod 3:14). Out of reverence, pious Jews never pronounce this name. In Hebrew the four lettered YHWH (meaning roughly, "I AM the One who causes to be") is written without vowel pointing, reinforcing that it is unpronounceable. In oral reading of a text where YHWH is written, a Jew would pronounce "Adonai," meaning "Lord." New Testament texts often refer to God as "Lord."[4] In one of Jesus' prayers he

---

[4] In Matthew's Gospel see 1:20, 22, 24; 2:13, 15, 19; 5:33; 21:9; 22:37; 23:39; 27:10; 28:2.

addresses God, "Father, Lord of heaven and earth" (Matt 11:25 // Luke 10:21).

A significant step was taken by early Christians after the resurrection when they applied the same term, "Lord," (*kyrios* in Greek; *mārê'* or *māryā'* in Aramaic) to Jesus.[5] However, the Greek address, *kyrie,* does not always carry a religious significance. It was a term of respect, proper for speaking to teachers. When people called Jesus *kyrie* during his earthly ministry, it was a polite form of address, such as "Sir," that did not carry connotations of divinity.[6] In a number of instances the evangelists retroject this postresurrection title into the phase of Jesus' earthly ministry.[7] It is likely that the title was first applied to Jesus in reference to his return at the parousia (as in Matt 24:42). We see this use in the early Christian Aramaic prayer, *māranā' thā',* "Our Lord come!" preserved in Greek form in 1 Corinthians 16:22.[8]

For contemporary believers "Lord" is still a very popular term of address both for God and for Christ. Yet today there are serious difficulties with this address.[9] In English, the term evokes an image of feudal times replete with lords and ladies and courtly airs. Although there is a certain romantic fascina-

---

[5] In Matthew 3:3; 4:7,10 the evangelist applies to Jesus texts from Isaiah and Deuteronomy where "Lord" had originally referred to God.

[6] For this reason the *NRSV* translates *kyrie* as "Sir," not "Lord" when addressed to Jesus at Mark 7:28; John 4:11, 15, 19, 49; 5:7; 12:21. In addition to these instances the *NAB* (with revised NT) translates *kyrie* as "Sir" at John 6:34; 8:11; 9:36; 20:15. Pilate is addressed as *kyrie,* "Sir," by the chief priests and Pharisees at Matt 27:63.

[7] In addition to the many gospel texts in which Jesus is addressed as *kyrie,* there are those in which the earthly Jesus is called "the Lord," e.g., Mark 5:19; 11:3; Luke 1:43; 7:13, 19; 10:1, 41; 11:39; 12:42; 13:15; 17:5, 6; 18:6; 19:8, 31, 34; 22:61; John 6:23; 11:2.

[8] As a christological title "Lord" was a favorite of the apostle Paul—it occurs some 250 times in the letters attributed to him! On the background of the title see further Joseph A. Fitzmyer, "New Testament *Kyrios* and *Maranatha* and Their Aramaic Background," in *To Advance the Gospel: New Testament Studies* (2d ed.; The Biblical Resource Series; Grand Rapids: Eerdmans, 1998) 218–35; "The Semitic Background of the New Testament *Kyrios*-Title," *A Wandering Aramean* (SBLMS 25; Chico, Calif.: Scholars Press, 1979) 115–42.

[9] See Gail Ramshaw, *God Beyond Gender. Feminist Christian God-Language* (Minneapolis: Fortress, 1995) 47–58.

tion with royalty, the question must be posed: What are the effects of using this language for God and Christ?

The original Anglo-Saxon word "lord" denoted the male authority figure who was obligated to provide food and protection for his community. In the Middle Ages it acquired its connotation of feudal power. What is problematic about using "Lord" for God or Christ today is that the term is androcentric, archaic, and domination-oriented. While the divine name YHWH or "I AM" has no gender, "Lord" is always male. Whereas all language about God is metaphorical, and no one term captures all that God is, it is vitally important which metaphors are used. When exclusively male terminology is used of God then God is less fully encountered and females are not perceived as equally made in God's image (Gen 1:27). Moreover, "Lord" derives from an economic system in which a powerful man was looked to as provider for his subservient vassals. More often medieval times found the reverse was true: powerful lords consumed disproportionately the produce of peasants. However, the issue is not whether lords were benevolent or abusive. The problem is that the term "Lord" reinforces patterns of inequality and domination.

The present day challenge is to find or create language that is able to express the idea of divine providence, mercy, and power in ways that do not support earthly systems of domination and submission. One proposal, offered by the National Council of Churches, is to use "the SOVEREIGN ONE" to render the Hebrew YHWH and "the Sovereign Jesus Christ" for *kyrios*.[10]

Another proposed title is "the Living One."[11] This phrase has the advantage of encompassing both genders and captures

[10] This proposal was made by the committee of the NCC in their inclusive language revision of the Revised Standard Version. See *An Inclusive-Language Lectionary*, ed. the Inclusive-Language Lectionary Committee, Division of Education and Ministry, National Council of the Churches of Christ in the U.S.A. (Atlanta: John Knox, 1984) 10–11. It should be noted, however, that this is not an entirely acceptable solution. Many African American Christians, for example, insist that calling both God and Jesus "Lord" is essential for their piety, and that for them it is liberating to address God, not white masters, as "Lord."

[11] Gail Ramshaw, *God Beyond Gender*, 54–57. She also suggests "the Name" and "I AM" as more moderate proposals (pp. 57–58).

the life-giving and life-sustaining power of "I AM." Further, it speaks of God's power to release all from suffering and death, expressed in and exercised by Christ, who is also well-named, "the Living One."

It is a delicate business to try to alter long-used, cherished names of God. It is extremely important for preachers to understand the genesis of our names for God and how language about God and Christ functions in the contemporary context. The preacher plays a critical role in either reinforcing the *status quo* or opening up new horizons. Attentive, consistent use of inclusive and liberating names for God and Christ in the liturgy works best when accompanied by respectful and clear adult education. The ideal is a community that can study together and wrestle jointly with misgivings and apprehensions, while clearly journeying toward liberating praxis in worship.

DOING THE WILL OF GOD

The positive pole in the contrast in Matthew 7:21 is doing "the will of my Father in heaven."[12] What, precisely, does this mean? How does a believer know what is God's will? There are four other times in which the Matthean Jesus speaks of the will of his "Father." The first is the episode in which Jesus teaches his disciples to pray, "Our Father . . . your will be done, / on earth as in heaven" (6:9-10). Phrased in a theological passive, the prayer asks that God accomplish the divine will on earth as in heaven, without giving specifics of how humans participate in this task.

In another episode Jesus' mother and siblings search him out and Jesus assures his disciples that "whoever does the will of my heavenly Father is my brother, and sister, and mother" (12:50). Here Jesus assures his disciples that doing God's will, not blood relationship, cements familial bonds with Jesus. Again, what constitutes doing the will of God is not spelled out.

The final two instances do speak more directly about what is involved in doing God's will. In Matthew 18:14 Jesus concludes the parable of the lost sheep, saying, "In just the

---

[12] See above, pp. 55–59 on "my Father in heaven."

same way, it is not the will of your heavenly Father that one of these little ones be lost." The Matthean context makes this parable an admonition to church leaders (disciples in 18:1) to seek after any "little ones" (v. 10) who go astray. Doing God's will is prizing the most insignificant one to such a degree that a Christian leader is willing to risk going away from the rest of the "flock" to search after the one who has wandered off. Upon gathering that one in, a joy of exponential proportion fills the person who does God's will.

The last example is a sobering one. In Gethsemane, three times Jesus prays, "My Father, if it is possible, let this cup pass from me; yet, not as I will, but as you will." (26:39, 42, 44). As the gospel reaches its climax, God's will is manifest in Jesus' passion and death. It is not that God desires suffering and death; rather, passion and death is the consequence of having lived a life relentlessly pursuing a ministry centered on God's desire for life and good for all. Just as Jesus alienated the powerful by preaching God's will for life for all, anyone following in his footsteps inevitably faces persecution, and even death. That God's will is always for life to the full is most dramatically seen in the power of The Living One over even death itself.

BOTH/AND

From the contrast set up in verse 21, it would seem that the way to assure a positive outcome at the final judgment is to do the kinds of things that Jesus did: prophesy, drive out demons, and other mighty deeds.[13] Yet verse 23 predicts a dire fate for those who do these things. "I never knew you"[14]

---

[13] That people regarded Jesus as a prophet is asserted in Matt 14:5; 21:11, 46. For Jesus' ministry of exorcising demons see Matt 4:24; 8:16, 28-34; 9:32-34; 12:22-32; 15:22; 17:14-21. His mighty deeds *(dynameis)* are spoken of in Matt 11:20, 21, 23; 13:54, 58. In Matt 10:5-15 Jesus commissions the Twelve to do likewise: proclaim the kingdom of heaven, cure the sick, raise the dead, cleanse lepers, and drive out demons.

[14] In Hebrew, to "know" another is to have sexual relations, e.g., Gen 4:1, 16, 25; Luke 1:34. Matt 7:23 speaks of no relationship, intimate or otherwise. The solemn declaration, "I never knew you" (v. 23) is also echoed in Peter's insistent denial, "I do not know the man!" (Matt 26:69-75).

indicates that though the outward deeds correspond to those that Jesus did, those performing them had no relationship with him.

The final verdict is, "Depart from me, you evildoers" (v. 23).[15] The phrase translated "evildoers" is literally, "doers of lawlessness" *(hoi ergazomenoi tēn anomian)*.[16] It is startling that those who appear to be doing good works (prophesying, driving out demons, doing mighty deeds) are actually doing evil. A similar charge is lodged against the scribes and Pharisees in Matthew 23:28. Jesus criticizes them because they appear righteous on the outside, but inside "are filled with hypocrisy and evildoing *(anomia).*" The inner disposition is what distinguishes between righteousness and lawlessness. But neither is it sufficient to have an inner disposition that acclaims Christ's sovereign power (v. 21). *Both* proclamation *and* doing God's will are necessary to enter into God's eternal realm.

In the context of Matthew's community, the charge of "lawlessness" relates to following Jesus' interpretation of the Law, not rampant disregard for the Law.[17] As Jesus found himself in conflict with religious leaders of his day over his interpretations of the Law, so too did his followers clash with Jews of the synagogue, and other Christians as well, over their various understandings of righteousness. Whereas other Jews would see Matthean Christians as "lawless," this gospel passage asserts that one who acclaims Jesus' authoritative power in word and deed is one who is truly observant of the Law.

---

[15] In Psalm 6:9 "Depart from me all evildoers" is a prayer of one in distress.

[16] The term *anomia* is unique to Matthew among the Gospels. It appears in Matt 13:41; 23:38; 24:12. Matt 13:41 is quite similar to 7:23. It describes how, at the end time, "doers of lawlessness" are collected and thrown into the fiery furnace by the angels of the Son of Humanity, in contrast to the righteous who "will shine like the sun in the kingdom of their Father" (13:43). Matt 24:12, speaking of the calamities that will occur at the end time, warns that because of the "increase of evildoing *(anomia)*" the love of many will grow cold.

[17] See above, pp. 39–41 on "The Role of the Law" in Matthew.

TWO BUILDERS

The parable of the Two Builders[18] (vv. 24-27) also contrasts two characters, but in it the point shifts from "saying and doing" to "hearing and doing." The simile is straightforward. Its meaning is not elusive. Everyone who hears and acts on Jesus' words is likened to a person who builds a house on a rock foundation (v. 24). Such an abode does not collapse when buffeted by rain, floods, and winds. But anyone who listens yet does not act on the words of Jesus is like a fool who builds a house on sand. When the storms come it is completely ruined.

"THESE WORDS OF MINE"

This parable brings the Sermon on the Mount to a close with a choice clearly set forth. One who has heard Jesus' interpretation of the Law now faces the decision of whether to accept or reject it. This choice lay before Jesus' original audience and still confronts every person to whom the sermon has been proclaimed. "These words of mine" in verses 24 and 26 are emphatic—it is *Jesus'* interpretation of Torah that is at issue. In his own lifetime Jesus' understanding of the Law was often at odds with that of other Jewish religious leaders. And in the first decades following his death, the conflicts continued as an inner-Jewish struggle.[19] This parable advises that a wise person will choose to act on Jesus' authoritative teaching; while a fool listens but does not heed.

HEARING AND DOING

The echoes from the First Testament are unmistakable. The same two actions—hearing and doing—are required of

---

[18] Other titles for this parable include "The Two Foundations" *(NAB)* and "The House Built Upon the Rock" (Aland, *Synopsis of the Four Gospels*, 70). The source for the simile is Q; the Lukan parallel in 6:46-49 (along with vv. 43-45) is the gospel assigned for Saturday of the Twenty-Third Week of Ordinary Time. There is also a similar rabbinic story in *m.* ʾ*Abot.* 3:18.

[19] This point is reinforced in the concluding verses of the Sermon on the Mount, which are not included in the Lectionary selection: "When Jesus finished these words, the crowds were astonished at his teaching, for he taught them as one having authority, and not as their scribes" (7:28-29; see Mark 1:22).

Israel at the giving of the Law. Their response was, "All that the LORD has said, we will heed and do" (Exod 24:7). The close connection between hearing and doing is again underscored in Moses' final instructions for the reading of the Law. He charges Joshua to read the law aloud in the presence of all Israel "that they may hear it and learn it, and so fear the LORD, your God, and carefully observe all the words of this law" (Deut 31:11-12). For Jesus' followers, it is his words that require the same response.

The choice is not neutral, that is, Jesus' interpretation is not one good option among many possible. One who hears Jesus' words but does not act on them comes to a ruinous end (v. 27). The choice is between life and death. And in the context of final judgment (vv. 21-23), it is eternal life or ultimate perdition.

BUILDING ON ROCK

As is often the case in the New Testament, language used of God in the First Testament is now applied to Jesus. The image of rock is used frequently in the Hebrew Scriptures to speak of God's steadfast faithfulness, strength, and protection (e.g., Deut 32:4, 18, 31; Pss 18:2, 31; 27:5; 28:1; Isa 17:10). In the Christian Scriptures Matthew 7:24 is one of several instances[20] where the rock is now said to be Jesus.

RAIN, FLOODS, AND WIND

In Matthew's version of this parable, the staccato of the short phrases, "the rain fell, the floods came, and the winds blew" (v. 25) gives the sense of a storm where nature's fury is

---

[20] E.g., Paul identifies the "spiritual rock" from which the Israelites drank during the Exodus as Christ in 1 Cor 10:4. The first letter of Peter invites Christians, "Come to him [Christ], a living stone . . ." (2:4-5). Closer still to the image in Matt 7:24-27 is 1 Cor 3:10-11 where Paul says, "According to the grace of God given to me, like a wise master builder I laid a foundation, and another is building upon it. But each one must be careful how he builds upon it, for no one can lay a foundation other than the one that is there, namely, Jesus Christ." Note that in each of these instances Jesus himself is the foundation, whereas in Matt 7:24-27 it is Jesus' teaching that is the foundation.

unleashed in relentless blasts of water and wind.[21] The storm is usually thought to represent the trials in the life of a disciple[22] or the tribulations that accompany the coming of the king-dom.[23] Yet each of these weather phenomena is also a symbol of God's action in the world.[24] In arid Palestine rain is a bless-ing, as in Matthew 5:45, where God's inclusive love is known because God makes rain to fall on the just and the unjust alike.[25] So too, was the flood in Noah's time a sign of God's purifying action in the world. Matthew 24:37-39 likens the time of the coming of the Human One to the days before the flood in Noah's time. Finally, wind is associated with the action of the Spirit. The Greek word *pneuma* means both "wind" and "spirit."[26] Thus, the rain, floods, and winds in Matthew 7:25, 27 may represent not trials and tribulations, but God's action in the world, whereby the upright are distinguished from the "lawless" (v. 23).[27] The former are seen to be set firmly on the "rock" foundation of hearing and doing Jesus' words, while the latter collapse in utter ruin.

---

[21] By contrast, Luke 6:48 gives more attention to the process of digging a deep foundation, and speaks only of a flood arising.

[22] E.g., Madeline Boucher, *The Parables* (NTM 7; Wilmington: Glazier, 1981) 129–31.

[23] Daniel Harrington, *Matthew* (SacPag 1; Collegeville: The Liturgical Press, 1991)109.

[24] Robert Winterhalter and George W. Fisk, *Jesus' Parables: Finding our God Within* (New York: Paulist, 1993) 188.

[25] See also Deut 11:10-17 for a description of the gift of rain that God will give Israel in the Promised Land.

[26] In Matt 7:25 the verb *epneusan,* "blew," is from the same root as the noun *pneuma,* "wind," or "spirit." "The winds" is rendered *hoi anemoi* in Matt 7:25. The close association between "wind" and "the Spirit" is seen in Acts 2:2, where the coming of the Spirit at Pentecost is accompanied by "a noise like a strong driving wind," *pnoēs biaias.* In Greek the term *pnoē,* "breath, or wind" passes over into the same meaning as *pneuma.* Another example is John 3:8, where there is a double word play on *tēn phōnēn* and *to pneuma:* "the voice of the spirit" or "the sound of the wind."

[27] In Ezek 13:10-16 there is a similar image of flooding rain and storm winds sent by God that lay bare the foundations of a whitewashed wall. This exposes the false prophets who have been wrongly predicting peace to Israel in the face of the Chaldeans.

RABBINIC PARALLELS

Several rabbinic parallels to this parable show that questions regarding the relationship between hearing and doing, wisdom and works, study and good deeds, were rife in developing Judaism and Christianity. A parable attributed to Rabbi Elisha ben Avuyah (ca. 110 C.E.) also tells of two builders: "A man who has good deeds to his credit and has also studied much Torah, to what is he like? To one who builds [a structure and lays] stones below [for the foundation] and bricks above, so that however much water may collect at the side it will not wash it away. But the man who has no good deeds to his credit, though he has studied Torah, to what is he like? To one who builds [a structure and lays] bricks first [for the foundation] and then stones above, so that even if only a little water collects it at once undermines it."[28]

This rabbinic story follows the same contours as the gospel parable, but the debate is framed in terms of Torah study plus good deeds. The conclusion is the same in both: action must result from study of Torah for the rabbis; from heeding Jesus' interpretation of Torah for Christians.

Another close rabbinic parallel is found in *Pirqe ʾAbot* 3.18: "He whose wisdom exceeds his works, to what may he be likened? To a tree whose branches are numerous but whose roots are few. The wind comes along and uproots it and sweeps it down. But he whose works exceed his wisdom, to what may he be likened? To a tree whose branches are few but whose roots are numerous. Then even if all the winds of the world come along and blow against it they cannot stir it from its place."[29]

Note that this parable formulates the question in quantitative terms. The issue is the balance between wisdom and works.[30] This is a different question than that posed by the gospel parable. The choice in Matthew 7:24-27 does not in-

---

[28] *ʾAbot R. Nat.* ver. a, chap. 24, quoted from Brad Young, *Jesus and His Jewish Parables* (New York: Paulist, 1989) 257.

[29] Boucher, *The Parables*, 129–31.

[30] Other rabbinic texts (e.g., *b.Sanh.* 74a; *b.Qidd.* 40b) formulate the question in terms of which is more important: study or action?

volve the correct proportion of action to hearing; the choice is whether one will act, once having heard.

PREACHING POSSIBILITIES

The choice set before those who hear Jesus' teaching in the gospel echoes that which Moses presents to the Israelites in the first reading (Deut 11:18, 26-28). Moses offers them blessing or curse. Blessing ensues when the Israelites obey God's commandments; curse is the consequence of disobedient turning aside to other gods. The same dynamic is operative in the gospel, with obedience now defined as following Jesus' interpretation of God's commands. Obedience involves both proclamation of Jesus' sovereignty and doing God's will after the example of Jesus and in intimate relationship with him (vv. 21-23). The preacher might highlight the element of choice: that being a disciple is not a matter of drifting along in a direction once set, but rather involves repeated conscious choice to both hear and act on the word. The preacher might give concrete examples to help the hearers recognize disjunctures in their Christian lives and help them move toward further conversion. For example, if someone says their family takes primacy of place, does the amount of time they carve out to spend with family as compared to their number of work hours reflect this? If I say I believe in standing with the poor, can I name concrete instances when I actually do this? If I say I value exercise and balanced diet, how is this evident in my daily practices? If I say I believe in prayer, how often and with whom do I actually make the space to pray? Which actions that identify a disciple remain on the level of ideals that I strive toward? What help would I ask from Jesus to further bring my words and deeds into line with the call of the gospel? What would I want to start doing or saying? What would I want to stop doing or saying? Conversely, what good actions do I do routinely but without my heart being in it? What admirable deeds do I do for show? What help would I ask from Jesus to conform my heart to his as I act visibly as his disciple?

The central metaphor in the parable is the image of Jesus and his word as rock. One who listens and acts on Jesus' teaching stands on an unshakable foundation. This is also the image of God in the responsorial psalm. For those who feel buffeted by the storms of life or by the demands of gospel living, the rock image in the parable offers reassurance and encouragement. There may be an opportunity to experience God's presence in a unique way in the very midst of the turbulence. The solidity that is offered by adherence to Jesus, however, should not lead to rigidity or self-righteousness. Disciples must also be able to bend, like trees in the wind, to the beckoning of the Spirit in new ways in every age.

The second reading also connects well with the message of the parable. Romans 3:21-25, 28 is the heart of Paul's famous thesis that right relation with God no longer depends on works of the Law, but is already accomplished by Christ. Consequently, one is saved not by deeds, but by faith in Christ. At first this reading appears to stand in direct contrast to the gospel's insistence on the necessity for action following upon hearing Jesus' teaching. However, Paul in no way disregards the need for good deeds. In every letter he exhorts Christians to loving actions that flow from the gift of God that they have received. In the letter to the Galatians for example, he speaks of "faith working through love" (5:6) and of the whole law being summed up in a single commandment, "You shall love your neighbor as yourself" (5:14). Paul's point in Romans 3 is that works of the Law do not earn salvation. This is not far removed from the point in Matthew 7:22, where prophesying, driving out demons, and doing mighty deeds are no guarantee that one will enter the eschatological realm of God. Paul is emphasizing that right relation with God is a gift, already accomplished for the believer by Christ, and that good deeds flow from the acceptance of this gift. The preacher might take the lead from Paul in emphasizing that one can never boast of good deeds. The ability to perform them comes as a gift, as does the grace of a heart that embraces the Giver.

CHAPTER SIX

Sower, Seed, Soil, Harvest
(Matt 13:1-23)[1]

Fifteenth Sunday of Ordinary Time

Wednesday of the Sixteenth Week of Ordinary Time
(Matt 13:1-9)

Thursday of the Sixteenth Week of Ordinary Time
(Matt 13:10-17)

Friday of the Sixteenth Week of Ordinary Time
(Matt 13:18-23)

[On that day, Jesus went out of the house and sat down by the sea.
Such large crowds gathered around him
  that he got into a boat and sat down,
  and the whole crowd stood along the shore.
And he spoke to them at length in parables, saying:
  "A sower went out to sow.
And as he sowed, some seed fell on the path,
  and birds came and ate it up.
Some fell on rocky ground, where it had little soil.
It sprang up at once because the soil was not deep,
  and when the sun rose it was scorched,
  and it withered for lack of roots.
Some seed fell among thorns, and the thorns grew up and choked it.
But some seed fell on rich soil and produced fruit,
  a hundred or sixty or thirtyfold.

---

[1] The Lectionary offers the option of using the short form, Matt 13:1-9.

Whoever has ears ought to hear!"]
The disciples approached him and said,
    "Why do you speak to them in parables?"
He said to them in reply,
    "Because knowledge of the mysteries of the kingdom of heaven
    has been granted to you, but to them it has not been granted.
To anyone who has, more will be given and he² will grow rich;
    from anyone who has not, even what he has will be taken away.
This is why I speak to them in parables, because
    they look but do not see and hear but do not listen or understand.
Isaiah's prophecy is fulfilled in them, which says:
    You shall indeed hear but not understand,
        you shall indeed look, but never see.
    Gross is the heart of this people,
        they will hardly hear with their ears,
        they have closed their eyes,
        lest they see with their eyes
        and hear with their ears
    and understand with their hearts and be converted,
        and I heal them.

"But blessed are your eyes, because they see,
    and your ears, because they hear.
Amen, I say to you, many prophets and righteous people
    longed to see what you see but did not see it,
    and to hear what you hear, but did not hear it.

"Hear then the parable of the sower.
The seed sown on the path is the one³
    who hears the word of the kingdom without understanding it,
    and the evil one comes and steals away
    what was sown in his heart.
The seed sown on rocky ground
    is the one who hears the word and receives it at once with joy.

---

² In the Greek text, the pronouns in v. 12 are masculine singular. It is preferable in proclamation today to use the gender-inclusive plural, as does the *NRSV*:
"For to those who have, more will be given, and they will have an abundance;
but from those who have nothing, even what they have will be taken away."

³ The Greek *pantos akouontos* is both masculine and neuter singular. A
gender-inclusive translation in vv. 19, 20, 22, 23 is, "the one who hears" (*NAB*,
rev. 1986), rather than "the man who hears" (*NAB*, 1970).

But he⁴ has no root and lasts only for a time.
When some tribulation or persecution comes because of the word,
    he immediately falls away.
The seed sown among thorns is the one who hears the word,
    but then worldly anxiety and the lure of riches choke the word
    and it bears no fruit.
But the seed sown on rich soil
    is the one who hears the word and understands it,
    who indeed bears fruit and yields a hundred or sixty or thirtyfold."

LITERARY CONTEXT

The greatest concentration of parables in the Gospel of Matthew is in chapter 13, the third of Matthew's five major discourses. There are seven parables, two allegorical explanations (vv. 18-23, 36-43), and a theory of Jesus' use of parables (vv. 10-17, 34-35, 51-52). The entire chapter is proclaimed over the course of three Sundays, the fifteenth through seventeenth Sundays of Ordinary Time in Year A, and is repeated in the weekday Lectionary in the sixteenth and seventeenth weeks of Ordinary Time.

Matthew 13:1-23 has three parts: the parable proper (vv. 1-9), a discussion about Jesus' reason for speaking in parables (vv. 10-17), and a secondary interpretation of the parable (vv. 18-23). The whole of vv. 1-23 follows the Markan source (4:1-20)⁵ fairly closely, though there are significant differences in Matthew's redaction of vv. 10-17. Almost all scholars agree that the explanation (vv. 18-23) was not part of Jesus' original parable. One of the distinguishing features of the gospel parables is that they are open-ended, allowing for a variety of interpretations.⁶ Only in the case of the parable of the Sower,

---

⁴ The *NRSV* translates v. 21 more inclusively: "yet such a person has no root, but endures only for a while, and when trouble or persecution arises on account of the word, that person immediately falls away."

⁵ Neither the Markan nor the Lukan version of the parable (8:4-15) appear in the Sunday Lectionary; Mark 4:1-20 is assigned for Wednesday of the Third Week of Ordinary Time; Luke 8:4-15 is the gospel for Saturday of the Twenty-Fourth Week of Ordinary Time.

⁶ See above, pp. 8–9.

Seeds, Soil, and Harvest (Matt 13:1-9,18-23 and pars.) and that of the Weeds and the Wheat (Matt 13:24-30, 36-43) is there an allegorical explanation given in the gospel text. These are likely representative of the meaning that early Christian communities construed, not Jesus' own words.

THE TEACHER

In the Matthean version of the parable Jesus assumes the position of teacher: he sits while a large crowd gathers around him. In the First Gospel the crowds play a generally favorable role until the passion narrative (26:47, 55; 27:20).[7] They follow Jesus (4:25; 8:1), listen to his teachings (4:1; 7:28), are healed by him (12:15), and glorify God when they witness Jesus' powerful deeds (9:8, 33). It is to them that this first parable is directed.[8]

The parable allows for a variety of interpretations, depending on which "character" is chosen as the focus. It can be: The Parable of the Sower;[9] The Parable of the Seed;[10] The Parable of the Soil (the focus of the allegorical explanation in vv. 18–23); and The Parable of the Harvest.[11]

THE PARABLE OF THE SOWER

The opening line of the parable draws attention to the sower, a familiar character in rural Palestine. If Jesus' original audience were peasant farmers, who saw the sower as their landowner, they might react with disdain toward the sloppy and wasteful manner of sowing.[12] Alternatively, if they saw the

[7] See Warren Carter, "The Crowds in Matthew's Gospel," *CBQ* 55 (1993) 54–67.

[8] Matt 13:3 is the first time that the term *parabolē* appears in Matthew.

[9] So *NAB, NJB, La Nueva Biblia Latinoamericana, The Christian Community Bible*.

[10] So 1970 edition of *NAB*.

[11] The *NRSV* wisely avoids titling the parable, allowing for any of the various interpretations. The *Revised English Bible* titles the whole of chapter 13, "Parables." There are no titles in the Greek text.

[12] There is some debate whether the custom was to plow after sowing, as this parable envisions. Some ancient texts refer to plowing before sowing: Isa 28:24-26; Jer 4:3; Ezek 36:9; *Gos. Thom.* §20; Pliny, *Nat.Hist.* 18.176. Others speak of plowing after sowing: *Jub.* 11.11; *m. Šabb.* 7.2; *b. Šabb.* 73a-b.

sower as a tenant farmer or a day laborer like themselves, their reaction would be sympathetic. They would know all too well the amount of seed and effort that is expended that never bears fruit because of the difficult conditions.[13]

The sower is usually interpreted as representing God or Jesus, and the seed is the word of God.[14] From this perspective the story centers on how God acts. God is like a profligate farmer, who indiscriminately sows seed on every type of ground. The story is an illustration of God's all-inclusive love, akin to Matthew 5:45, where God is said to make the sun rise on the bad and the good, and cause rain to fall on the just and the unjust. The point is that God knowingly scatters the seed on all types of soil. God offers the word to every person, regardless of their potential for accepting it. Although not all will accept the word and bring it to fruition, it is offered to all. If the sower is Jesus, the point is the same. Jesus preaches the word to all, offering God's inclusive love indiscriminately to all kinds of people.

The exhortation to hear (v. 9)[15] recalls the *Shema*ꜥ, the prayer from Deuteronomy 6:4-5, prayed by observant Jews three times daily, "Hear, O Israel! The LORD is our God, the LORD alone! Therefore, you shall love the LORD, your God, with all your heart, and with all your soul, and with all your strength" (quoted also in Matt 22:37).[16] While this prayer underscores Israel's unique relationship with God, Jesus' parable widens the audience to whomever God now extends the graciousness that was formerly directed to Israel alone.

---

[13] John J. Pilch, *The Cultural World of Jesus. Sunday by Sunday, Cycle A* (Collegeville: The Liturgical Press, 1995) 109–11; Bruce J. Malina and Richard L. Rohrbaugh, *Social Science Commentary on the Synoptic Gospels* (Minneapolis: Fortress, 1992) 202.

[14] Mark 4:14 is clearer than Matthew in equating the seed with the word.

[15] Matthew's redaction reduces this emphasis from the Markan source. In Mark the parable begins, "Hear!" (v. 3) and concludes, "Whoever has ears to hear ought to hear" (v. 9), so that the exhortation to hear frames the whole parable.

[16] See B. Gerhardsson, "The Parable of the Sower and Its Interpretation," *NTS* 14 (1968) 165–93. For him the seed devoured by birds represents those who do not love God with their whole heart; those on rocky ground are those who do not love God with their souls; those choked by thorns are those who fail to love God with their whole might.

In the first-century Palestinian world of Jesus this crossing of boundaries and mixing of peoples would be shocking.[17] If Jesus' peasant audience has regarded the sower with hostility, seeing in him the figure of a wasteful landlord, there is a challenge to them that God can be manifest even in the one they regard as despicable. If they were to exercise God's all-inclusive love, it must extend even to one who exploits them. Note, however, that as Matthew 5:38-48 makes clear, inclusive love does not mean that exploitation goes unchallenged. Rather, it creates an opportunity for an oppressor to repent; it does not simply cut such a one off as unredeemable. Alternatively, if the peasants identify with the sower as one like themselves, the challenge is for them to understand that in their own actions they emulate God whenever their actions of sowing God's word extend beyond their own circles of friends and relations.

From the narrative perspective of the gospel text, the invitation to the crowds who are not yet followers of Jesus is to receive and respond to the gracious word he preaches. If they are Jews who think they already know and are obedient to God, Jesus invites them to expand their perception of who it is God invites to be among the chosen ones. For people in the crowd who see themselves outside the bounds of Israel, or not addressed by Israel's God, a door is now opened to them.

From the standpoint of Matthew's community the parable justifies the inclusion of marginal Jews and Gentile members among the faithful. The sower has scattered seed among those formerly not regarded as "good soil." For contemporary Christian communities that struggle with inclusivity, the parable can function the same way.

THE PARABLE OF THE SEED

If the seed is the focus of the parable, then the point shifts to the reliability of the seed to bring forth a yield. Though it appears at first that there will be no harvest, the end result confirms

---

[17] Malina and Rohrbaugh, *Social Science Commentary*, 192–94; David Rhoads, "Social Criticism: Crossing Boundaries," in *New Approaches in Biblical Studies*, ed. J. C. Anderson and S. D. Moore (Minneapolis: Fortress, 1992) 135–61.

the seed's efficacy. The parable assures that God's word does accomplish its purpose, even though much of it falls on deaf ears.

The parable may well be a recasting of Isaiah 55:10-11: "For as from the heavens the rain and the snow come down from heaven, / and do not return there until they have watered the earth, / making it bring forth and sprout, / giving seed to the sower and bread to the eater, so shall my word be that goes forth from my mouth; / it shall not return to me empty, / but it shall accomplish that which I purpose, / and succeed in the thing for which I sent it" *(NRSV)*.[18]

In the context of Jesus' ministry, the parable encourages his disciples that, despite the lack of an overwhelmingly positive response, Jesus' preaching of God's word does, finally, achieve God's purpose. In the context of Matthew's community, who question why many do not accept Jesus' interpretation of the Law as they understand it, the parable makes the same assurance of reliability. If any want to blame the quality of seed for the fact that not all of it matures (as in 13:27) the parable makes clear that the seed is not at fault. Christians today can take the same assurance from the parable; despite lack of apparent initial results, their efforts at spreading God's word will eventually bring forth fruit.

THE PARABLE OF THE HARVEST

Another point emerges if the focus of the parable is the harvest. The narrative creates a dynamic in which expectations rise with each arena of sowing. From the footpath, hopes of harvest are immediately dashed as the birds instantly devour the seed. From the rocky ground, hope springs up immediately with the sprouting seed, but, again, is short-lived. From the thorn patch, hopes endure a bit longer, as, presumably, the seed and the thorns both "grow up," only to have the thorns triumph. Finally, from the good soil comes grain that reaches maturity.

[18] C. A. Evans ("A Note on the Function of Isaiah 6:9-10 in Mark 4," *RB* 99 [1981] 234–35) analyzes the Markan version of the parable as a midrash on Isa 6:9-13 and Isa 55:10-11. See also J. W. Bowker, "Mystery and Parable: Mark 4:1-20," *JTS* 25 (1974) 300–17, who sees Mark 4:1-20 as a midrash on Isa 6:13.

But the story does more than build to an expected climax. It is not simply an assurance of eventual success in the face of repeated failure. The staggering amounts of the harvest shatter open the parable, and propel the hearer into an eschatological scenario. The image of harvest is often used to speak of the end time,[19] as is hyperbole.[20] The amounts of the harvest are astronomical. If a good harvest for a Palestinian farmer yields up to tenfold, one that produces one hundred or sixty or thirtyfold is unimaginable.[21] This abnormal tripling symbolizes the overflowing of divine fullness, which surpasses all human measure.[22]

Considered from this perspective, whether the context is Jesus' preaching, or Matthew's community, or contemporary proclamation of the gospel, the parable leaves the hearer overwhelmed at the inconceivable abundance of God's graciousness manifest in the end-times. It evokes awe and praise of God, as the miraculous harvest is clearly the work of God, surpassing anything that is possible from human efforts. A peasant farmer who has labored mightily against adverse conditions hears in this story good news of God's loving providence toward those in need and assurance of great reward in the end-time.[23]

---

[19] So also Matt 13:30, 39; 21:34, 41; Mark 4:29. The explanation of the parable of the weeds and the wheat explicitly says "the harvest is the end of the age" (Matt 13:39).

[20] Irenaeus (*Adv. Haer.* 5.33.3-4) asserts that Papias foretold that in messianic times "a grain of wheat shall bring forth 10,000 ears, and every ear shall have 10,000 grains." The rabbinic tractate *Ketub.* 111b-112a says it will take a ship to carry one grape in the messianic age.

[21] Jeremias (*The Parables of Jesus* [2d rev. ed.; New York: Scribners, 1972] p. 150, n. 84) asserts that a good harvest yields up to tenfold; an average one seven and a half. Pilch (*The Cultural World of Jesus. Cycle A,* 109) puts it at four- or fivefold for a good yield. Davies and Allison (*Matthew,* 385) question whether the amount of the harvest is meant to be fantastic. They cite Varro, *R.R.* 1.44.2, who attests that seed in Syria could yield one-hundredfold, and other texts (*Sib. Or.* 3.263-4; Theophrastus, *Hist. Plant.* 8.7.4; Strabo 15.3.11; Pliny, *N.H.* 18.21.94-5) that point in the same direction.

[22] A similar point is found in Gen 26:12, "Isaac sowed seed in that land, and in the same year reaped a hundredfold. The Lord blessed him."

[23] Pilch (*Cultural World. Cycle A,* 109) notes that if Jesus' audience heard the parable as telling of a wasteful owner who realized such an enormous profit, it

In light of Jesus' proclamation that the reign of God is already at hand (Matt 4:17), some scholars read the abundant harvest as articulating the hopes of oppressed people for a present reordering of relationships.[24] It is not just wishful dreaming for the future, but has a subversive function in the present. The bumper crop could shatter the vassal relationship between peasant and landlord. With such a surplus a farmer who formerly struggled just to eat and pay his debts could think outrageous thoughts of even buying the land himself. His oppressive servitude to the landowner could come to an end.

One detail that Matthew has altered from his source is that he speaks about the amounts of the yield in descending order: "a hundred, or sixty, or thirty-fold" (v. 8). In Mark 4:8 the scale moves upward and the dynamic in the story is explosive. Matthew's style is akin to that of Sirach 41:4 which speaks of a person living "a thousand years, a hundred, or ten."[25]

REASON FOR SPEAKING IN PARABLES (13:10-17)

Framed by the parable proper (vv. 1-9) and the allegorical explanation (vv. 18-23) is a discussion with Jesus and his disciples about his reason for speaking in parables.[26] It is this section that deviates most from the Markan source. In Mark

---

would hardly be good news. We would wonder, then, why Jesus would tell such a story that depicts the way things are in an oppressive situation without offering any hopeful alternative.

[24] E.g., Ched Myers, *Binding the Strong Man* (Maryknoll: Orbis, 1988) 177.

[25] Jeremias, *Parables*, 150. Gundry (*Matthew*, 254) suggests that Matthew puts one hundred first as the best example. The early Church Fathers allegorized the numbers. Jerome equated the one-hundredfold with chaste women, sixtyfold with widows, and thirtyfold with those married (*PL* 26.89). So also Augustine, with the exception of the hundredfold, who for him were martyrs (*PL* 35.1326). See also Theophylact in *PG* 123.532.

[26] Davies and Allison (*Matthew*, 387) note that Matt 13:1-23 follows a pattern found in the Old Testament, Jewish apocalypses, rabbinic literature, and Hermetic and Gnostic texts: (1) teaching; (2) change of scene or audience; (3) question; (4) reproach; (5) interpretation or clarification. See Zechariah 4; Mark 7:14-23; 2 Baruch 13–15; *Gos. Thom.* 42-43; *Ap. Jas.* 6–7; *Corp. Herm.* 10.6-7. In Matt 13:1-23 there is no reproach, although v. 9 may hint at it.

4:10-12 those who were around Jesus, along with the Twelve ask him about the parables (v. 10). Jesus' reply contrasts insiders with outsiders. The former are given "[t]he mystery of the kingdom of God," but to those outside, everything is in parables (v. 11). The result is that, as with the prophets, only those properly disposed hear and heed (v. 12). In Mark's Gospel, the contrast is not between Jesus' disciples and the crowd; "insiders," include any who are "around" Jesus, who hear and heed his teaching. Markan disciples are fallible followers; they constantly struggle to understand. Mark 4:1-20 warns disciples that they can become outsiders; more is required than an initial decision to follow Jesus.

Matthew, by contrast, has drawn a clear division between Jesus' disciples and the crowd in 13:10-17. It is the disciples *(hoi mathētai)* that approach Jesus, not "those present along with the Twelve" (Mark 4:10). In Matthew the disciples' request is not for Jesus to explain the parables to them; rather they ask, "Why do you speak to them [i.e., the crowd] in parables?" (v. 10). It is implied that the parables are not even directed to the disciples. Not until 13:36, where the disciples ask Jesus to explain the parable of the weeds in the field, do the disciples seem to be part of the listening audience of chapter 13. Verse 34 clarifies that the audience in vv. 24, 31, 33, is the crowd.

Jesus' reply (vv. 11-12) explains why disciples have understanding, but the crowds do not. God is the implicit subject in the theological passive construction, "to you it has been given" *(hymin dedotai)*. The knowledge that disciples have is a gift from God. Matthew then transposes and expands a verse that appears later in the Markan parables discourse (Mark 4:25), that drives the wedge even further: to one who has more, will be given, and such a one will have an abundance; but from the one who has not, even that will be taken away (v. 12).

In the context of Matthew 13:10-17 what is "given" is "knowledge of the mysteries of the kingdom of heaven" (v. 11). This is the only time that the word "mysteries" appears in the gospels (Matt 13:11 and pars.). It is the presence of God's realm in Jesus and his ministry that constitutes the "mystery."

In other Jewish sources "mystery" is associated with God's purposes for the end-times.[27]

The focus then shifts in v. 13 to the reason[28] why Jesus speaks to the others in parables. Whereas vv. 11-12 focus on God's disposition, vv. 13-17 emphasize human responsibility. Matthew quotes more fully than Mark the text from Isaiah 6:9-10, which he sees now fulfilled.[29] The effect is that the crowd is to blame for their lack of understanding. Their dull hearts, heavy ears, and closed eyes block any possibility of hearing and heeding Jesus' words. It is *because* of their unbelief that Jesus speaks in parables to those who do not heed his teaching.

Another shift occurs in vv. 16-17, with a beatitude taken from the Q source (par. Luke 10:23-24). That the disciples have received a special grace to see and hear frames the discussion of why Jesus speaks to the others in parables. Another eschatological note is sounded as Jesus contrasts the blessedness of what his disciples see and hear with what former prophets and righteous people longed for. It is a new in-breaking of the realm of God.

PARABLE OF THE SOIL (vv. 18-23)

Most scholars believe that the explanation of the parable in vv. 18-23 is a secondary interpretation by the early Church.[30] A linguistic analysis shows this to be the only instance in the Gospels of the absolute use of *ho logos*, "the

[27] E.g., Dan 2:27-28; *1 Enoch* 68.5; 103.2; 4 Ezra 10:38; 14:5; *2 Bar.* 81:4; *b. Meg.* 3a; *Tg. Ps.-J.* to Gen 49:1. See also Rom 11:26-26; 2 Thess 2:7; Rev 10:7; 17:5-7.

[28] Matthew changes Mark's *hina*, "so that," to *hoti*, "because." Mark's emphasis is on the result or the consequence of Jesus' parabolic speaking, not the reason for it.

[29] Citations from the First Testament, particularly from Isaiah, that interpret Jesus' words and actions as a fulfillment of prophecy are very frequent in Matthew. It is unusual, however, to find the citation on the lips of Jesus; it is more often the authorial narrator who interprets with the quotes.

[30] See Allison and Davies, *Matthew,* 396–99 for a detailed analysis of the arguments pro and con. They are among the few scholars who are less certain of the secondary character of vv. 18-23. They find that both sides fall short of definitive proof.

word," a technical term for "the gospel" that occurs often in the Pauline letters and Acts.[31] Another signal that vv. 18-23 were composed by the early Church is the use of *speirein*, "to sow," with reference to "the word" (similarly, 1 Cor 9:11). In addition, the parallel in *Gos. Thom.* §9 does not have the interpretation, a sign that at one time the parable circulated without it.[32] Moreover, the interpretation misses the eschatological point of the parable; it becomes, instead, an exhortation to self-examination.[33] With the exception of the weeds in the field (Matt 13:24-30, 36-43), no other gospel parable has an allegorical explanation. It is more likely that Jesus left his stories with open-ended challenges.

Nonetheless, these verses offer an important insight into how the early Church preached this parable of Jesus, and they give one direction for how it might yet be preached. The audience for vv. 18-23 remains the disciples. The exhortation at the outset to hear (v. 18) and Matthew's framing the whole explanation with hearing *and understanding* (vv. 19 and 23)[34] makes it clear that the disciples do comprehend (vv. 11, 16), but not fully. They must still listen to and heed Jesus.

The allegorical explanation in vv. 18-23 clearly focuses on the varying levels of receptivity of the four different types of soil, that is, four types of hearers of the word. The kinds of obstacles that a farmer would face from birds, rocks, thorns, and overexposure of seedlings to sun, are likened to stumbling blocks one faces, once having received the word. Deficient understanding, the work of the evil one, lack of rootedness, tribulation and persecution on account of the word, worldly

[31] E.g., 2 Cor 11:4; 1 Thess 1:6; 2:13; 2 Thess 1:6; 2 Tim 1:8; 2:9; Col 1:6, 10; Acts 6:7; 12:24; 17:11; 19:20.

[32] Davies and Allison (*Matthew,* 398) note that it is just as possible that the explanation was originally part of the parable and that the author of *Gos. Thom.* dropped the explanation to keep the story esoteric.

[33] Jeremias, *Parables,* 28. Davies and Allison (*Matthew,* 402–03) observe that for Matthew the main point was not exhortation, but rather, an explanation of why the majority of Jews had not accepted Jesus as the Messiah. The root of this failure does not lie with God, but with people, who are free to harden their hearts.

[34] Matthew alone adds "understanding" to "hearing" in vv. 19 and 23.

concerns, and the lure of riches, all stand in the way of God's word taking deep root and bearing fruit.[35]

The emphasis in this approach to the parable is on the hearer; each is exhorted to cull out all impediments and become "good soil." The parable not only explains why some hearers of the word "bear fruit" and others don't, but it calls those who hear to cultivate themselves for maximum receptivity and understanding. For Matthew's community it addresses the question of why all Israel has not embraced Jesus as the Messiah.

PREACHING POSSIBILITIES

The task of the preacher is to discern which of the many possible points, the four outlined above, or others still, conveys the message that their congregation needs to hear at this time and place. Does the community struggle with inclusivity? Then the preacher would do well to focus on the sower's profligate and indiscriminate sowing of the word. Is there discouragement over lack of results from efforts toward evangelization and justice? Then the parable could provide a word of encouragement about the assured efficacy of the seed, the word, and the bountiful harvest at the end-time. Support for these two lines of interpretation can also be drawn from the first reading, Isaiah 55:10-11, an announcement of salvation to Israel. It paints a picture of God's word that is cyclic. Just as rain and snow originate from clouds suspended above the earth, water the ground, and evaporate again, so does God's word come forth, accomplishing its life-giving purposes with humankind, and drawing all back to God. In juxtaposition with the parable in Matthew 13:1-9, it underscores both the inclusivity and the efficacy of God's word.

Another direction might be to focus on the harvest. If there are people in the congregation who are caught in impossible

---

[35] There is a similar passage in the Mishnah that speaks of four different kinds of hearers as: those who are slow to hear and swift to lose; those who are slow to hear and slow to lose; those who are swift to hear and slow to lose; and those who are swift to hear and swift to lose (*m.ʾAbot* 5.10-15).

webs of oppression then the revolutionary image of an out-of-bounds harvest can give hope to an upturning of systems of domination. This interpretation intersects well with the second reading (Rom 8:18-23) on the Fifteenth Sunday of Ordinary Time, in which Paul speaks eloquently of the eschatological glory to be revealed in those who suffer in the present.

For an assembly that is growing lax in their efforts to cultivate themselves as receptive "soil" for the word an exhortation to clear away the "rocks" and "thorns" and all other obstacles would be in order. The parable warns disciples that their initial good reception of the word can falter in the face of deterrents to faith. More is required than an initial decision to follow Jesus.

If the preacher chooses to address the question of why some do not understand and others do (vv. 10-17), he or she should not lose sight of the two parts of the discussion. On the one hand, understanding is a gift from God (vv. 11-12, 16-17); on the other hand one must respond to the gift with human endeavor (vv. 13-15). Likewise, if the preacher focuses on the end-time harvest, he or she would do well not to lose sight of this second point, that of human responsibility. The parable with its explanation does not advocate passive waiting for the future harvest, but exhorts hearers to have open eyes and ears and hearts. The preacher should also emphasize, not the exclusivity of the gift of understanding given to a choice few, but rather the responsibility to share that gift in the same profligate and indiscriminate way that the sower scatters the seed.

CHAPTER SEVEN

Weeds and Wheat, Mischievous Mustard, Hiding Yeast
(Matt 13:24-43)[1]

Sixteenth Sunday of Ordinary Time

Saturday of the Sixteenth Week of Ordinary Time
(Matt 13:24-30)

Monday of the Seventeenth Week of Ordinary Time
(Matt 13:31-35)

Tuesday of the Seventeenth Week of Ordinary Time
(Matt 13:36-43)

[Jesus proposed another parable to the crowds, saying:
"The kingdom of heaven[2] may be likened
to a man[3] who sowed good seed in his field.
While everyone was asleep his enemy came
and sowed weeds all through the wheat, and then went off.
When the crop grew and bore fruit, the weeds appeared as well.
The slaves of the householder came to him and said,
'Master, did you not sow good seed in your field?
Where have the weeds come from?'
He answered, 'An enemy has done this.'

---

[1] The Lectionary offers the option of reading a short form: Matthew 13:24-30.

[2] See above, pp. 41–42 on "the kingdom of heaven."

[3] The Greek word *anthrōpos* should be translated inclusively, "someone," as in the *NRSV*.

His slaves said to him,
    'Do you want us to go and pull them up?'
He replied, 'No, if you pull up the weeds
    you might uproot the wheat along with them.
Let them grow together until the harvest;
    then at harvest time I will say to the harvesters,
    "First collect the weeds and tie them in bundles for burning;
    but gather the wheat into my barn."'"]
He proposed another parable to them.
"The kingdom of heaven is like a mustard seed
    that a person took and sowed in a field.
It is the smallest of all the seeds,
    yet when full-grown it is the largest of plants.
It becomes a large bush,
    and the 'birds of the sky come and dwell in its branches.'"

He spoke to them another parable.
"The kingdom of heaven is like yeast
    that a woman took and mixed with three measures of wheat flour
    until the whole batch was leavened."

All these things Jesus spoke to the crowds in parables.
He spoke to them only in parables,
    to fulfill what had been said through the prophet:
    "I will open my mouth in parables,
    I will announce what has lain hidden from the foundation
    of the world."

Then, dismissing the crowds, he went into the house.
His disciples approached him and said,
    "Explain to us the parable of the weeds of the field."
He said in reply, "He who sows good seed is the Son of Man,
    the field is the world, the good seed the children of the kingdom.
The weeds are the children of the evil one,
    and the enemy who sows them is the devil.
The harvest is the end of the age, and the harvesters are angels.
Just as weeds are collected and burned up with fire,
    so will it be at the end of the age.
The Son of Man will send his angels,
    and they will collect out of his kingdom
    all who cause others to sin and all evildoers.
They will throw them into the fiery furnace,
    where there will be wailing and grinding of teeth.

Then the righteous will shine like the sun
  in the kingdom of their Father.
Whoever has ears ought to hear."

LITERARY CONTEXT AND STRUCTURE

This selection is from the center of Matthew 13, the parables discourse, the third of five major blocks of teaching in the gospel. It includes the lengthy parable of the weeds and the wheat (vv. 24-30), its explanation (vv. 36-43), two short parables: one about mustard seed (vv. 31-32); one about yeast hidden in flour (v. 33); and another explanation of why Jesus speaks to the crowd only in parables (vv. 34-35). The preaching possibilities are myriad!

The structure of Matthew 13:24-43 mirrors that of Matthew 13:1-23, the gospel from the previous Sunday. In both selections a parable and its allegorical explanation frame an explanation for Jesus' use of parables. The audience for all three parables in Matthew 13:24-33 is the crowds. Verses 34-35 are a narrative aside explaining Jesus' use of parables. In v. 36 the audience shifts to the disciples, who ask for an interpretation of the parable of the weeds in the field after Jesus has dismissed the crowds.

THE WEEDS AND THE WHEAT

In the canonical Gospels, the parable of the weeds in the wheat field (vv. 24-30) and its secondary explanation (vv. 36-43) are unique to Matthew.[4] They echo, in many respects, the parable of the sower/seed/soil/harvest and its allegorical interpretation (13:1-9,18-23). Motifs that have already appeared in 13:1-23 recur: sowing, seeds, soil, God's realm, impediments

---

[4] The *Gos. Thom.* §57 has this version: "Jesus said: the father's kingdom is like a person who had [good] seed. His enemy came at night and sowed weeds among the good seed. The person did not let them pull up the weeds, but said to them, 'No, or you might go to pull up the weeds and pull up the wheat along with them.' For on the day of harvest the weeds will be conspicuous and will be pulled up and burned." (translation from Marvin Meyer, *The Gospel of Thomas* [HarperSanFrancisco, 1992] 45). Most scholars consider this abbreviated version to be a secondary compression of the canonical form.

to growth. Both speak of a positive outcome at the harvest. However, the emphasis of 13:24-30 is different from 13:1-9. In Matthew 13:1-9 the primary question is why all who hear the word do not respond to it fully. The parable of the weeds among the wheat addresses the broader issue of the coexistence of good and evil, and poses two difficult questions: Who is responsible for evil? (vv. 27-28a) and What is to be done about it? (vv. 28b-30). The answers that emerge from this parable are partly determined by whether the hearer takes up the position of the householder or the slaves.

"THE KINGDOM OF HEAVEN IS LIKE . . ."

The three parables in 13:24-33 all use a simile to make an explicit comparison. Each begins, "The kingdom of heaven[5] is like . . ." Note, however, that in each case the story compares God's realm to the whole situation described in the parable. It is not that God's reign is like the person who sows good seed, or like the mustard seed, or the yeast. The whole of what happens in the parable is what God's realm is like.[6] The translation of the Revised English Bible captures this well: "The kingdom of Heaven is like this. A man sowed his field . . ."

THE STORY

The story presumes an audience familiar with agricultural practices. They are people who know from experience that weeds always crop up among wheat. The narrative begins with a landowner who sows good seed in a field (v. 24). An enemy sabotages the farm while all are unaware (v. 25).[7] A cri-

---

[5] See above, pp. 41–42 on "the kingdom of heaven."

[6] Jeremias (*Parables*, 101) notes that the formula introducing the parable reflects the Aramaic *lᵉ*, and the meaning is not "it is like" but "it is the case with . . . as with . . ." The content of the parable itself reinforces this understanding.

[7] W.O.E. Oesterley (*The Gospel Parables in the Light of their Jewish Background* [New York: Macmillan, 1936] 60) argues for the realism of this detail. He cites a Roman law that treats of sowing weeds in another's field. Jeremias (*Parables*, 224) alludes to a similar occurrence in modern Palestine. Others (e.g., Schweizer, *Matthew*, 303) find the introduction of an enemy sowing

sis arises when weeds appear along with the wheat as the crop grows and begins to put forth its fruit (v. 26). The ensuing dialogue between the slaves and the householder first asks the source of the weeds (vv. 27-28a) and then questions what course of action to take (vv. 28b-30).

STANDING WITH THE SLAVES

If Jesus' original audience were peasant farmers they would most likely identify with the slaves in the story. They would hear the query about the source of the weeds with some trepidation. Presuming that it was the slaves who did the actual sowing, and that they have also been the ones tending the field, they may fear being blamed for the appearance of the weeds. The question of the slaves to the householder, "Did you not sow good seed in your field?" (v. 27) seeks to deflect blame from themselves and to cast it on the quality of seed they were given to sow. The householder's reply (v. 28) relieves the slaves of responsibility and points the finger at an enemy. From a narrative perspective, the hearer already knows that the cause of the weeds is the work of an enemy (v. 25).[8]

The householder's reply to the second question, concerning the course of action to take with the weeds, is startling, since the best method is to cull out the weeds as early as possible. Commentators identify the weed *(zizania)* in the parable as darnel, a poisonous weed that is common in Palestine. It closely resembles wheat in the early stages, though an

---

weeds an implausible touch that ruins an otherwise realistic story. See also A. J. Kerr, "Matthew 13:25: Sowing *zizania* among another's wheat: realistic or artificial?" *JTS* ns. 48/1 (1997) 106–09; David H. Tripp, "*Zizania* (Matthew 13:25): Realistic if Also Figurative," *JTS* 50 (1999) 628.

[8] Douglas Oakman *(Jesus and the Economic Questions of His Day* [SBEC 8; Lewiston: Mellen, 1986] 114–23) explains that weeds can infest a field by many different means. If the field is not clean fallowed in the summer after the harvest, weeds of all types grow rapidly and deplete the water reserves. If the weed is darnel, a poisonous weed, its seed is unsavory to rodents and birds, and so remains in the field and is plowed in with the stubble. Humans, animals, and wind can carry the seeds of weeds onto a field.

experienced farmer can distinguish the two by the width of the leaves. Because the grains of darnel carry a strong toxin, it is not wise to harvest it together with wheat. The mixing ruins the quality of the grain and poses a health hazard. Moreover, separating the two at harvest time is very difficult. Darnel is similar to wheat in size and appearance, but different in weight. The farmer could hope to separate the two by winnowing or with a sieve, but without modern technology, these methods are not completely effective. The preferred course of action is to pull out the weeds as early as possible, and repeatedly, if necessary. This eliminates danger to the wheat seedlings, whose roots may become intertwined with those of the darnel, and who no longer have to compete with the darnel for space, soil nutrients, moisture, and light.[9]

THE UNDOING OF AN EXPLOITIVE LANDOWNER

The decision of the householder to wait until harvest to separate the weeds from the wheat, then, seems a poor one. This twist in the story leaves the hearer in a quandary about what to think and how to respond. If the hearer stands with the slaves, one reaction is to question the wisdom of the householder. The workers who are directly involved in the farming are well aware of the difficulties at hand. Seeing the householder as removed from the real situation, they may find him foolishly optimistic about the harvest. They may perceive the proprietor as greedy, thinking that even the weeds can bring an unexpected benefit—they can be burned for fuel.[10]

From this perspective, the parable portrays the lack of farming knowledge and the imprudence of an acquisitive landowner. The good news for the slave would be that the householder's exploitation is curtailed by the sabotage of an

---

[9] The above information is taken from Oakman, *Economic Questions*, 114–23.

[10] Davies and Allison (*Matthew*, 415) note that there is disagreement as to whether it was normal to gather weeds and to use them for fuel (so Jeremias, *Parables,* p. 225 n. 37) or whether the custom was to burn the whole field after the wheat stalks had been cut off (so Gundry, *Matthew,* 265). Texts from antiquity do not resolve the issue, and both practices are known from modern times.

enemy—perhaps a rival from the same landed class. The peasants would cheer the downfall of landowners at the hands of one of their own. To envision the reign of God as the undoing of those who profit from an exploitive system is good news for those on the underside of the system.[11]

From the perspective of an unwise householder, this parable presents a warning not to underestimate the threat that the weeds present. If the landowner cannot properly assess this situation, out of greed, lack of knowledge, or inability to take good advice from his underlings, he may likewise be caught short at the coming of the reign of God.

PATIENT TRUST

The point of the parable depends as well on how one envisions the ending. The parable does not tell whether the owner's plan worked, or whether the harvest was, indeed, disappointing. If the householder's method succeeded, then other interpretive possibilities arise. If the landowner's unconventional decision turns out to be a wise one, then the parable becomes one of assurance that the forces of good (the wheat) are always able to withstand the forces of evil (the weeds). To the field workers, it advocates patient trust in the one whose job it is to do the separating at the end-time. It counters the desire of the slaves to act prematurely and reminds them that it is not their task to do the judging.[12]

REFUSAL TO RETALIATE

John Pilch takes this line of interpretation a step further and sees the story as depicting the vindication of one who refuses to retaliate against an enemy. Within a first-century Mediterranean culture of honor and shame the householder is depicted as a man of status whose enemy makes him the

[11] Oakman, *Economic Questions*, 122–23.

[12] So Philippe Bacq and Odile Ribadeau Dumas, "Reading a Parable: The Good Wheat and the Tares (Mt 13)," *LumVit* 39 (1984) 181–94; W. G. Doty, "An Interpretation: Parable of the Weeds and Wheat," *Int* 25 (1971) 185–93.

object of laughter of the entire village when the weeds appear. The peasants expect him to retaliate, lest he be bested by his enemy. But the householder is savvy. He knows that the wheat is strong enough to prevail. His refusal to act in kind against his enemy is vindicated when at the harvest he has not only the grain, but extra fuel. The landowner and his servants have the last laugh.[13]

Note that this interpretation presumes a favorable outcome at the harvest and a positive portrayal of the householder. It also presumes that the enemy is known to the landowner, a detail that is not clear in the text. This interpretation would also link the parable of the weeds and the wheat with Matthew 5:38-48, a text that speaks against exacting "an eye for an eye and a tooth for a tooth." However, a very important difference is that in Matthew 5:38-48 the alternative to retaliation is not inaction. Rather, that text presents three examples of creative, nonviolent, direct actions that confront and destabilize an oppressive situation, offering the possibility of conversion and transformation.[14]

JESUS' PRACTICE OF INCLUSION

The most likely interpretation of the parable from a situation in the life of Jesus,[15] is that it justifies Jesus' practice of inclusivity. In view of other groups of Jews, such as the Pharisees, the Qumran community, the Zealots, or even John the Baptist (see Matt 3:12), who were intent on strictly delimiting their groups of devout believers, the parable champions Jesus' open-

---

[13] John Pilch, *Cultural World. Cycle A*, 112–14.

[14] See Walter Wink, *Engaging the Powers. Discernment and Resistance in a World of Domination* (Minneapolis: Fortress, 1992) 175–93.

[15] A number of scholars doubt that the parable comes from Jesus himself and believe that it has been composed by Matthew, perhaps under the influence of Mark 4:26-29 (the parable of the seed growing secretly) that Matthew eliminates. Others find the vocabulary to be characteristic of the M source and have no trouble envisioning a setting in the life of Jesus. See Davies and Allison (*Matthew*, 409–11) for a summary and evaluation of various attempts to analyze the tradition history of the text.

ness to all.[16] All are invited in; only at the end-time, the harvest,[17] is there judicious separation.

Further, this parable proclaims that the reign of God is not monochromatic. In its initial manifestation in this world, God's reign is a mixture of "wheat" and "weeds." It is in the midst of the mess of conflictive coexistence that God is revealed, not in some hypothetical situation where "good seed" grows in pure isolation. This parable rests on the notion that goodness is only identifiable in contrast to evil, and only grows through struggle with opposition.

ALLEGORICAL EXPLANATION (vv. 36-43)

The explanation of the parable in vv. 36-43 takes the meaning in another direction. In the text there is a shift in audience at v. 36, from the crowds to Jesus' disciples, as they once again become privy to special understanding. That the allegorical explanation is secondary, not from the lips of Jesus, is evident for many of the same reasons as for Matthew 13:18-23.[18] It takes on a parenetic tone, becoming an exhortation to hear in light of the coming judgment.

Each detail is assigned a symbolic meaning: The sower is the Son of Humanity; the field is the world; the good seed are the children of the kingdom; the weeds are the children of the evil one; the enemy is the devil; the harvest is the end of the age, and the reapers are angels. The tone is apocalyptic as the future judgment is depicted in fiery terms. The patient forbearance found in vv. 24-30 is gone; the moment of crisis is not the appearance of the "weeds," but their final horrible demise. The conclusion is cast in dualistic terms: evildoers are separated

[16] Davies and Allison, *Matthew,* 410.

[17] See above, pp. 83–85 on the frequent use of harvest as an image for the end time. See Joel 3:13; Hos 6:11; Jer 51:33; Rev 14:15-16; 4 Ezra 4:28-29; 2 Bar 70:2; Matt 13:40.

[18] See Jeremias, *Parables,* 81–85. For him the allegorical interpretation in vv. 36-43 misses the point of the parable as an exhortation to patience; it contains expressions that, on linguistic grounds, Jesus would not have used, such as *ho kosmos,* meaning "the world." Moreover it has some thirty-seven stylistic peculiarities of Matthew and the parallel story in *Gos. Thom.* §57 does not have it.

once and for all from the righteous, and their opposite fates are sealed.

With these interpretative verses the parable becomes a warning to all who hear that they be found among the "children of the kingdom" and not among the "children of the evil one." There is a notable shift from Matthew 13:16, where the disciples were assured, "But blessed are your eyes, *because* they see, and your ears, *because* they hear" (emphasis added). Now, in v. 43, the possibility lies open that a disciple may not hear.

The allegorical explanation points to a struggle of the Matthean community to understand the coexistence of the "children of the kingdom" and the "children of the evil one" in the world. Believing that the Messiah had already come in the person of Jesus, questions for them were: Why are there still "children of the evil one" in the world? Why has not Satan's power yet been defeated? And why must the "children of the kingdom" still suffer at the hands of the "children of the evil one"? Verses 36-43 answer these questions by pointing to the endtime. It is at the final judgment that all will obtain their reward: evildoers will be thrown into the "furnace of fire"; the righteous will "shine like the sun." The parable gives assurance of final reward to the upright who are persecuted and encourages them to endure with patience and faith. To those who are not upright, it is a warning to move away from the realm of the evil one and join the ranks of the "children of the kingdom" before that final moment strikes.

The parable proper (vv. 24-30) could also have been used in the Matthean community to address problems of inclusion within the Church, e.g., the admission and full participation of Gentiles or other identifiable "sinners." The allegorical explanation in vv. 36-43, however, points outside the Christian community, to "the world" (v. 38) as the ground of conflict. Nonetheless, the later Church did use this parable to address problems of "weeds" within the Church. Augustine, for example, used it to argue against the Donatists that heretics or the lapsed should not be cut off from the Church. Hippolytus (*Haer.* 9.12.22) records bishop Callistus as saying, "Let the tares grow along with the wheat; or, in other words, let sinners remain in the church."

SON OF HUMANITY

In v. 37 the farmer who sows good seed is equated with the Son of Humanity. This expression is an enigmatic one, found in the Gospels only on the lips of Jesus. It occurs in contexts where Jesus speaks of his earthly ministry, his passion, and his future coming and role as judge at the end time.[19] The origin of the phrase *huios tou anthrōpou* ("son of man") is disputed. Some scholars hold that it was an expression used in pre-Christian Jewish apocalyptic writings that was taken over by Christians to refer to Jesus. It is found in Daniel 7:14 and in *The Similitudes of Enoch* (*1 Enoch* 37–71) to denote an end-time agent of salvation and judgment.

Other scholars argue that *The Similitudes of Enoch*, which do not appear in early versions of *Enoch*, are not pre-Christian, and therefore its use of *huios tou anthrōpou* does not antedate Christian use of the term for Jesus. For them Daniel 7:14 is the only pre-Christian example, and there the expression denotes Israel as a corporate identity. For these scholars, the examples in Daniel and *Enoch* shed no light on the meaning of the expression as used of Jesus.

The meaning of the phrase *huios tou anthrōpou* is likewise debated. It may be understood to reflect a Semitic expression, *ben ʾādām* in Hebrew, or *bar ʾĕnāsh* in Aramaic (literally "son of man"), a phrase that individualizes a noun for humanity in general by prefacing it with "son of," thus designating a single member of the human species. An example of this is found in Psalm 8:5, "What are humans that you are mindful of them, / mere mortals[20] that you care for them?" Jesus may have used

[19] In reference to his earthly ministry see Matt 9:6; 11:19; 12:8, 32; 13:37; 16:13; in regard to his passion and resurrection see Matt 12:40; 17:9, 12, 22; 20:18, 28; 26:2, 24, 45; in reference to his future coming see Matt 10:23; 13:41; 16:27, 28; 19:28; 24:27, 30, 37, 39, 44; 25:31; 26:64. See further, Reginald H. Fuller, "Son of Man," in *Harper's Bible Commentary* (ed. Paul J. Achtemeier; SanFrancisco: Harper & Row, 1985) 981; Joseph A. Fitzmyer, "The New Testament Title 'Son of Man' Philologically Considered," in *A Wandering Aramean: Collected Aramaic Essays* (Missoula, Mont.: Scholars Press, 1979) 143–60; Douglas R. A. Hare, *The Son of Man Tradition* (Minneapolis: Fortress, 1990).

[20] The Hebrew *ben ʾādām* and the Greek *huios anthrōpou* in the LXX are singular, i.e., "son of man," translated more inclusively here in the *NRSV*.

this phrase as a way of speaking of himself simply as a human being. It could be translated, "a certain person," or "someone" or when used as a self-designation, simply, "I."

Some scholars who hold that there was a pre-Christian concept of an apocalyptic "son of man," believe that Jesus used the phrase of a coming figure other than himself. In Mark 8:38 and Luke 12:8 Jesus appears to be talking about the "son of man" as someone other than himself who would vindicate his present ministry. In this view, it was Jesus' followers who attributed to him the title from a postresurrection stance of faith.

Other scholars hold that Jesus did not use the term of himself at all and that all the references to him as *huios tou anthrōpou* arise from the post-Easter insight of his followers. This theory posits that they first applied it to Jesus in an apocalyptic sense, in sayings about his future coming and his role as judge and savior. From this developed the application of the expression to Jesus' earthly ministry and to his passion.

Whatever the provenance and original meaning of the expression, it is clearly used as a christological title in the Gospels. A further difficulty is posed when translating this term into English. There is no felicitous translation that allows for the ambiguity in meaning in the original phrase, nor one that satisfactorily avoids using exclusively male terminology. Some use "Son of Humanity" or "the Human One," but in any case there is not a satisfactory way to capture what it would have originally conveyed.

MISCHIEVOUS MUSTARD (vv. 31-32)

This parable appears in all three Synoptic Gospels.[21] Both the Matthean and the Lukan versions conflate the Markan and Q sources.[22] From the latter come the details of the shrub be-

---

[21] The Markan parable (4:30-32) is assigned for the Eleventh Sunday of Ordinary Time and Friday of Week Three of Ordinary Time in Year B. The Lukan version (13:18-19) is used on Tuesday, Week Thirty of Ordinary Time in Year C.

[22] There is also a version in *Gos.Thom.* §20: "The followers said to Jesus: 'Tell us what heaven's kingdom is like.' He said to them: 'It is like a mustard seed. [It] is the smallest of all seeds, but when it falls on prepared soil, it produces a large

coming a tree and the birds nesting in the branches. In the Markan version the birds nest in the shade of the "shrub." In addition, Matthew and Luke make the sowing of the mustard seed a deliberate action of a man who plants it in his own field.[23] In Mark the passive voice is used and the ground on which the grain of mustard is sown is indefinite.

FROM SMALL TO LARGE

The most common interpretation is that the parable emphasizes the contrast between the small seed[24] and the resulting large tree. Just so the realm of God grows enormously from small beginnings. The modest success of Jesus' preaching and that of the tiny band of his original followers would eventually have universal impact. The Jesus movement would grow to greatness, offering refuge to all peoples. In Ezekiel 17:22-24 the same image is used to speak of the restoration of the Davidic dynasty to Israel: a small shoot becomes a great tree and offers a dwelling beneath the shade of its boughs to every winged thing (see also Ezek 31:1-18; Dan 4:10-27). The birds finding refuge in the boughs of the tree is a metaphor for the Gentiles who are gathered into Israel.[25] With the rise of evolutionary science in

---

plant and becomes a shelter for birds of heaven'" (translation from Marvin Meyer, *The Gospel of Thomas* [HarperSanFrancisco, 1992] 33). This form follows the Markan tradition more closely, but omits making the mature mustard into a shrub (Mark 4:32) or a tree (Matt 13:32; Luke 13:19). This rendition is probably a later development, dependent on the Matthean (as reflected in the use of "heaven's kingdom") and Markan traditions. For analyses of the tradition history see J. D. Crossan, "The Seed Parables of Jesus," *JBL* 92 (1973) 244–66; H. K. McArthur, "The Parable of the Mustard Seed," *CBQ* 33 (1971) 198–210.

[23] Matthew's *espeiren en tǭ agrǭ autou* shows his redactional touch as he makes the phrase similar to other verses (vv. 3, 24, 27, 44) in chapter 13.

[24] Although botanically mustard is not the smallest of all seeds, it was proverbial for its small size, as is seen from the Q saying about faith the size of a mustard seed in Matt 17:20 and Luke 17:6.

[25] Davies and Allison, *Matthew*, 420; Jeremias, *Parables*, 147. But Harrington, *Matthew*, 205 notes that this point is not emphasized in the parable. The image of birds dwelling among tree branches and sending forth their song is found in Ps 104:12, a hymn in praise of the Creator. Pss 1:3; 92:13-15 also use a tree as a symbol of God's favor.

the nineteenth century the interpretation of the mustard seed parable as representing the slow, but inevitable growth of the Church as the locus of the reign of God became prominent.

FROM SHRUB TO TREE

It is perhaps owing to these references from the Hebrew Bible that in Matthew and Luke the mustard plant becomes a "tree," a botanical impossibility. But there is another possible twist to this story. Commentators often note that mustard is not a plant in which birds build nests. Although mustard bushes reach a height of eight to ten feet in Palestine, they are not sturdy enough to support birdnests. Birds eat the seeds, or may find shelter under the bush (so Mark 4:32), but do not dwell in this garden herb. Rather than an unrealistic detail,[26] it may be the guide to the very point of the parable. It is possible that the simile is a burlesque of the image found in Ezekiel 17, 31, and Daniel 4. Rather than think of the coming reign of God as a majestic cedar tree that is imported from Lebanon, Jesus uses the image of a lowly garden herb, that grows right in one's own back yard. God's realm is not like a dominating empire, but its power erupts out of weakness. Its transformative power comes from unpretentious ventures of faith by those who would choose such an unlikely venue as the Jesus movement in which to build their nests.[27]

MIXED ALLUSIONS

These explanations, however, do not completely resolve the tension created by the mixed allusions in the parable. The hearer faces a predicament: how can a parable about a mustard seed be concluded with allusions that more properly belong to the cedar of Lebanon?[28] One solution is that in Jesus'

---

[26] So Davies and Allison, *Matthew*, 420. For Jeremias (*Parables*, 147) features that transcend the bounds of actuality are meant to point toward divine realities.

[27] Robert Funk, "The Looking Glass Tree is for the Birds," *Int* 27 (1973) 3–9.

[28] B. Brandon Scott, *Hear Then the Parable* (Minneapolis: Fortress, 1989) 385.

original parable he spoke only of the mustard becoming a large shrub, not a tree, as in Mark 4:32. Not appreciating the irony in this parable, the tradition brings it more in line with the story of the cedar.[29]

If we stay, however, with the tensions in the text as we have it in Matthew, how is one to fit together a mustard plant that aspires to the greatness of a Lebanon cedar? When one probes further the image in Daniel 4 and Ezekiel 17 and 31, it is notable that the cedar represents an enemy of Israel. The metaphor is that God brings low the powerful empires of Babylon and Egypt that once stood proudly like tall cedars. When Israel is the small sprig become a lofty cedar (Ezekiel 17) can it be exempt from such humbling?

DELIBERATE PLANTING AND UNCONTROLLABLE SPREADING

A further tension in the parable is the deliberate planting of the mustard seed and the question of its desirability. In Matthew's version of the parable, a person actively sows a grain of mustard seed in his field (v. 31). The term *agros*, "field," connotes a plot of ground used mainly for agriculture.[30] Jewish hearers of Jesus' parable would raise an eyebrow as this farmer plants mustard in a field in which other crops are also growing. Is he violating the prohibition against mixing diverse classes of plants?[31] Leviticus 19:19 specifies: "do not sow a field of yours with two different kinds of seed" (see also Deut 22:9-11). The purpose for such separation is to maintain the order of creation (Gen 1:11-12, 21, 24-25), because order signifies holiness. The Mishnah tractate *Kilayim* further spells out regulations for the planting of mustard. It can be planted next to vegetables, for example, but not wheat. The danger from mixing and confusion of the two is less with vegetables. Moreover, mustard is sown only in a patch or two of a field. The amount is strictly limited, since it tends to grow wild and take over other patches (see *m.Kil.* 2.9).

---

[29] John Dominic Crossan, *The Dark Interval* (Niles: Argus, 1975) 95.

[30] BDAG, s.v., ἀγρός.

[31] Scott, *Hear Then the Parable*, 373–87.

From this perspective, the impact of the parable is that the reign of God is associated with uncleanness, where boundaries are too porous, where separation cannot be maintained. It is an apt image to describe Jesus' association with the unclean. In Matthew's community, the uncontrollable way that mustard crosses over the established boundaries of the field, mixing with other sown crops, could be likened to the manner in which Gentiles and Jews intermingle in the Christian community.

Pressing this point further, Crossan notes that there is the ever-present danger that mustard will destroy the garden.[32] The point of the parable is not one of hopeful encouragement that the small seed will produce a large shrub, but rather it is "like a pungent shrub with dangerous takeover properties."[33] It is uncontrollable and crosses into plots where it is not wanted. Moreover, it attracts undesirable birds in cultivated areas.[34]

Moreover, mustard is a tenacious herb, very difficult to eradicate once it infests a field. When this parable is told in tandem with that of the weeds and the wheat, one might hear the message that any endeavor to weed out the reign of God will never succeed. God's realm will always overcome antagonistic forces.

DEATH AND NEW LIFE

A slightly different interpretation is that the seed and the tree represent a contrast between death and life. It is from the seed that appears dead in the earth that new life comes. Thus, the seed is a symbol of resurrection, the mystery of life that comes out of death.[35] This meaning for a seed metaphor is more evident in Paul's use of it in 1 Corinthians 15:35-38 and in the Fourth Gospel at John 12:24 than in the mustard seed parable.

---

[32] J. D. Crossan, *The Historical Jesus* (HarperSanFrancisco, 1991) 276–80.
[33] Ibid., 279.
[34] Oakman, *Economic Questions*, 127, observes that birds are the natural enemies of the sown.
[35] Jeremias, *Parables*, 148–49.

HIDING LEAVEN (v. 33)

Matthew, like Luke, pairs the parable of the mustard seed with that of the leaven. In Mark's Gospel the parable of the mustard seed is linked with that of the growing seed (Mark 4:26-34). Mark does not have the parable of the leaven; this tradition comes from the Q source. It is likely that the parables of the mustard seed and the leaven were already paired in Q, but the fact that they have parallels in the *Gospel of Thomas* (§20 and §96) that are not joined indicates that at one time they circulated independently.

Because the parable of the mustard seed, with its contrast of small-to-large, is linked with the leaven parable the most common interpretation of the latter also focuses on the small amount of yeast that one would mix with flour to produce a loaf of bread. The point would be the astonishing growth of something small into something that permeates a large entity. In this interpretation, the leaven is thought to be Jesus' preaching, or the word of God, which grows phenomenally in its efficacy throughout time and history.[36] In the version of the saying found in *Gospel of Thomas* §96 there is such a contrast, between the "bit of leaven" used and the "big loaves" it made.[37] However, there is no reference in either the Matthean or Lukan versions of the parable to the amounts involved. Knowledge of Paul's proverbial statement, "A little yeast leavens the whole batch of dough" (Gal 5:9; similarly 1 Cor 5:6), may also influence one to read a contrast of amounts into the parable.

CORRUPTION

Important to the meaning of the parable is the fact that in every other instance in Scripture in which leaven occurs, it represents evil or corruption. In Exodus 12:15-20, 34 the Passover

---

[36] E.g., Joachim Jeremias, *Rediscovering the Parables* (New York: Charles Scribner's Sons, 1966) 116–17.

[37] *Gos.Thom.* §96 reads, "The father's kingdom is like [a] woman. She took a little yeast, [hid] it in dough, and made it into large loaves of bread. Whoever has ears should hear" (transl. from Meyer, *Thomas*, 61).

ritual prescribes that unleavened bread be eaten for seven days. This recalls the Israelites' hasty departure from Egypt, with no time to wait for dough to be leavened. Eating unleavened bread becomes a sign of membership in God's holy people. Grain offerings are to be unleavened (Lev 2:11), equating unleavened with sacred. In Matthew 16:6 Jesus cautions his disciples, "Look out, and beware of the leaven of the Pharisees and Sadducees." In vv. 11-12 the disciples comprehend that this is a warning against their false teaching (similarly Mark 8:15; Luke 12:1). Twice Paul uses leaven as a symbol for corruption. He admonishes the Corinthians, "Do you not know that a little yeast leavens all the dough? Clear out the old yeast, so that you may become a fresh batch of dough, inasmuch as you are unleavened. For our paschal lamb, Christ, has been sacrificed" (1 Cor 5:6-7). To the Galatians he quotes the proverb, "A little yeast leavens the whole batch of dough," warning them not to be misled by those preaching a different message from his own.[38]

For some interpreters such a singular positive use of leaven in Jesus' parable constitutes the unexpected twist in the story. However, if leaven is meant to connote corruption, the startling message is that the reign of God is like a batch of dough that has been permeated by what societal standards would consider a "corruptive yeast." In other words, Jesus' story presents an image of God's realm as one that reverses previous notions of holiness: no longer unleavened, but leavened is the locus of the sacred. It proclaims that God's realm thoroughly incorporates persons who would have been considered corrupt, unclean, or sinners according to prevailing interpretations of the Jewish purity regulations.

To understand the parable this way accords well with Jesus' other teachings and actions, in which Jesus continually extends himself to people who are poor, outcast, or marginalized. The challenge of the parable for those who are on the fringes is to begin to see themselves as "leaven," a vital com-

---

[38] In other Greek writers, e.g., Plutarch, *Mor.* 289 E-F; 659 B, leaven also connotes corruption.

ponent of the believing community. For those who are privileged, it is a summons to change their attitude toward those they consider "corrupt" and to see them as the very ones who provide the active ingredient for the growth of the community of God's people.[39]

For Matthew's predominantly Jewish community, the parable may have provided an apt image for their experience of how Gentile Christians, who began as a hidden minority in Jewish Christian communities, were now beginning to permeate the whole. To Jewish Christians, this "corrupting" influence would have had a disturbing effect on their prevailing theology and praxis. Having let a few Gentiles mix in, these now were changing the character of the whole community!

HIDDENNESS

An odd detail in this parable is the hiddenness of the leaven. The parable says that the woman took and hid *(enekrypsen)* leaven in three measures of flour. The verb *enkryptō* is nowhere else attested in a recipe for "mixing" dough.[40] Some scholars understand the point of the parable to be that the reign of God, like leaven, works silently, imperceptibly within, surely bringing about transformation.[41] This interpretation is not far removed from that of the small-to-large contrast. But there is something more to be explored in this detail.

Forms of the verb *kryptō* ("to hide") occur several other times in Matthew. In one instance, Jesus assures the disciples

[39] So e.g., Robert W. Funk, "Beyond Criticism in Quest of Literacy: The Parable of the Leaven," *Int* 25 (1971) 149–70; Susan Praeder, *The Word in Women's Worlds. Four Parables* (Zacchaeus Studies: New Testament; Wilmington: Glazier, 1988) 32; Scott, *Hear Then the Parable*, 329.

[40] Praeder, *Women's Worlds*, 35. Elizabeth Waller, "The Parable of the Leaven: A Sectarian Teaching and the Inclusion of Women," *USQR* 35 (1979–80) 99–109, proposes that the verb *enkryptō*, "to hide," came into the leaven parable by its similar sound to the noun *enkrypsias*, "cakes," found in Gen 18:6. Waller asserts that the story in Gen 18:1-10 stands behind the leaven parable. Both concern a woman who mixes three measures of dough for an epiphany.

[41] E.g., C. H. Dodd, *The Parables of the Kingdom* (rev. ed.; New York: Charles Scribner's Sons, 1961) 155–56.

that "Nothing is concealed that will not be revealed, nor secret *(krypton)* that will not be known" (10:26). In another
place, Jesus rejoices in the holy Spirit and says, "I give praise
to you, Father, Lord of heaven and earth, for although you
have hidden *(ekrypsas)* these things from the wise and the
learned you have revealed them to the childlike" (11:25). In
the verses that elaborate on why Jesus spoke only in parables,
he explains that it was "to fulfill what had been said through
the prophet:[42] 'I will open my mouth in parables, / I will announce what has lain hidden *(kekrymenna)* from the foundation (of the world)'" (13:35). In another parable Jesus likens
the kingdom of heaven to treasure hidden *(kekrymennō)* in a
field (13:44).[43]

These texts speak about the paradox of hiddenness and
revelation with regard to Jesus and his message. Understanding of God's realm is revealed to disciples, but remains hidden from others. Through Jesus' preaching and that of his
disciples, it is gradually becoming revealed. The parable of
the leaven may be understood as God "hiding" Jesus in human
form in the midst of God's people, the bread dough. The startling thing is that God is concealing rather than revealing
plainly.

Perhaps this parable reflects the struggle of the early
Christian communities to explain the paradoxes which framed
their faith. They declared that a crucified criminal was the
Messiah (Acts 2:36), that death was the way to life (Acts 17:3),
and that suffering was the path to glory (Luke 24:26). For
people who readily attributed all things to God, the incompre-
hensibility of these seeming contradictions could be explained
in terms of God concealing their full meaning until the propitious time of revelation.

---

[42] While some manuscripts of Matthew add "Isaiah the prophet," the quotation is actually from Ps 78:2.

[43] Other instances include: Matt 5:14, where the disciples are told that they
are like a city built on a hill that cannot be hidden *(krybēnai)*. The parable of the
talents features a slave who hid *(ekrypsen)* his master's money in the ground
(25:18, 25).

A FEMALE IMAGE OF GOD

Another startling thing in this parable is that it presents a female image of God.[44] Although God does not have a gender, when we picture a personal God, our human experience of persons being either male or female enters into our imagination. All language about God is metaphorical; no image adequately expresses who God is.[45] God is like a woman hiding leaven in bread dough, a woman searching for a lost coin, a shepherd going after a lost sheep, but God *is* not any of these. But the language and images we use for God are extremely important because they work in two directions: what we say about God reflects what we believe about human beings made in God's image. Genesis 1:27 asserts that male and female are made in God's image. But when we use predominantly male metaphors for God, then being male is equated with being God-like. Consequently, women are not thought to be like God, and are regarded as less holy than men.

Jesus' teaching and praxis contradicts such a notion and invites believers to envision God in such a way that women and men are both seen to reflect God's image equally. When the parable of the woman mixing bread dough is paired with that of the man who sowed mustard seed in his field it shows that women and men both act in the divine image to bring about the reign of God.

[44] The other two parables that feature female figures for God are the parable of the woman searching for the lost coin (Luke 15:8-10) and that of the widow confronting the unjust judge (Luke 18:1-8). See Barbara E. Reid, *Parables for Preachers. Year C* (Collegeville: The Liturgical Press, 2000) 186–91; 227–36. Interestingly, in *Gos. Thom.* §96 the focus of the leaven parable is clearly on the woman. Waller ("Leaven," 102–3) believes that Thomas's version of the introduction is earlier than that of Matthew or Luke. Her arguments for such are not convincing. Her desire to make the figure of the woman central to the story can be achieved without resorting to an earlier date for the version of *Gos. Thom.*

[45] See Elizabeth Johnson, *She Who Is. The Mystery of God in Feminist Theological Discourse* (N.Y.: Crossroad, 1992); Rosemary Radford Ruether, *Sexism and God-Talk* (Boston: Beacon, 1983); Sandra Schneiders, "God is More Than Two Men and a Bird," *U.S. Catholic* (May 1990) 20–27; *Women and the Word* (N.Y.: Paulist, 1986); Sallie McFague, *Models of God* (Philadelphia: Fortress, 1987).

EPIPHANY BAKING

One other startling element in the story is the grandiose amount of flour—three measures—approximately fifty pounds! The woman is preparing bread for a feast fit for a manifestation of God. In fact, the very same amount of flour is used by Sarah when she bakes for Abraham's three heavenly visitors (Gen 18:6). Gideon uses this amount, too, when preparing for an angel of God (Judg 6:19), as does Hannah when making the offering for the presentation of Samuel in the Temple at Shiloh (1 Sam 1:24). In each of these instances, the large-scale baking prepares for an epiphany. So too, the parable in Matthew 13:33 portrays the work of a woman as a vehicle for God's revelation.

CROWDS ON THE OUTS (vv. 34-35)

Matthew concludes this cycle of parables with verses similar to Mark 4:33-34, explaining again (as at 13:10-17) that Jesus' disciples have a privileged place of understanding, whereas to the crowds he speaks in enigmatic parables, keeping his message hidden. With his addition of a quotation from Psalm 78:2, Matthew advances that the hiddenness of the message to those who are not disciples of Jesus is already spoken of in the Scriptures. Ordinarily he quotes the prophet Isaiah 6:9-10 to this end (as at 13:14-15), as do many other New Testament authors (see Mark 4:11-12; Luke 8:10; Acts 28:26-27; Rom 11:8; John 12:40).

PREACHING POSSIBILITIES

This gospel selection presents myriad possibilities for preaching. The homilist would do well to develop only one of them as the central image. If the preacher decides to focus on the first parable, that of the weeds and the wheat, it may be preferable to proclaim the short version of the gospel (vv. 24-30). One of the first things to determine is what the "good seed," the "weeds," and "the field" represent. Are the "weeds" personal shortcomings, vices, or sins that grow along with virtues in one's own garden? Are the plants people who are good and people who do evil? Or does the wheat represent impersonal forces for growth and goodness while the weeds stand for all that impedes growth? Is the "field" the family, the Christian community, or the global village? Is it the whole world or even the cosmos? Further, is the householder a positive character who makes a wise decision? Or is he foolish and greedy? Does his plan work?

Having wrestled with the various possible outcomes, the preacher must also carefully assess the needs of his or her congregation. Does the community struggle with racism, sexism, or any other type of discrimination toward people different from themselves? Then the parable of the weeds can serve as an invitation to the inclusivity that Jesus practiced toward those on the margins. The parables of the mustard seed and leaven likewise can serve to make this point: they are two other uncontrollable substances that permeate boundaries and overturn categories of what is good and what is not.

Do people in the congregation struggle with dualistic tendencies, seeing the world in clear categories of right and wrong, good and evil, and themselves as the champions of right? Then the parable of the weeds and the wheat can invite them into a less judgmental and less self-righteous stance. It opens up a worldview in which ambiguity exists[46] and where God's realm is revealed in the midst of conflictive situations, i.e., while the "weeds" and the "wheat" are growing together, not only in their resolution, at the "harvest" when the separation occurs.[47] It invites the hearer to compassionate forbearance which would allow people of differing ideologies and theologies to remain together in the same community. Other methods than excommunication would be engaged for conflict resolution and other solutions than capital punishment would be sought for "evildoers." Similarly, for people who struggle with scrupulosity or perfectionism within themselves, the parable can be an invitation to accept God's graciousness and patience. The first reading, from Wisdom 12:13,

[46] Bacq and Dumas, "Reading a Parable," 192.
[47] See David Buttrick, *Speaking Parables* (Louisville: Westminster, John Knox, 2000) 93–100.

16-19 also articulates trust in God whose might is manifest in lenience toward all.

If members of the community tend to unwisely underestimate corruptive forces such as greed, consumerism, hedonism, and individualism around them, then the parable can be preached as a warning. It would be an exhortation not to be like the overconfident, avaricious householder, whose foolish plan becomes his undoing.

For people who jump to conclusions or try to usurp the role of one in authority, the parable can be a reminder to them to have patience until the larger picture emerges. It advises against hasty decisions made by those who may not be in the position to discern wisely. If the landowner is a figure for God, then the parable advises against taking over God's role as judge.

If there are persons in the community inclined toward discouragement or despair about the inability to eradicate evil by their work of justice and gospel preaching, the parable of the weeds can serve as a story of encouragement that the "wheat" is strong enough in the end to withstand all the adversarial forces. God's realm will triumph ultimately. Or if a community of "good seed" is distraught by persecution from "evildoers" the parable assures them future reward.

The parable of the mustard seed can likewise be a parable of encouragement to those who are weary and who are tempted to think that their puny efforts on behalf of the gospel are to no avail. Like the tiny seed that becomes the greatest of plants, the ineradicable faith and actions of all the "nobodies" who believe have the potential to transform the world. The mustard seed parable can likewise stir into action one who is reluctant to put faith into practice, thinking their small efforts won't make any difference.

The parables of the mustard seed and the leaven can speak of the great subversive potential of little seeds and pinches of yeast. The messianic symbol is not the majestic cedar of Lebanon, but the lowly garden herb. God's reign will not arrive with traditional symbols of might and power, but will infest the world through the faith of ordinary believers.

The hiddenness of the seed sown or the leaven mixed into the dough could be the central image. The preacher might focus on assurance that God is at work, even when the divine action seems imperceptible or unintelligible. In its original setting these parables may have assured followers of Jesus that the word he preached would eventually become impressive in the visible growth of the body of the believers, even if the beginnings seemed very modest.[48]

From the mustard parable the preacher could also choose to focus on the locale of the reign of God and its manner of coming. It is not imported from far off, but comes with every small venture of faith by ordinary believers who act in the power of the crucified and risen Christ. Such ventures pose a challenge to oppressive systems of power just as mustard run wild can overtake cultivated fields. These kinds of efforts also shelter the little ones who, like the birds of the air, depend on God's benefaction for existence (Matt 6:26). This subversive power of radical faith, like mustard gone to seed, is impossible to root out once it has taken hold and is impossible to control within confined plots of land.

The parable of the leaven likewise poses a challenge about crossing boundaries. As Matthew's community may have understood the parable to speak to their experience of including "corrupt" Gentiles, for believers today the message may be a challenge to discard attempts at keeping the faith community a flat, "unleavened," mass of homogenous people, and to enthusiastically embrace an image of God's reign that includes persons of diverse races, ethnic origin, class, gender, age, sexual orientation, differing physical and mental abilities, who energize and transform the whole.

The parable of the leaven provides a rare opportunity for the preacher to speak of God in female terms and of the ministry of women as leaven, the critical ingredient for vitality and transformative action in the life of the church and the reign of God. It is still difficult for many contemporary Christians to embrace a female image of God, even though there are ample instances in the Scriptures. In Deuteronomy 32:18

---

[48] Herman Hendrickx, *The Parables of Jesus* (rev. ed.; San Francisco: Harper & Row, 1986) 40.

and Isaiah 42:14 God is portrayed as a mother giving birth. Isaiah speaks of God's tenderness as that of a mother consoling her child (Isa 49:15; 66:13). Isaiah 66:9 and Psalm 22:10-11 portray God as a midwife, drawing Israel forth from the womb. The Psalmist talks of God's care for humans like that of a mother eagle for her brood (Ps 91:4). Jesus uses this same image in Matthew 23:37 to express his care for Jerusalem. He also tells a parable about a woman searching for a lost coin (Luke 15:8-10) to speak about God's willingness to expend every effort to bring back those who are lost. By entering into the figurative world of the parable of the woman mixing dough, the preacher can invite both female and male believers to expand their repertoire of God images and more fully apprehend the divine mystery.

The image of the agitating action of leaven could be a vehicle to articulate how for some people women's entry into ministries traditionally reserved for males and the use of female images of God is the ruination of the unleavened bread, the Church. Others will thrill with the fermentation that causes the whole loaf to rise and be transformed into fulfilling fare for the whole community of believers. The preacher might lead the congregation in reflecting how it was that leaven, a good thing, which brings taste and texture to the loaf, came to be used exclusively as a symbol of corruption and evil. Similarly, we may ask how it was that women's leadership in ministry, so vital to the Church's early life, came to be regarded as a corrosive element and increasingly restricted. To have leavened bread is what is normal. It was the crisis situation of having to flee hastily from Egypt, with no time to wait for bread to be leavened (Exod 12:15-20, 34) that gave rise to the Jewish custom of eating unleavened bread in remembrance at Passover. Likewise, the restriction of women from the ministry of presiding at the breaking of the bread might be considered to have arisen from a crisis situation in the first Christian decades, where for the survival of the fledgling communities in a patriarchal and imperial world, these roles were taken over by men. What would be needed to return to a situation of leavened bread, where the mix of women with men in the same ministerial roles is considered "normal"?

The context of these parables shows that these are not peaceful stories about birds and plants and baking bread. Rather, they pose difficult challenges and invite conversion. The hearer is faced with a choice to side with those for whom everything remains hidden (13:35) or with those who become Jesus' followers, to whom understanding is given.

CHAPTER EIGHT

Buried Treasure, Precious Pearls, Indiscriminate Dragnet
(Matt 13:44-52)

Seventeenth Sunday of Ordinary Time

Wednesday of the Seventeenth Week of Ordinary Time
(Matt 13:44-46)

Thursday of the Seventeenth Week of Ordinary Time
(Matt 13:47-53)

[Jesus said to his disciples:
    "The kingdom of heaven is like a treasure buried in a field,
    which a person finds and hides again,
    and out of joy goes and sells all that he has and buys that field.
Again, the kingdom of heaven is like a merchant
    searching for fine pearls.
When he finds a pearl of great price,
    he goes and sells all that he has and buys it.]
Again, the kingdom of heaven is like a net thrown into the sea,
    which collects fish of every kind.
When it is full they haul it ashore
    and sit down to put what is good into buckets.
What is bad they throw away.
Thus it will be at the end of the age.
The angels will go out and separate the wicked from the righteous
    and throw them into the fiery furnace,
    where there will be wailing and grinding of teeth.

"Do you understand all these things?"
They answered, "Yes."

And he replied,
> *"Then every scribe who has been instructed in the kingdom of heaven*
> *is like the head of a household*
> *who brings from his storeroom both the new and the old."*

LITERARY CONTEXT

These three pithy parables and final remarks about understanding them complete Matthew's parables discourse that comprises the whole of chapter 13. The audience is the disciples, not the crowds, who Jesus dismissed in v. 36. The parables of the buried treasure (v. 44) and the pearl of great price (vv. 45-46) probably circulated together as a pair. They offer two different ways of coming upon the reign of God but end with the same message about the total response that is required to obtain it. The parable of the net (vv. 47-48) and its explanation (vv. 49-50) mirror that of the weeds and the wheat and its interpretation (13:24-30, 36-43) both in wording and in theme. The final verses (vv. 51-52) refer to the whole complex of parables in Matthew 13 and the disciples' ability to understand.

BURIED TREASURE (v. 44)

While the image of a person stumbling unexpectedly upon buried treasure may be foreign to contemporary hearers of this gospel, such was fairly common in ancient Palestine.[1] The threat of loss of land, either through invasion or indebtedness, was a constant one and it was commonly thought that one of the best ways to protect valuables was to bury them in the ground. A number of scenarios can be imagined for what would prevent a person from retrieving their goods. They might have died before having the opportunity to unearth them. Or they may have died without telling their heirs about the treasure. Or the precise locale may have been forgotten if too many years intervened. Or the land may have passed into the possession of foreign powers or a wealthy landowner and the former owner may not have

---

[1] See Matt 25:25, where the servant given one talent buries it in the ground.

been able to reclaim it. However the treasure got there, the parable presumes that the present owner does not know about it.

The circumstances in which the finder comes upon the treasure are not spelled out. It could have happened during the course of plowing the field, although more likely it would be discovered while doing work that was not routine, such as digging out a clogged well, or repairing a terrace wall, or excavating a new foundation. The finder could have been a day laborer, a tenant farmer, one who leased the land, or an independent contractor. In each of these cases the finder does not take the treasure out of the ground, since anything that would be lifted out would belong to the owner as long as the finder is in his employ.[2] In order for the finder to benefit from the treasure, he must purchase the field and the rights to all that it contains.

ENTITLEMENT

One detail in the parable that has caused some speculation is whether the finder who purchases the field is entitled to the treasure. There are detailed regulations spelled out in the Mishnah and Talmud for all sorts of scenarios in which a treasure is found and whether it can be legally acquired.[3] While these writings postdate the New Testament by several hundred years it is possible that they or similar ones were in force in Jesus' day.

A further question is whether or not the finder acted morally by buying the field. Was he dishonest in not telling the owner of the treasure? In one section of the Talmud the law specifies that one is obliged first to look for the treasure's owner, or in the case of newly purchased land, the treasure belongs to the previous owner, not the new one. Only after one has had the land for seven years and if the owner cannot be found can the new owner claim the treasure.[4] From this perspective the question arises as to whether the parable presents a positive

---

[2] J. Duncan M. Derrett, "Law in the New Testament: The Treasure in the Field (Mt. XIII,44)," *ZNW* 54 (1963) 31–42.

[3] See Derrett, "Law," 31–42, who details these regulations and who concludes that the finder acted morally.

[4] Bernard Brandon Scott, "Lost Junk, Found Treasure," *TBT* 26 (1988) 31–34.

image that is to be emulated or a warning about behavior that is to be avoided.[5]

JUST JUBILATION OR GREEDY GLEE?

Presuming that the finder is in the employ of the owner of the field, his joy at the unexpected find is realistic. The found treasure is the way out of servitude and ratchets the new owner into a whole other social and economic world from the one he knows. What is not clear is whether or not this is a good thing. A look at the literary echoes in the parable may help determine its meaning.

While references to joy are not plentiful in the Gospel of Matthew, there are two other parables in which joy features. In the parable of the sower/seed/harvest/soil, the one who receives the word at once with joy is the seed that is sown on rocky ground, but then, being rootless, is short-lived (13:20-21).[6] The other example is in the parable of the talents. A share in the master's joy is the reward for the two servants who doubled the talents entrusted to them (25:21, 23). In these two parables, the meaning of joy is ambiguous. In the first, joy is the proper response to reception of the word, but it is accompanied by rootlessness and it fizzles out. In the latter instance joy may be the glee of greediness,[7] and therefore not an exemplary response. Likewise, the joy in 13:44 can be understood as the reaction of a person who sees a way out of servitude, and takes it, despite the risk and dishonesty that it entails.[8] The plan may be disastrous for a poor person: if it goes awry after he has sold everything, he will have nothing to fall back on.[9] Or

[5] Charles W. Hedrick (*Parables as Poetic Fictions* [Peabody: Hendrickson, 1994] 117–41) examines how the imprecision in the story creates a polyvalence that purposely leaves it open to many possible readings, none of which exhausts the story.

[6] See above, chapter 6.

[7] See below, chapter 15.

[8] J. D. Crossan (*Finding is the First Act. Trove Folktales and Jesus' Treasure Parable* [Philadelphia: Fortress, 1979] sees the buying as unjust.

[9] John J. Pilch, *The Cultural World of Jesus. Sunday by Sunday. Cycle A* (Collegeville: The Liturgical Press, 1995) 115.

the lure of treasure is such that it corrupts a person into taking narcissistic illegal actions that taunt, "Finders keepers, losers weepers." If we presume the Talmudic laws, the finder would remain paralyzed and impoverished since he dare not dig up the treasure, for then all will know it is not rightfully his. In seeking to possess the treasure, he actually forfeits its use.[10]

In this vein the parable coheres with Jesus' warnings in the Sermon on the Mount against storing up for oneself treasures on earth, "where moth and decay destroy, and thieves break in and steal." Rather, Jesus advises, "store up treasures in heaven, where neither moth nor decay destroys, nor thieves break in and steal. For where your treasure is, there also will your heart be" (6:19-21). This saying is echoed in the episode where Jesus invites the rich young man to sell his many possessions, give it all to the poor, thereby having treasure in heaven (19:21). He goes away sad and does not follow Jesus.

On the other hand, the parable can be understood as a positive example of the total response that is asked of a disciple who rightly abandons all in order to follow Jesus. There are verbal echoes with the previous cycle of parables, where the same root word is used for hiddenness. The treasure is hidden (*kekrymmenō*) in the field and hidden (*enekrypsen*) again by the finder (13:44), recalling the leaven that is hidden (*enekrypsen*) in three measures of flour (13:33).[11] And Jesus had declared that by his speaking in parables he is announcing what has lain hidden (*kekrymmena*) from the foundation of the world (13:35). In this context, the hidden treasure is something to be sought.

There are also echoes of the response of the first disciples to Jesus' invitation to follow him. Simon Peter, Andrew, James, and John all leave their nets, their boats, their father, and their prosperous business to follow Jesus (4:18-22). The toll collector, Matthew, similarly leaves his customs post to follow Jesus (9:9). When Peter later questions Jesus about what there will be for those who have given up everything to follow him, Jesus assures them they will sit on twelve thrones judging the twelve tribes of Israel and that everyone who has given up houses or

---

[10] Scott, "Lost Junk," 32–33.
[11] See above, chapter 7.

family or lands for his sake will receive a hundred times more, and will inherit eternal life (19:27-29). In this context, the selling all by the finder of the treasure is the desired total response of a disciple to the discovery of the reign of God as proclaimed by Jesus.[12] The emphasis is not on how much such a one gives up, but rather on the immense gain and the joy that comes from the complete investment of self and resources to God's realm.[13]

PRECIOUS PEARLS (vv. 45-46)

This parable replicates that of the found treasure, except that the image is that of a person deliberately seeking the item of great value, rather than one who comes upon it unexpectedly. Another difference is that the merchant may be rich, in contrast to the finder of the treasure, who was more likely a poor peasant.

The same ambiguities are present as with the previous parable. A buyer of pearls can evoke an image of ostentatiousness and corruption. Most of the references to merchants in the Scriptures are negative.[14] Ben Sirah remarks that a merchant "can hardly remain upright, nor a shopkeeper free from sin" (Sir 26:20). Isaiah prophesies that God will bring down the traders, "the earth's honored men" (Isa 23:8). A denunciation of Tyre's merchants is found in Ezekiel 27. In 1 Timothy 2:9 the pastor advises that women should adorn themselves with proper conduct and not with gold ornaments, pearls, and expensive clothes. In the book of Revelation the harlot of Babylon is decked out in opulent purple, adorned with gold, precious stones, and pearls (17:4; 18:16). In Revelation 18:15 the merchants who deal in such luxury items, "who grew rich from her, will keep their distance for fear of the torment inflicted on her." The pearl merchant, then, could embody avaricious acquisitiveness. He could be a ruthless businessman who uses cut-throat tactics to assure his own social and economic en-

---

[12] Donald Senior, *Matthew* (ANTC; Nashville: Abingdon, 1998)156.

[13] Daniel J. Harrington, *Matthew* (SacPag1; Collegeville: The Liturgical Press, 1991) 207.

[14] Warren Carter, *Matthew and the Margins. A Sociopolitical and Religious Reading* (The Bible and Liberation Series; Maryknoll: Orbis, 2000) 296.

hancement. To poor divers who labor to find his pearls he would not be a sympathetic figure. The merchant's occupation is fraught with temptations. His seeking can result in misdirection or corruption, like Herod, who seeks *(zētein)* to destroy the child Jesus (2:13), or like evil and unfaithful generations who seek signs (12:39; 16:4), or the chief priests and Sanhedrin who seek to put Jesus to death (21:46; 26:59). The point of the parable may be that even such a one can come upon the reign of God, and can be moved to sell off all his holdings, to dedicate himself to the only pearl worth pursuing.

The merchant could also be an image for a righteous rich person who earnestly seeks God. He puts a human face on the sayings in the Sermon on the Mount that underscore the importance of seeking the reign of God (6:32-33) and that assure disciples that when they seek they will find (7:7-38). Such seeking reaches its culmination in the gospel when the Galilean women seek the crucified Jesus at the empty tomb (28:5); instead, they encounter him alive and are commissioned by him to tell the others where to seek for him (28:9-10).

The two parables highlight the single-hearted response that is demanded when one finds God's reign, whether it is through active seeking, or by accidental discovery. If the treasure finder and the merchant are not at first blush, entirely upright characters, the next parable wrestles with the way that Jesus has attracted such a motley mix of folk.

NETTING ALL KINDS (vv. 47-50)

The third parable in the trio and its explanation parallels to a great extent the parable of the weeds and the wheat and its interpretation (vv. 13:24-30, 36-43). Verbal echoes include collecting (vv. 40-41, 47), what is good (vv. 37, 48), the end of the age (vv. 40, 49), angels separating (vv. 41, 49), the righteous (vv. 43, 49), throwing the rejected into the fiery furnace (vv. 42, 50), weeping and gnashing of teeth (vv. 42, 50).[15] It is likely that

---

[15] Jan Lambrecht, *Out of the Treasure. The Parables in the Gospel of Matthew* (Louvain Theological and Pastoral Monographs 10; Grand Rapids: Eerdmans, 1991) 172.

Matthew composed the concluding interpretive verses (49-50) on the pattern of 13:36-43.[16]

The parable advances the image introduced in the call of the first disciples, where Jesus told Peter and Andrew that they would henceforth be fishers of people (4:19).[17] Fishing was sometimes done with lines and fishhooks (17:27), but professional fishermen would have used either a circular sweep-net *(amphiblēstron)* that was weighted along the edges, or a dragnet *(sagēnē)* that was weighted at one end and had floats on the other. The former was used for fishing in deep water (4:18); the latter for surface fishing or for fishing from shore. It is the latter that is envisioned in Matthew 13:47.[18] It is indiscriminate in its gathering; the catch is sorted after it is hauled ashore.

As at the harvest of the weeds and the wheat, what is good is kept and what is bad *(sapra)* is thrown out and burned, not thrown back into the sea. The word *sapra* ("bad") is used elsewhere to refer to what is decayed or rotten (Matt 7:17; 12:33). It is possible that this word evokes a delay in the sorting (akin to the parable of the weeds and the wheat) and so some of the fish spoils in the elapse of time. But it is also possible that Matthew has in mind the netting of both clean and unclean fish (see Lev 11:10-12) as a metaphor for his mixed community of Jews and Gentiles. But the dynamics of the narrative point toward it being an image for the mingling of everyone from good, upstanding people to flagrant sinners, all attracted to Jesus and his movement.[19] Until the end time good and evil in people and in structures coexist, even within the Christian community.

In the explanation (vv. 49-50) the sorting of good and bad is equated with the separation of the righteous from the wicked at the end of the age. There is an eschatological moment when there can be no more blurring of the lines or mix-

---

[16] Harrington, *Matthew,* 207. Note that the fiery furnace makes more sense for burning weeds than it does as a way to dispose of rotten fish.

[17] Warren Carter and John Paul Heil, *Matthew's Parables* (CBQMS 30; Washington, D.C.: CBA, 1998) 90.

[18] John Pilch, *The Cultural Dictionary of the Bible* (Collegeville: The Liturgical Press, 1999) 188.

[19] John P. Meier, *Matthew* (NTM 3; Wilmington: Glazier, 1980) 153.

ing of the two. This parable points ahead to the stark reality sketched in the parables in Matthew 25 where one is either included or not; there is no in-between space. A favorite Matthean expression, "weeping and gnashing of teeth," captures the anguish of exclusion.[20]

UNDERSTANDING (vv. 51-52)

The concluding verses tie together the whole of the discourse in chapter 13. "These things" (v. 51) refers to all the preceding parables and all that they reveal about God's reign. The disciples in Matthew's Gospel do have a certain privileged level of understanding (13:11-12, 16-17), but as subsequent episodes reveal, their comprehension of Jesus and his words is by no means complete. There is a certain irony to their straightforward affirmative reply.[21]

The final saying, about scribes who have been instructed *(mathēteutheis),* is often thought to be a self-portrait of the evangelist,[22] but actually characterizes every educated disciple. Elsewhere in Matthew scribes are not favorable characters.[23] In contrast to the Jewish scribes who are members of the religious elite and opponents of Jesus, his disciples *(mathētai)* who are schooled in his interpretation of the Law know how to preserve what is essential from the old for a new reality (see also 5:17; 9:17).

PREACHING POSSIBILITIES

The first two parables offer divergent ways of finding in God's realm the one thing worth total dedication and the all-encompassing response that is expected. The preacher might sketch in contemporary images ways in which this happens

---

[20] Matt 8:12; 13:42; 22:13; 24:51; 25:30.

[21] Here the gospel intersects with the first reading, where Solomon prays for an understanding heart, one that is able to discern right from wrong.

[22] Harrington (*Matthew,* 208) observes that the verb *mathēteutheis* even sounds like "Matthew."

[23] Carter, *Matthew and the Margins,* 297. See 2:4; 5:17; 7:29; 8:19; 9:3; 12:38.

today. Some people are actively seeking God through prayer, study, reading, questioning, conversing, ministering. Others are just trying to deal with the ordinary demands of life, not looking for anything unusual to happen, when out of the blue God touches them in an unexpected way. It can be through a marvelous event like a birth or a sudden tragedy. An unanticipated visit or a stray remark from someone at work can be the vehicle of a startling revelation of God's gracious goodness in such a way that it transforms one's whole life.[24] The homilist might invite the congregation into a stance of receptivity for the moment of finding. She or he might offer concrete avenues by which those who are actively seeking God's reign might bring it to expression by participation in education or service opportunities.

One pitfall that the preacher will want to avoid is to speak of the reign of God as if it were something that could be bought or possessed. The element of surprise in the first parable helps underscore the way in which participation in the realm of God is first and foremost, a gift, not something that can be earned.[25] Acceptance of the gift means giving everything in return. It is the opposite of what happens when we go bargain-hunting: this great find costs everything we have—and it is worth it! Joy results not in having gotten something for nothing, but rather in the freedom that comes from finding oneself in Christ and his realm.

The preacher might focus on the parable of the net as an invitation to suspend all judgmentalness in the present incarnation of God's realm. Those who are involved in the work of evangelization might find this message particularly apt. Even a wily merchant or a scheming treasure-hunter can be a potentially good "catch." The parable can offer an image for the patience required of disciples with the imperfect mix of things in the present. There is room in the Christian community both for

---

[24] Thomas G. Long, *Matthew* (WBC; Louisville: Westminster John Knox, 1997) 156–57.

[25] Another misdirection would be to link the second reading (Rom 8:28-30) with the gospel in a such a way that would convey the message that finding treasure unexpectedly is the way God makes things work out for people who love God.

people who are serious in their quest for God and for those who are just looking for a nice church in which to get married.[26] Who knows whether the latter may someday become drawn in more deeply to the point of "selling all" by those who have already done so?

There is a note of judgment at the end of this parable, however, that is important not to gloss over. There is a point at which the toleration of the mix of good and evil comes to an end. At the end time there will be a separation, and as other parables emphasize, a disciple will want to be found among the "good." One pitfall the preacher will want to avoid is to depict the world or people in dualistic contrasts between good and evil. Such ways of thinking can close off the wellsprings of compassion, pitting "us" against "them" in ways that blind us to the mix of both good and bad in persons and structures. Furthermore, the promise of total joy and fulfillment may go further than the threat of a fiery furnace in turning a listener's heart toward God.

Finally, a preacher may take his or her direction from the saying at the conclusion of the gospel. The task for Christians of every age is to interpret the "old" of the tradition in new circumstances, places, and times. Just as Matthew helped his community to understand themselves as faithful to their traditions and to the God of their ancestors, in their way of following Jesus, so preachers today help the community interpret the Good News both newly and faithfully for this age.

[26] Long, *Matthew*, 158.

CHAPTER NINE

Forgiveness Aborted
(Matt 18:21-35)

Twenty-Fourth Sunday of Ordinary Time

Tuesday of the Third Week of Lent

Thursday of the Nineteenth Week of Ordinary Time
(Matt 18:21–19:1)

Peter approached Jesus and asked him,
  "Lord, if my brother sins against me,
  how often must I forgive?
As many as seven times?"
Jesus answered, "I say to you, not seven times but seventy-seven times.
That is why the kingdom of heaven may be likened to a king
  who decided to settle accounts with his servants.
When he began the accounting,
  a debtor was brought before him who owed him a huge amount.
Since he had no way of paying it back,
  his master ordered him to be sold,
  along with his wife, his children, and all his property,
  in payment of the debt.
At that, the servant fell down, did him homage, and said,
  'Be patient with me, and I will pay you back in full.'
Moved with compassion the master of that servant
  let him go and forgave him the loan.
When that servant had left, he found one of his fellow servants
  who owed him a much smaller amount.
He seized him and started to choke him, demanding,
  'Pay back what you owe.'
Falling to his knees, his fellow servant begged him,
  'Be patient with me, and I will pay you back.'

But he refused.
Instead, he had the fellow servant put in prison
    until he paid back the debt.
Now when his fellow servants saw what had happened,
    they were deeply disturbed, and went to their master
    and reported the whole affair.
His master summoned him and said to him, 'You wicked servant!
I forgave you your entire debt because you begged me to.
Should you not have had pity on your fellow servant,
    as I had pity on you?'
Then in anger his master handed him over to the torturers
    until he should pay back the whole debt.
So will my heavenly Father do to you,
    unless each of you forgives your brother from your heart."

LITERARY CONTEXT

This dramatic parable comes as the conclusion and climax of the discourse on Church life that comprises the whole of Matthew 18. The parable is preceded by an outline of the steps that should be taken in a situation in which one member of the community sins against another (vv. 15-20).[1] Highlighted are the hard work and persistence that are necessary for achieving reconciliation. The first step in the process is direct confrontation initiated by the one offended (v. 15). A readiness to forgive is the first requisite, and a willingness to approach the sinner from such a stance. This demands that the one offended be willing to relinquish the role of victim and the satisfaction of telling everyone else about the other's fault. Sometimes this first confrontation brings about the needed repentance and reconciliation results. But if not, the second step is to involve one or two others (v. 16). The point is not to gang up on the sinner, but rather, with the help of an objective voice, or a facilitator who is outside the conflict, the truth may be established, and forgiveness and reconciliation occur.

---

[1] See further William G. Thompson, *Matthew's Advice to a Divided Community, Mt. 17,22–18,35* (Rome: Biblical Institute, 1970); Dennis C. Duling, "Matthew 18:15-17: Conflict, Confrontation, and Conflict Resolution in a 'Fictive Kin' Association," *BTB* 29 (1999) 4–22.

If this does not work, then the matter is taken before the whole community *(ekklēsia)*.[2] If that effort fails, then the person is to be treated like a Gentile or a toll collector (v. 17). At first blush this last line may seem to mean that the person should be expelled. But in light of Jesus' treatment of Gentiles and toll collectors,[3] it may, rather, connote a willingness to sit at the same table and break bread together, while working toward oneness with God and one another.[4] Other episodes in the gospel point in this direction. When Jesus called Matthew, a toll collector, to be a disciple (9:9) he then went to eat at his house with many other toll collectors and sinners. When the Pharisees challenge his disciples about this, Jesus responds, "Those who are well do not need a physician, but the sick do. Go and learn the meaning of the words, 'I desire mercy *(eleos)*, not sacrifice.' I did not come to call the righteous but sinners" (9:12-13). By recalling Jesus' stance of mercy toward toll collectors at 18:17, Matthew sets the stage for the parable in 18:23-35, where the king demands to know why his slave has not shown mercy *(eleēsai, v. 33)*.

Following the three-step program for reconciliation (vv. 15-17) are sayings that underscore the lasting ramifications of forgiveness, the role of prayer in achieving reconciliation, and the role of the community in mediating, praying, and forgiving. The whole Church is involved in prayer (vv. 19-20) and in binding and loosing (v. 18).[5] The saying in v. 18 about what is bound or loosed on earth is likewise bound or loosed in heaven points forward to the concluding verse of the parable,

[2] Among the evangelists, only Matthew uses the word *ekklēsia*, "church" (Matt 16:18; 18:18 [2x]).

[3] Despite the sayings in Matthew that Jesus has come to save only the lost sheep of the house of Israel (10:5-6; 15:24), there are episodes in which he heals Gentiles (8:5-13; 15:21-28) and there are sayings on the lips of Jesus which point toward a mission to the Gentiles (12:18, 21; 28:19). Jesus calls a toll collector to be a disciple and eats with him and other toll collectors (9:9-13), thus becoming known as their friend (11:19).

[4] Of course the scenario in Matt 18:15-20 does not indicate the nature of the sin. Such a strategy would not be tolerable for certain kinds of offenses.

[5] The verbs *dēsēte* ("you bind") and *lysēte* ("you loose") in v. 18 are in the second person plural.

which speaks of how forgiveness of a brother or sister has ramifications on the heavenly Father's[6] forgiveness (v. 35).

ENDLESS FORGIVENESS (vv. 21-22)

Immediately preceding the parable is a query by Peter: how many times does a disciple have to forgive?[7] Is the process described in vv. 15-20 to be followed for every offense? Peter proffers, "As many as seven times?" (v. 21). In the Bible seven is symbolic for a full number. Jesus' response, "not seven times but seventy-seven times" (v. 22) stretches the boundaries of forgiveness to astronomical and limitless proportions. There may be a contrast intended with Lamech, who vowed vengeance "seventy-sevenfold" (Gen 4:24). A person who forgives foregoes vengeance, in order to short-circuit the cycles of violence and to initiate a different direction in the relationship, toward reconciliation. Both the leaders of the community and the whole body are to exercise forgiveness over and over so as to lead to transformation of heart (v. 35).[8]

A CALCULATING KING (vv. 23-27)

The parable plays out in three acts. The first scene places us in a world of elites and court intrigues.[9] A king, perhaps

---

[6] See above, pp. 55–59 on heavenly Father.

[7] Matt 18:21-22 has a parallel in Luke 17:4, but the context is different. The parable in Matt 18:23-35 is unique to Matthew.

[8] John Pilch ("Forgiveness," in *Cultural Dictionary of the Bible* [Collegeville: The Liturgical Press, 1999] 62–63) sees a different pattern in vv. 15-20 than in vv. 21-35. In the first part the offense is between equals and the dynamics of challenge and riposte are allowed. That is, one who is insulted by an equal responds in kind or else they will incur a loss of honor. The parable and the exchange with Peter, however, describe the dynamics between superior and inferior. An inferior cannot challenge a superior, therefore a superior can overlook a debt and still maintain honor for benevolence. I question, however, whether Peter is meant to be seen as superior to the other disciples, in light of sayings such as Matt 20:26-27, where Jesus asserts that whoever wishes to be first among the disciples shall be the slave.

[9] The following interpretation follows that of William Herzog (*Parables as Subversive Speech* [Louisville: Westminster John Knox, 1999] 131–49) and of Warren Carter (*Matthew and the Margins*, 370–75).

evocative of the client-king Herod, stands at the top of the whole social, political, economic, and religious system. The parable zeroes in on his exercise of control of financial matters, as he has brought before him one of his slaves *(doulos)*. The latter is a high level bureaucrat, not someone in poor circumstances. Most likely he is responsible for exacting tribute from other subjects of the realm, and has achieved his high place in the king's employ through calculating and cunning tactics. He has built networks and worked the system to both his advantage and that of the king. That he is dubbed "slave" in the parable connotes his subservience to the king. It serves to highlight that no matter how good he is at his job, it is always done at the king's bidding. And if he falters, there are other power-hungry servants ready to step into his shoes.[10]

A crisis moment ensues when the king suddenly decides to call in his "loan" *(daneion)*, that is, the amount of money due him from the tribute this functionary is collecting. That the latter is operating in the world of high finance is clear from the "huge amount" (v. 24). Literally, it is *myriōn talantōn*, ten thousand talents.[11] This equals somewhere between six thousand and ten thousand denarii when one denarius was a day's wage (20:2).[12] The amount is astronomical. It is the same as the amount Josephus says that Rome extracted from all of Judea in the 60s B.C.E. (Jos. *Ant*. 14.78). In whatever way the servant has spent or re-invested the money, he has overreached and cannot retrieve all that is due the king.

[10] Jennifer Glancy, "Slaves and Slavery in the Matthean Parables," *JBL* 119 (2000) 67–90 shows that slaves who were managers of their masters' funds had the opportunity of amassing their own fortunes, which they frequently used to purchase their freedom or that of their family members. A slave's purpose, however, is to advance the interests of his or her owner.

[11] Herzog, *Subversive Speech*, 144, argues on the grounds of verisimilitude that the original contrast in Jesus' parable was between one hundred talents and one hundred denarii. Matthew has inflated the first figure.

[12] Pilch (*Cultural World*, 137) observes that at this rate ten thousand talents would require more than 164,000 years of work, seven days a week to pay off. But that calculation would be in terms of a day laborer, who would never have incurred a debt of this amount in the first place. The slave involved is a high-ranking bureaucrat, with large sums of money under his control.

In a pure display of power, the master threatens to make an example of him: to remove him from his position, sell him into slavery,[13] along with his family and all his property. The purpose of this is not so that the servant can work off his debt and thus repay it, for not only is the sum beyond repayment, but repayment would be impossible to do while incarcerated. To collect all that is owed him, the servant needs the freedom to manipulate among the web of clients. Rather, the purpose of the accounting is for the king to reassert his power. It is to keep his subordinates aware that at a moment's notice the king can reduce his high-level bureaucrats to slavery.

The servant's response is exactly what is required. He falls down and worships the king (v. 26), begging patience and assuring his full loyalty and intent to pay the king everything. The verb *proskyneō* ("worship," "do homage") designates the custom of prostrating oneself before a person and kissing his feet, the hem of his garment, or the ground.[14] Elsewhere in the gospel this action is directed only to Jesus. The Magi come to do homage to the newborn king (2:2, 11; in contrast to Herod who voices a false intention to do so in 2:8). People who come to Jesus with requests prostrate themselves before him: a leper (8:2); an official whose daughter has just died (9:18); a Canaanite woman (15:25); and the mother of the sons of Zebedee (20:20). Disciples worship Jesus after he rescues Peter from sinking in the sea (14:33); and after the resurrection (28:9, 17). The devil tempts Jesus to fall down and worship him, to which Jesus replies, "The Lord, your God, shall you worship and him alone shall you serve" (4:10).

---

[13] Some commentators take this detail as an indication that Matthew envisions a Gentile king, since Jewish law forbade both the selling of a fellow Jew into slavery as well as torture. As Herzog (*Subversive*, 130, 138–39) points out, however, this is a moot point, since whether or not these things were lawful, the king stands outside the law and can do exactly what he pleases. This is not a constitutional monarch, who is subject to the law, but one who can exert authoritarian control as arbitrarily as he pleases. Glancy ("Slaves and Slavery," 86) notes that the king is not selling a free man *into* slavery; he is already a slave, and the king plans to sell him to another owner.

[14] BDAG, s.v., προσκυνέω.

The king is moved to change his tactics. But, as the ending of the parable shows, it is not from heart-felt compassion.[15] In the honor and shame game, the king has won. He has made his point and has exacted homage and acknowledgment of his power. He has put the bureaucrat in his place. The servant may have overstepped his bounds, but he has proven his loyalty and worth. He knows the system and has shown his ability. The king decides to retain him for his service. He does not demand repayment of all the money owed, but allows him to return to his position to continue his financial machinations for the benefit of the king. The immediate payback for the monarch will be that word of this confrontation will spread among the other functionaries and will keep them conscious of the vulnerability of their position. In addition, he will receive adulation for his generosity and benefaction.

MISDIRECTED VENGEANCE (vv. 28-30)

The scene shifts and the next act begins with an almost exact repetition of the previous one. This time the forgiven slave is in the role of the superior. His motive for initiating his own day of reckoning is not given. Perhaps his intent is to redouble his collection efforts to reassure the king of his worth and efficiency. Or, having been shamed before the king, he needs to reassert his own power with his clients.[16] He finds one of his subordinates,[17] and with physical violence demands payment of what is owed.[18] This servant owes only one hundred denarii (*hekaton dēnaria,* rendered "a much smaller amount" in the *NAB*). The point is not that this is a payable debt in contrast

---

[15] Elsewhere in the gospel the verb *splagchnizomai* ("to have pity") is used of Jesus, to describe his compassion for crowds to whom he ministers (9:36), by curing and feeding them (14:14; 15:32; 20:34).

[16] Carter, *Matthew and the Margins*, 373.

[17] The Greek word *syndoulos* means "fellow slave." They are both slaves as regards their standing in relation to the king, but as the next verses show, the fellow slave is a subordinate of the first one.

[18] Glancy ("Slaves and Slavery," 67–90) shows that the emphasis on the vulnerability of slaves to violence, pervasive in Matthew's parables, is consonant with the reality of the Greco-Roman world.

to an unpayable one in act one. In the world of this middle level slave, the debt may as well be ten thousand talents.[19] He is just as unable to pay as the first servant was.

The underling replicates the same response as his superior made to the king. He falls to his knees in obeisance, pleads for patience, and assures his master of honor and payment. It is at this juncture that the first slave makes a fatal mistake. Rather than imitate his master and forgive the debt, he refused and threw the debtor into prison. From prison he would be able to pay the debt if he can secure another patron. But who would be willing to take him on if there is doubt of his trustworthiness? His reprieve will come from solidarity displayed by his fellow servants.

SHOCKING REVERSAL (vv. 31-34)

In the final act of the drama other slaves on the same rung of the social and economic ladder are grieved at the turn of events and decide to report it all to their master. To gain the ear of the king they may have secured a new patron. Given the precarious situation with their shamed patron and his brutal treatment of one like themselves, it is likely they have shifted allegiances.

When the king summons the high ranking official for the second time, he denounces him as wicked and details the action he expected from him: he should take direction from the king's actions. If he is loyal to the king and understands the monarch's message to him, then he should have replicated what the king did. If the slave wants to ensure loyalty, adulation, and recognition of power for himself, the king showed him how it was to be done. Instead he has shamed the king by not imitating him. His actions have sent the message that the king's way of exerting power is not effective. If the slave thinks that physical throttling, imperviousness to debasement, and

---

[19] Herzog (*Subversive Speech*, 143) notes that one hundred denarii represented one-half of a Roman legionnaire's annual salary and more than a full year's wages of a day laborer. Few peasants would see such an amount at one time in their lifetime.

brutal imprisonment is the way to do it, then the king will show him just that.[20]

ETHICAL CONCLUSION (v. 35)

It is probable that this concluding verse was added to the parable by the evangelist.[21] It is typical of Matthew to bring to the fore a reference to judgment.[22] It is an allegorizing conclusion that relates the godless machinations of ruling elites to the anticipated response of the divine toward those who are unforgiving. The parable begins as an answer to a question posed by Peter, but in the end is addressed to all disciples.[23] The parable has created a scenario in which the king is not like God, but the dynamic of the story is like what happens to disciples when they do not learn to imitate God's actions as exemplified by Jesus. Just as the king's underlings are expected to understand his comportment and to replicate it, so with disciples of Jesus.

Disciples of Jesus, like the first slave, owe everything to God who has graciously endowed it. The debt is beyond what can ever be paid, and it has all been eliminated by Jesus. The only response to such mercy is to let it transform one's heart and so be able to act with the same kind of mercy toward others. Unlike the king in the parable, God does not act this way for self-aggrandizement, but for the well-being of all creation. A different kind of power is at work in Jesus and his disciples: instead of gaining honor through avenging wrongs with violence and vengeance, Jesus shows the way of power through vulnerability. Potency is evident in willingness to forego vengeance and

---

[20] See, Carter, *Matthew and the Margins*, 374. Herzog (*Subversive*, 146–47), taking direction from J.D.M. Derrett (*Law in the New Testament* [London: Darton, Longman & Todd, 1970] 42), proposes that the king's anger is because the slave misunderstood the release as a personal beneficence, when it was intended to be the first in a series of actions to "oil all the wheels" for the well-being of all the kingdom. The slave's subsequent actions make the king look like a fool, so the monarch reverts with a vengeance to business as usual.

[21] See Lambrecht, *Out of the Treasure*, 53–68, for a more detailed analysis of the tradition history of the parable.

[22] See 8:12; 13:42, 50; 22:13; 24:51; 25:30.

[23] "You" (*hymin*) in v. 35 is plural.

to engage in the hard work of reconciliation. Such depends on a transformation of heart that impels one to begin from a stance of willingness to forgive when wronged. If disciples do not learn to imitate these godly ways in their dealings with one another, then they can expect to be treated by God with their own preferred method. Matthew is ever insistent on the ethical demands of discipleship. Forgiveness is freely given by God, but the price tag is to go and do likewise.

PREACHING POSSIBILITIES

The preacher can get into a bind if he or she tries to interpret the images in the parable as straightforward equations in which God is the king and the slaves are human beings. The preacher would then have to answer questions like: How could God rescind loving kindness? How could God be so heartless? Can human behavior determine God's conduct? Moreover, the analogy of a king with his slaves is a poor one for trying to speak of God's power and infinite mercy as revealed in Jesus.[24] The model of imperial might was far removed from the manner in which Jesus expressed the divine longing to bring all into reconciled relation. Moreover, the notion of falling at the feet of a monarch to implore beneficence can too easily slip into the sentiment that groveling is pleasing to God.

The preacher might highlight that the prayer we recite together most frequently incorporates the very same message as this parable. When, at the end of the Our Father, we pray, "forgive us our trespasses[25] as we forgive those who trespass against us," we are asking God to let the experience of being forgiven so transform our hearts that we may likewise forgive others.[26] It would be a foolish person who would pray the other

---

[24] See above, pp. 41–42 on the "kingdom of heaven" and the metaphor of God as king.

[25] In Matthew's version of the Our Father the word "debts" *opheilēma* (6:12) is used, rather than "sins," *hamartia* (Luke 11:4).

[26] In Deut 15:1-2 the relaxation of debt in the sabbatical year is justified by the same principle: one must act thus toward the neighbor because God has done the same toward Israel.

way around, asking God to forgive us only in the puny measure we are able to forgive others. What 18:35 as well as 6:14-15
express is that the extent to which disciples learn to forgive in
this life has ramifications for eternal life.[27]

Further, it is not sufficient that forgiveness be mouthed:
transformation of heart is necessary (v. 35). For the ancients,
the heart is the center not only of emotions and passions, but
also the source of thought and understanding. From the heart
also comes will and conscience. It is the source of obedience
and devotion. It is the place where one meets God and is transformed. In short, it represents the whole human person.[28]

The preacher might also point out to the congregation
how easy it is to revert to ways of strict accounting and punishment for failure even when one has been the recipient of
lavish mercy. One might ask the hearers, did you cheer when
the unforgiving servant got what he seemed to have coming?
Or did your heart break with compassion for him, over his
having missed the mark? Would you give him seventy-seven
chances to learn to be transformed by mercy? The homilist
might invite the congregation to reflect on whether there is
anyone they have given up on because of hurts that seem to be
too old or too deep to heal. The gospel this Sunday could be an
invitation to hold out to Jesus the woundedness of our hearts
and pray for God's mercy to heal the wounds and move us to
approach an offender with forgiveness to begin the process of
reconciliation. The preacher can encourage prayer, too, for the
strength to persevere an infinite number of times in letting our
hearts be molded into the pattern of divine mercy.

It is interesting that Matthew uses a scenario of financial
accounting and release of debt as a metaphor for sin. The
preacher might take direction from this to speak about forgiveness not only in interpersonal terms, but in the realm of
global finances. How might this parable help us know what
response to make in the face of astronomical unpayable debts
of developing countries owed to rich nations? Or on a local

---

[27] Similarly, at Matt 5:7, "Blessed are the merciful for they will be shown
mercy."

[28] See Matt 5:8, 28; 6:21; 9:36; 11:29; 12:34; 13:15, 19; 14:14; 15:18, 19, 32; 22:37.

scale, what outstanding debts, both metaphorical and actual, could be written off in a spirit of jubilee? How can disciples initiate debt release that would have a rippling effect as each one forgiven would imitate the mercy they were shown?

One thing that the preacher should stress clearly is that this parable does not advocate unlimited forgiveness by victims for their unrepentant abusers. This parable has often been misinterpreted to advocate that forgiveness over and over again is the way for a victim of domestic violence, for example, to follow the way of the Cross of Jesus. Homilists should highlight that in contrast to 18:22, the parable actually shows that there *are* limits to forgiveness. The one who has been forgiven and does not in turn act toward another cannot receive boundless forgiveness. The parable holds in tension both unlimited grace and the demands of forgiveness. It is also important to note that in the wider context of Matthew 18, where forgiveness is a communal responsibility, not an individual action, the aspects of truth-telling, acceptance of responsibility, and repentance, also play a critical role in the process of reconciliation.[29]

Finally, a further, more subtle lesson of the parable is that as hearers take the stance of the fellow servants in the last act of the parable, it can implicate them in the very sin of the unforgiving servant—their sin is identical to his.[30] The preacher might reflect on how "the narrative leads to a parabolic experience of evil, not intentional evil but implicit, unanticipated, systemic evil. The ability to acknowledge one's entanglement in evil is part of the experience of the kingdom."[31] From this stance, the parable calls the community not only to recognize sin in others and bring them to repentance, but to see the same in ourselves and to seek forgiveness and reconciliation.[32]

---

[29] See Susan E. Hylen, "Forgiveness and Life in Community," *Int* 54 (2000) 146–57, who articulates these insights from her experience of work with victims of domestic abuse.

[30] Ibid., 157.

[31] B. B. Scott, "The King's Accounting: Matthew 18:23-34," *JBL* 104 (1985) 442.

[32] Hylen, "Forgiveness," 157. See also David Buttrick, *Speaking Parables* (Louisville: Westminster John Knox, 2000) 107–13.

CHAPTER TEN

Workers and Wages
(Matt 20:1-16a)

Twenty-Fifth Sunday of Ordinary Time
Wednesday of the Twentieth Week of Ordinary Time

Jesus told his disciples this parable:
*   "The kingdom of heaven is like a landowner*
*   who went out at dawn to hire laborers for his vineyard.*
After agreeing with them for the usual daily wage,
he sent them into his vineyard.
Going out about nine o'clock,
*   the landowner saw others standing idle in the marketplace,*
*   and he said to them, 'You too go into my vineyard,*
*   and I will give you what is just.'*
So they went off.
And he went out again around noon,
*   and around three o'clock, and did likewise.*
Going out about five o'clock,
*   the landowner found others standing around, and said to them,*
*   'Why do you stand here idle all day?'*
They answered, 'Because no one has hired us.'
He said to them, 'You too go into my vineyard.'
When it was evening the owner of the vineyard said to his foreman,
*   'Summon the laborers and give them their pay,*
*   beginning with the last and ending with the first.'*
When those who had started about five o'clock came,
*   each received the usual daily wage.*
So when the first came, they thought that they would receive more,
*   but each of them also got the usual wage.*

And on receiving it they grumbled against the landowner, saying,
  'These last ones worked only one hour,
  and you have made them equal to us,
  who bore the day's burden and the heat.'
He said to one of them in reply,
  'My friend, I am not cheating you.
Did you not agree with me for the usual daily wage?
Take what is yours and go.
What if I wish to give this last one the same as you?
Or am I not free to do as I wish with my own money?
Are you envious because I am generous?'
Thus, the last will be first, and the first will be last."

LITERARY CONTEXT

This parable is uttered by Jesus while on his way to Jerusalem. In the preceding chapter Jesus has addressed a question posed to him by Pharisees about divorce (19:1-12), and then has welcomed children (19:13-15). He has invited a rich young man to follow him, but he goes away sad (19:16-22). This gives Jesus occasion to address his disciples about how difficult is it for one who is rich to enter the reign of God (19:23-24). Peter, always the spokesman in Matthew's Gospel, asks Jesus what there will be for those who have given up everything and followed him (19:27). Jesus assures them a role in judging the twelve tribes of Israel, as well as a hundredfold reward and eternal life (19:28-29). The parable is followed by the third prediction of Jesus' passion (20:17-19) and the request by the mother of James and John for places at either side of Jesus in his kingdom (20:20-28). The chapter concludes with the healing of two blind men (20:29-34) as Jesus enters Jerusalem (21:1).

The parable of the workers in the vineyard is unique to Matthew. In its literary context, it continues Jesus' answer to Peter's query about what disciples will get for all they have given up.[1] On the heels of this question, the payment of the la-

---

[1] Not evident in the Lectionary translation is that the parable begins with the conjunction *gar*, "for," which ties it to the previous section. See Michael L. Barré, "The Workers in the Vineyard," *TBT* 24 (1986) 173–80 for a more detailed analysis of the literary links between the parable and 19:16-30 as well as to 6:19-34.

borers in the vineyard would seem to speak about God's manner of giving of rewards to those who have worked for the reign of God.[2] Tying the parable to the previous section and framing it, is the final verse (16:20), which exactly repeats 19:30. Though not the main point of the parable,[3] it alerts the hearer to an unexpected conclusion.[4] In relation to the request of James and John that follows the parable (20:20-28), the parable points to equal rewards for disciples, with no special distinctions.

HIRING

The drama unfolds in two acts (vv. 1-7, 8-15). The first depicts the hiring of the laborers, the second is their payment and the ensuing conflict. Act one unfolds with five hirings. The householder goes out at dawn (vv. 1-2), at the third hour (nine o'clock, vv. 3-4), at the sixth hour (noon, v. 5a), at the ninth hour (three o'clock, v. 5b), and finally at the eleventh hour (five o'clock, vv. 6-7). Although it is not specified in the story what is the motive for the multiple hirings, a possible scenario is that it is harvest time and there is urgency to bring in the crop before the grapes spoil. Possibly he has miscalculated at the beginning of the day how many workers will be needed, and so he continues to bring in more laborers to finish the work. A detail that is not true to life in the parable is that a vineyard owner would not be going out to the marketplace to hire the workers; this is the job of his manager (who appears in

---

[2] On "the kingdom of heaven" (v. 1) see above, pp. 41–42.

[3] The saying about the last being first and the first last is a free-floating proverb that appears in various contexts in the other Synoptic Gospels as well: Mark 10:31; Luke 13:30.

[4] That this verse is a Matthean creation is generally agreed by most all New Testament scholars. See, J. Lambrecht, *Out of the Treasure. The Parables in the Gospel of Matthew* (Louvain Theological and Pastoral Monographs 10. Grand Rapids: Eerdmans, 1991) 71. J. D. Crossan (*In Parables* [New York: Harper & Row, 1973] 113–14) advocates that the parable as Jesus spoke it concluded with v. 13. B. B. Scott (*Hear Then the Parable* [Minneapolis: Fortress, 1989] 185–86) and Dan O. Via ("Parable and Example Story: A Literary-Structuralist Approach," *Semeia* 1 [1974] 125) think v. 14a was the original conclusion.

v. 8). Literarily, his involvement at the beginning of the drama sets the stage for his role in the confrontation at the end.[5]

The vineyard owner is obviously a rich man. He has a manager (*epitropos*, v. 8), and presumably numerous other servants, as well as the means to hire many day laborers. It is possible this is only one of many estates he owns. Vineyards belonged to the wealthy, since they required significant initial investment. It took four years of careful tending before a vineyard would bear fruit. The payoff was worth it, though, as grapes could then be converted into wine, a product with a higher return than mixed grains grown by subsistent peasant farmers.[6]

Day laborers are at the opposite end of the economic spectrum. They congregate in the marketplace (*agora*, v. 3) each day, hoping to be hired. When they are not employed they are reduced to begging. They are in a most vulnerable position, since their work is sporadic and they have no ongoing relationship with a patron or employer. Even slaves are better off, since it is in their owners' interest to feed and care for them to make them profitable. When there is a surplus of day laborers they have little bargaining power. The last four groups sent into the vineyard (vv. 3-7) are dependent on whatever the owner thinks is just (*dikaios*) compensation (v. 4). Life for these workers is precarious and unpredictable. Malnutrition, hunger, disease, separation from family, dependency, and begging were their constant companions. Some may see in the face of the vineyard owner one who had stripped them of their own small peasant farm, a wealthy landowner foreclosing on a debt.[7] Having fallen into the class of expendables, they could expect to meet death in a matter of a few years.[8]

That some remain idle in the marketplace all day (v. 6) is not unexpected. They are not there because of lack of willingness to work, but rather, because no one has hired them (v. 7). They are the ones who would be bypassed for those who looked

---

[5] Warren Carter, *Matthew and the Margins* (Maryknoll: Orbis, 2000) 396.

[6] William R. Herzog II, *Parables as Subversive Speech* (Louisville: Westminster John Knox, 1994) 85; Carter, *Matthew and the Margins*, 395.

[7] Herzog, *Subversive Speech*, 88–89; Carter, *Matthew and the Margins*, 396.

[8] Herzog, *Subversive Speech*, 90.

more vigorous—the ones deemed more able to produce more work in less time. Those left behind would be the older ones, those with infirmities, those with physical disabilities. With the first group of workers the vineyard owner bargains and they agree on one denarius (v. 2).[9] With the second group, he promises to give them "what is just" (*dikaios,* v. 4), and does likewise (v. 5) for the remainder.

PAYDAY

At the end of the day the foreman begins to dole out one denarius to each of the workers, beginning with those hired at the end of the day. The point is not that the last will be first and the first last, but rather, the last hired have to be paid in the presence of the first hired or there is no story. The level of expectation rises as the reader anticipates that the first hired will be paid more than the last hired.

The first hired begin to grumble[10] against the landowner, because he has made those who worked only one hour "equal" to those who labored all day in the heat (v. 12). Readers whose

---

[9] It is difficult to know the precise value of a denarius. It is generally thought to have represented the amount needed to support a worker and his family at a level of subsistence as a peasant. So Scott, *Hear Then,* 291. F. Heichelheim ("Syria," in *An Economic Survey of Ancient Rome* [ed. Tenney Frank, 4:121–258; Baltimore: Johns Hopkins Press, 1938] 79–80) calculates that an adult in second-century C.E. Palestine needed about a half a denarius a day for food, not including other necessities. Douglas Oakman ("The Buying Power of Two Denarii," *Forum* 3 [1987] 33–38) estimates that a denarius would provide a 3–6 day supply of food for a family. Herzog (*Subversive Speech,* 90) finds this excessive, since it assumes the silver denarius of Roman vintage rather than local variations of it. But recent studies suggest that a denarius a day would not be enough to sustain a day worker, since he did not work every day. Nor is it reasonable to imagine that a day laborer could support a family on such wages. Other references in the New Testament to the buying power of a denarius are: in the Gospel of Mark the disciples estimate that it will take two hundred denarii to feed five thousand people (6:37). In the Johannine version of the episode, Philip thinks this will not be enough (John 6:7). When the Samaritan traveler entrusts the wounded man to the innkeeper, he gives him two denarii for his care with the promise of more if it is needed (10:35).

[10] The verb *gonguzō* (v. 11) recalls the grumbling of the Israelites in the desert (Exod 17:3; Num 11:1; 14:27, 29).

sense of fairness demands that people get compensated proportionately for what they earn easily sympathize with the
first hired. Instead of giving different levels of pay for different
amounts of work, the owner has recompensed all equally,
erasing the economic distinctions.

The owner replies to one of the grumblers,[11] "My friend, I
am not cheating you" (v. 13). There is no question of friendship between the owner and the workers. They belong to two
vastly different worlds. Friendships are formed only among
equals. There is an irony that if the vineyard owner were to
truly become a friend of the workers, he would have to follow
the directives given by Jesus to the rich young man in the previous chapter, "[g]o, sell what you have and give to (the) poor,
and you will have treasure in heaven. Then come, follow me"
(19:21).[12]

In the final exchange the vineyard owner fires off four
accusatory questions, none of which can be countered by the
workers. He did not cheat them. He gave them the wage they
agreed on. The injustice is perceived only in comparison with
what he gave the others. If the rich owner wants to give the
last ones hired the same as the first he has every power to do
so. There is no question but that a rich man can do exactly
what he pleases with his own money.

The last question that the owner asks is often mistranslated. Literally, he queries, "Is your eye evil *(ponēros)* because
I am good *(agathos)*?" Note that the translation of *agathos* as
"generous" misses the mark. The meaning of *agathos* is "good,"
a word Matthew frequently pairs with *ponēros*, "evil."[13] Moreover, there is nothing "generous" in providing merely a subsistence wage to a day laborer. Matthew is fond of creating

---

[11] Herzog (*Subversive Speech*, 93) sees this as a divide-and-conquer tactic in
which the landowner has humiliated, isolated, and definitively dismissed the
spokesperson so that he will not find work in the vicinity again.

[12] In the other two instances in the Gospel in which a person is addressed
as *hetaire*, "friend," it highlights their wrong deeds: the guest lacking a wedding garment (22:12) and Judas at the moment of betrayal (26:50).

[13] Contrasts between *ponēros* and *agathos* are found in Matt 5:45; 7:11, 17-
18; 12:34-35; 22:10.

contrasts between evil and good. In some cases he personifies evil and speaks of the role of *ho ponēros*, "the evil one," as the one who prompts equivocation (5:37), tempts people (6:13), and steals the word that is sown in their hearts (13:38). Only once does Matthew speak of *ho agathos*, "the good One" (19:17). It is in the episode in which Jesus is responding to the rich young man who asked him what good he must do to gain eternal life (19:16). Jesus' reply, "Why do you ask me about the good? There is only One who is good" (19:17), clearly indicates God as "the One who is good." In two instances "your heavenly Father" is associated with giving good: sun that rises on the bad and the good (5:45) and giving good things to those who ask (7:11).

While in many respects the owner of the vineyard is not like God,[14] in light of these other references, there is a resonance in the final verses between the vineyard owner and God. God *is* free to dispense beneficence or recompense as God pleases. If God wishes to treat all alike (5:45) God can do so. The problem is not that God is good, the difficulty comes when God's egalitarian distribution is perceived as unjust. Like the vineyard owner who declares that he will give the workers "what is just" (*ho dikaios*, v. 4),[15] so God, who is good, gives what is just. Justice (*dikaiosynē*) is not, however, about

---

[14] Herzog (*Subversive Speech*, 94) sees the landowner as having blasphemously arrogated to himself the prerogatives of Yahweh, who then engages in blaming the victim, and in condescension. The function of the parable, as he sees it, is to expose an oppressive reality that moves the victims to solidarity toward change (95–96). Carter (*Matthew and the Margins*, 398) also sees the landowner as using elitist strategies, but who nonetheless does do something good. For him the landowner is a cartoon figure who, ironically, would have the most to lose and to gain from consistently enacting the principle of egalitarian treatment which he has demonstrated. While Herzog and Carter's evaluation of the character of the vineyard owner is appropriate to a real life setting, I read him as a metaphor for God. As with all metaphors, there is always both a certain "is" and "is not" quality about the comparison.

[15] The adjective *dikaios* ("just") and its related words are favorites of Matthew. It occurs only twice in the Gospel of Mark; eleven times in Luke, three times in John, and sixteen times in the Gospel of Matthew: 1:19, 5:45; 9:13; 10:41; 13:17, 54, 59; 20:4; 23:28, 29, 35; 25:37, 46; 27:4, 19, 24. On the use of the verb *dikaioō* see chap. 18 on Matt 11:16-19.

each getting what they deserve,[16] or each gaining what they have earned. The parable represents divine justice as evident in that each person, regardless of their capacity to work or to produce, has what is necessary to sustain life at the end of the day. Not only does this parable turn upside down notions of what is just *(dikaios)*, but so does the very person of Jesus, who is labeled *dikaios* ("righteous") at his trial before Pilate 27:19, who fulfills all righteousness *(dikaiosynē*, 3:15), who teaches his disciples that their righteousness must surpass that of the scribes and Pharisees in order to enter into God's realm (5:20), and who vindicates *(dikaioō)* Wisdom by his works (11:19).[17]

The accusation of having an evil eye *(ophthalmos ponēros*, v. 15) is a serious one.[18] Both ancient as well as many modern cultures believe that certain individuals, animals, demons, or gods have the power to injure with a glance. Protective amulets and devices to distract such a look were commonly used. Many of the biblical references to the evil eye connect it with envy and covetousness (e.g., Deut 15:9; Wis 4:12; Sir 14:8). Within a first-century Palestinian worldview in which all goods were thought to be limited, any gain by one person necessarily meant a loss by another. Thus, evil eye envy or covetousness was one of the most pernicious of character flaws, destructive both for the person and for the community. Ben Sira, for example, warns, "Evil is the one with an evil eye; he averts his face and disregards people; a greedy eye is not satisfied with a portion and mean injustice withers the soul" (LXX Sir 14:8-9). The vineyard owner in the parable is publicly accusing the

---

[16] The term *dikaiosynē* is most often associated with Paul, but it also occurs seven times in Matthew: 3:15; 5:6, 10, 20; 6:1, 33; 21:32 (as compared to only once in Luke, twice in John, and not at all in Mark). Paul's famous assertion in Rom 3:21-26 describes justification *(dikaiosynē)* as something incapable of being achieved by human beings; it is a free gift from God, accomplished by Christ, and appropriated by the believer through faith and not through works of the Law.

[17] On the latter, see below, chap. 17.

[18] See further John H. Elliott, "Matthew 20:1-15: A Parable of Invidious Comparison and Evil Eye Accusation," *BTB* 22 (1992) 52–65; Bruce J. Malina and Richard L. Rohrbaugh, *Social Science Commentary on the Synoptic Gospels* (Minneapolis: Fortress, 1992) 125.

grumblers of evil eye envy. In the Sermon on the Mount Jesus had warned, "The lamp of the body is the eye. If your eye is sound, your whole body will be filled with light; but if your eye is bad *(ophthalmos sou ponēros)*, your whole body will be in darkness. And if the light in you is darkness, how great will the darkness be" (6:22-23). Twice Jesus advises, "If your right eye causes you to sin, tear it out and throw it away. It is better for you to lose one of your members than to have your whole body thrown into Gehenna" (5:29; 18:9).

The parable ends with this question facing the hearer: do you have evil eye envy because of God's goodness that makes all equal to one another?

PREACHING POSSIBILITIES

If, at the climax of the story, the landowner is a cipher for God, then the preacher may pursue the question of the nature of divine goodness and justice and how we respond to egalitarianism and unearned rewards. The homilist might begin by touching into experiences that people have had of grace or benefaction which was undeserved, and then speak about the gratuitous nature of every gift from God. He or she might explore how God loves each person equally, offers the same invitation to all[19] (though at different times and with different demands), and desires the same good for each one. When Christians live in this awareness with gratitude at the heart of their faith lives, then desire for good for each brother and sister flows from the heart, rather than evil eye envy.

Gospel justice, then, is experienced not as everyone getting proportional recompense for what they have earned, but rather, all being in right relation. A leveling of relationships among human beings is part of the biblical view of justice, which is manifest in harmonious relation of all creation with the Creator. This does not mean there are no distinctions among believers or no differentiation of ministries, but there are no

---

[19] Scott, *Hear Then*, 297–98. See also David Buttrick, *Speaking Parables* (Louisville: Westminster John Knox, 2000) 113–19.

distinctions in the measure of divine love or goodness toward God's creatures. Further, if one reads the "evening" of the day (v. 8) eschatologically, there is only one "payment" at the end: either one gets the full reward or one doesn't.[20] There is no half-salvation.

For Matthew's community the parable may have been a vehicle for challenging any sense of entitlement that Jewish Christians may have harbored in relation to Gentile members of the community. The image of a vineyard could call to mind Israel as God's vineyard, an image that recurs in the Hebrew Scriptures.[21] Having a longer claim on God's promises, Jewish Christians may have been challenged by the parable to relinquish any sense of propriety or priority and to embrace the newcomers as having equal status in God's eyes and attendant equal status in the Christian community. In a contemporary context there may a similar dynamic with regard to immigrant ethnic groups who are newcomers to a parish community, or attitudes toward neophytes in the faith as opposed to those who are lifelong members. The preacher might pose the question: In what ways does the parable unmask attitudes of privilege and entitlement and challenge Christians to regard each equally?

The homilist may want to pursue what are contemporary manifestations of covetousness that destroy both the person and the community. How do competition and acquisitive desires fuel inequities among us? How can Christians respond counterculturally to the barrage of advertising that assails us from radio, television, Internet, newspapers, and mail order catalogues? In what ways can we short-circuit envy and greed? To what do I think I am entitled? What do I think I have earned? How does this gospel help a disciple answer these difficult questions?

The literary context of the parable connects it with the episode in which Peter wants to know what disciples who have given up everything will have (19:27-29). In answer, the par-

---

[20] Matthew frequently paints scenarios in his parables in which inclusion or exclusion at the end-time are painted in stark contrast (e.g., 13:30, 49-50; 25:1-13; 31-46).

[21] Isa 5:1-7; Jer 12:10; Ezek 19:10-14; Hos 10:1.

able assures that God will see to it that they will be cared for: each will have what they need one day at a time. If there is hesitation to sell all and give to the poor so that one can be free to follow Jesus (19:21), the parable gives encouragement that dependence on God's goodness is not ill-placed.

While the point of the parable in its original setting may not have been about fair labor practices and just wages, it may be opportune for the preacher to speak about such as concrete ways in which God's equalizing love is visible. Might the parable prompt the parish or business people who are part of the community to explore the use of a "living wage" for their employees? How would such affect our notion of measuring worth by working ability and pay scale? What ramifications might this have on our relations with one another? How do we view those who are unemployed? What about workers who agree to accept a pittance rather than negotiate for a share in the profits?

CHAPTER ELEVEN

Saying and Doing
(Matt 21:28-32)

Twenty-Sixth Sunday of Ordinary Time
Tuesday of the Third Week of Advent

Jesus said to the chief priests and elders of the people:
  "What is your opinion?
A man had two sons.
He came to the first and said,
  'Son, go out and work in the vineyard today.'
He said in reply, 'I will not,'
  but afterwards changed his mind and went.
The man came to the other son and gave the same order.
He said in reply, 'Yes, sir,' but did not go.
Which of the two did his father's will?"
They answered, "The first."
Jesus said to them, "Amen, I say to you,
  tax collectors and prostitutes
  are entering the kingdom of God before you.
When John came to you in the way of righteousness,
  you did not believe him;
  but tax collectors and prostitutes did.
Yet even when you saw that,
  you did not later change your minds and believe him."

LITERARY CONTEXT

This is the first of three parables that are aimed at the religious leaders of Israel. They come on the heels of a challenge to Jesus' authority by the chief priests and elders (21:23-27) in

Jerusalem. In that episode Jesus' opponents pose a question about the source of his authority (v. 23), to which he responds with a question about the origin of John's baptism and a promise to answer their question if they answer his (vv. 24-25). After a debate among themselves they reply that they do not know (v. 27). Jesus wins the exchange and declares that neither will he disclose the source of his authority (v. 27). He then poses three parables to them, the first two of which indirectly answer the question about his authority.

In this first one, Jesus uses a technique much like that of the prophet Nathan when he confronts king David about his sin with Bathsheba (2 Sam 12:1-12). He tells a story and asks the listeners to give the answer.[1] In the reply, the hearer pronounces judgment on his or her own self. A moralizing conclusion on the lips of Jesus (vv. 31-32) is then followed by the parables of the wicked tenants (22:33-46) and that of the wedding feast (22:1-14).

SAYING YES

At first the parable seems a simple, straightforward one. Both children[2] fall short of the ideal, but when Jesus asks which of the two *did* the father's will, the answer seems easy: the first. In a culture that highly prizes honor, however, it is not so very clear which child is the more laudable. The first one shamed his father by refusing to go. The second says the honorable thing, even if his actions do not conform.

The fact that there are two other known variant versions[3] of this parable attests that in antiquity it was not entirely evident which one responded more honorably. Some manuscripts have the parable reversed: the first child says "yes" but

---

[1] Similarly, Matt 17:25; 18:12; 22:42. See also Luke 7:41-43; 15:1-32.

[2] In the Greek text the word that is used both times in v. 28 is *teknon*, "child," not *huios*, "son."

[3] For more detailed analysis of the transmission of the tradition see Bruce Metzger, *Textual Commentary on the Greek New Testament* (New York: United Bible Societies, 1971) 55–56 and J. Ramsey Michaels, "The Parable of the Regretful Son," *HTR* 61 (1968) 15–26.

does not go to the vineyard while the second says "no" but then goes. The answer that the hearers give is that the second child is the one who does the will of the father. This version is essentially the same as the one in the Lectionary, only the order is inverted. But a third version exists in which the first child says "no" and then goes while the second one says "yes" and then does not go (as our version in the Lectionary). But the startling thing is that it concludes with the declaration that the second child is the one who did the will of the father! When given a choice between being publicly honored and privately shamed or publicly shamed and privately honored, the honorable choice is for public saving of face.[4] Text critical analysis shows that it is more likely that this third version does not represent the original form of the parable, but its existence helps us to keep in mind that the parable's meaning is not as self-evident as we might think.

DOING THE FATHER'S WILL

The parable sets up a similar contrast to that of 7:21-27,[5] where Jesus spoke to his disciples about how only those who do the will of his father[6] will enter the kingdom of heaven, not those who say to him, "Lord, Lord" (7:21). There is, in fact, a verbal link between the two parables. In 21:30 the second son responds, "Yes, sir," using the same word (*kyrie*, "sir," or "lord") as in 7:21, an odd way of addressing one's father. Another link is that after the sayings concerning the importance of both doing and saying in 7:21-27, the evangelist remarks on the astonishment of the crowds because Jesus "taught them as one having authority" (7:28). In 21:23-27 the questioning of Jesus' authority is what prompts the ensuing parables. In chapter seven it is disciples who are instructed to have their words and actions cohere. In chapter twenty-one the message is aimed at the Jewish religious leaders.

---

[4] See Metzger, *Textual Commentary*, 55–56; B. B. Scott, *Hear Then the Parable* (Minneapolis: Fortress, 1989) 84.

[5] See above, chapter five.

[6] See above, pp. 68–69 on "the will of God."

The theme is played out further in Matthew 23, where Jesus warns the crowds and his disciples, "do and observe all things whatsoever they [the scribes and Pharisees] tell you, but do not follow their example. For they preach but they do not practice" (23:3). Matthew is ever keen to underscore the ethical implications: one who hears the word must act on it; saying "yes" must be accompanied by correspondent actions. Leaders who instruct correctly must also exemplify what they teach. The next verses move away from the fictional world of the parable, where Jesus' opponents easily understood the point. The real test is whether in actuality they can understand and act on it.

BELIEVING (vv. 31-32)

There is a certain disjuncture between the parable (vv. 28-30) and the interpretation (vv. 31-32).[7] In the parable the emphasis is on doing as well as saying, whereas the explanation focuses on believing John the Baptist. Three times in v. 32 the phrase "believe him" recurs.[8] This also clearly links vv. 31-32 to vv. 23-27, where the same phrase occurs in the question to the authorities: "why did you not believe him?" (v. 25).

For Matthew the connection between believing John the Baptist and recognizing the authority of Jesus is clear. The two cooperate at Jesus' baptism "to fulfill all righteousness (*dikaiosynē*)" (3:15), and they both perform the deeds by which Wisdom is justified (*edikaiōthē*, 11:19). There is an echo of these

---

[7] Verses 28-30 are unique to Matthew, whereas vv. 31-32 are derived from Q. The Lucan parallel to vv. 31-32 is at Luke 7:29-30, in the episode of the children in the marketplace, where the subject is also the identity of Jesus and John as prophets who exemplify righteousness. On this parable, see below, chapter 18. It is likely that vv. 28-30 represent a parable uttered by Jesus, to which Matthew secondarily appends vv. 31-32 to link it with 21:23-27. See Jan Lambrecht, *Out of the Treasure. The Parables in the Gospel of Matthew* (Louvain Theological and Pastoral Monographs 10; Grand Rapids: Eerdmans, 1991) 93–98.

[8] In the Greek text the threefold repetition is more evident: ". . . you did not believe him *(ouk episteusate autǭ)*; but tax collectors and prostitutes did believe him *(episteusan autǭ)* . . . you did not later change your minds and believe him *(pisteusai autǭ)*."

texts in v. 32, "John came to you in the way of righteousness." Both prophets proclaimed the coming reign of God (3:2; 4:17). Both emphasized the importance of producing "good fruit" (3:8-10; 7:17-19; 12:33; 21:43) and both confronted Jewish religious leaders as a "brood of vipers" (3:7; 23:33). Both were recognized by the people as prophets (21:11, 26, 46). Both are arrested and executed (14:3-10; 26:47-56; 27:45-56). Some mistakenly identify Jesus as John the Baptist or Elijah (16:14). But Matthew clearly distinguishes at 11:14 and 17:10-13 that it is John who is to be identified with Elijah, the forerunner of God's reign (Mal 4:5-6 [3:32-24 Heb]). Those who believed in John would be led to belief in Jesus.

The religious leaders' lack of belief in John is contrasted with the positive response of toll collectors[9] and prostitutes. While Matthew does not portray tax collectors repenting at John's preaching in the way that Luke does (3:12-13), he does show Jesus' association with them (9:9-11; 10:3) and the criticism he incurs as a "friend of tax collectors and sinners" (9:11; 11:19). It is curious that the stock phrase "tax collectors and sinners"[10] is converted here to "tax collectors and prostitutes." The only references to prostitutes being associated with the ministries of Jesus or John are found at Matthew 21:31-32. It is not a statement about the actual makeup of the retinue of

[9] There is a distinction between tax collectors and toll collectors. Direct taxes, such as the land tax and the poll tax, were under the direct supervision of Herod Antipas in Galilee and the Roman prefects and procurators in Judea. Collectors of these taxes were bureaucrats who were accountable to the government. The *telōnai* of the Gospels, however, were toll collectors, in charge of indirect taxes, such as tolls, imposts, customs, and tariffs (as Matthew at 9:9). These positions were leased out by contract and the amount to be collected had to be paid in advance. The toll collector had to then secure that amount and make some profit for his own survival. Because the system was open to extortion and greed, the Talmud most often groups toll collectors with robbers. The reason for hatred of toll collectors is more for their thievery than the fact that they are quislings of Rome or that their work makes them ritually impure. What offended other Jews was that Jesus evidently offered forgiveness to sinners and admission into his community without making the normal demand of restitution and commitment to the Law. See E. P. Sanders, *Jesus and Judaism* (Philadelphia: Fortress, 1985) 174–211.

[10] Matt 9:10, 11; 11:19; Mark 2:15, 16; Luke 5:30; 7:34; 15:1.

Jesus' followers,[11] but is a hyperbolic declaration intended to contrast the best and the worst imaginable. The point of the statement is that the religious leaders who should most exemplify uprightness do not, while those who are thought least able to do so, do believe and do enter God's realm.

CHANGING YOUR MIND

The interpretive verses (31-32) make this parable more than a simple repetition of the one in 7:21-27 that emphasized the importance of both doing and saying. In the context of Jesus' debates with the Jewish religious leaders this parable has a polemical dimension. The leaders pronounce judgment on themselves with their response in v. 31, a judgment that is confirmed with the ironic contrast between them and tax collectors and prostitutes. But there is yet the possibility of repentance. The interpretive verses affirm that those who initially refuse to respond affirmatively to Jesus can still change their minds[12] and believe.[13] Change of mind, of course, for Matthew,

---

[11] The only other references to prostitutes in the New Testament are at Luke 15:30 where the older brother complains that his brother has squandered the family inheritance with prostitutes, and in 1 Cor 6:9, 15, 16, where Paul lists prostitutes among those who will not inherit the reign of God, and he exhorts Corinthian Christians to avoid such immorality. The popular notion that Mary Magdalene was a prostitute has no basis whatsoever in Scripture. Nor is it clear that the woman who had been a sinner who anointed Jesus' feet in the home of Simon the Pharisee was a prostitute. On the latter text see Barbara E. Reid, *Choosing the Better Part? Women in the Gospel of Luke* (Collegeville: The Liturgical Press, 1986) 107–34.

[12] Michaels, "Regretful Son," 15–26, proposes that the verb *metamelomai* in vv. 29, 32 (as also 27:3, where it is used of Judas) carries the connotation of futile regret, not repentance, which would be indicated with *metanoeō*. This, along with other changes in the text, results in a parable in which the son who said no and regretted his decision when it was too late represents the Jewish priests and elders. As intriguing as his reconstruction of the text is, there is no manuscript evidence for his reading. Moreover, there does not appear to be as significant a difference in the meaning of the two verbs as Michaels would advocate. See BDAG, s.v., μεταμέλομαι, μετανοέω.

[13] So, e.g., John R. Donahue, *The Gospel in Parable* (Minneapolis: Fortress, 1988) 88–89; Warren Carter and John Paul Heil, *Matthew's Parables* (CBQMS 30; Washington D.C.: CBA, 1998) 159. In contrast, other scholars see in the parable

also implies that the change is manifest in fruitful deeds. In typically parabolic fashion the challenge is made and the opportunity to respond is left open.

PREACHING POSSIBILITIES

For Matthew's community the challenge directed to the chief priests and elders was most likely understood by them as a summons to the Jewish leaders of their day to imitate the first child and join them in believing in Jesus. Not only was it an invitation to those who were hardened opponents, but also to those Christians who had initially said "yes" and then wavered.[14] The preacher might reflect on how easy it is to say "yes," in the first fervor, but then how demanding it is to live a life of faithful obedience when one is committed for the long haul. But like a good marriage in which the fire of love burns less brightly, but more hotly as the embers are fanned with every loving deed, so the easy first infatuation of "yes" in a disciple is solidified into a habit of being, as it is acted on day after day. The "yes" is not something pronounced only once, but embraced anew each day. After years of acting out such transformative love the words need hardly even be spoken as the loving deeds say it all.

The parable may also provide an opportunity for the preacher to reflect on the ambiguities of living with imperfection as disciples. Neither child had it all together. But the one who had the humility to change their mind and do what was asked was the exemplary one. Are there ways in which, both as individuals and as a community, we are being asked to admit we were wrong and then embark on a new course of action?

---

a condemnation of the Jews and an explanation of the transfer of divine approval from them to the church. See, e.g., J. Drury, *The Parables in the Gospels* (New York: Crossroad, 1985) 96; Lambrecht, *Out of the Treasure,* 104. That Matthew has reached the conclusion that the mission to Israel is finished and hope is no longer held out to Jews is not at all clear in the text. See further discussion on this in the following chapter.

[14] Donahue, *The Gospel in Parable,* 89; Lambrecht, *Out of the Treasure,* 99. See also David Buttrick, *Speaking Parables* (Louisville: Westminster John Knox, 2000) 119–24.

CHAPTER TWELVE

Treacherous Tenants
(Matt 21:33-43)

Twenty-Seventh Sunday of Ordinary Time

Friday of the Second Week of Lent (Matt 21:33-43, 45-46)

Jesus said to the chief priests and the elders of the people:
    "Hear another parable.
There was a landowner who planted a vineyard,
    put a hedge around it, dug a wine press in it, and built a tower.
Then he leased it to tenants and went on a journey.
When vintage time drew near,
    he sent his servants to the tenants to obtain his produce.
But the tenants seized the servants and one they beat,
    another they killed, and a third they stoned.
Again he sent other servants, more numerous than the first ones,
    but they treated them in the same way.
Finally, he sent his son to them, thinking,
    'They will respect my son.'
But when the tenants saw the son, they said to one another,
    'This is the heir.
Come, let us kill him and acquire his inheritance.'
They seized him, threw him out of the vineyard, and killed him.
What will the owner of the vineyard do to those tenants when he comes?"
They answered him,
    "He will put those wretched men to a wretched death
    and lease his vineyard to other tenants
    who will give him the produce at the proper times."
Jesus said to them, "Did you never read in the Scriptures:
    The stone that the builders rejected
        has become the cornerstone;

by the Lord has this been done,
    and it is wonderful in our eyes?
Therefore, I say to you,
    the kingdom of God will be taken away from you
    and given to a people that will produce its fruit."
[When the chief priests and the Pharisees heard his parables,
    they knew that he was speaking about them.
And although they were attempting to arrest him,
    they feared the crowds,
    for they regarded him as a prophet.]

LITERARY CONTEXT

This is the second of three parables directed to the chief priests and elders (21:23). Preceding it is the parable of the two children, which confronts the Jewish leaders with their lack of response to John the Baptist, a failure which is compounded by subsequent lack of faith in Jesus. That parable issues a summons to change their minds and believe in Jesus before it is too late. The parable of the tenants is more pointedly christological. Matthew reworks the Markan tradition (12:1-12),[1] making the parable even more allegorical. His redaction also imports one of his favorite themes, the necessity of bearing fruit (vv. 41, 43). Another important theme is the identity of Jesus as the last in a long line of prophets sent from God. The theme is clearer in the weekday Lectionary when vv. 45-46 are included in the reading. On the lips of Jesus a form of this parable may well have been a summons to the religious leaders of Israel, but in its Matthean form it is a warning to Christians to be bearers of fruit at the proper time.[2]

---

[1] On the Markan version, see Barbara E. Reid, *Parables for Preachers. Year B* (Collegeville: The Liturgical Press, 1999) 111–20.

[2] Many scholars think that the allegorical nature of the parable and its narratively illogical elements point to its composition by the early Church, rather than being a parable told by Jesus. For different analyses of the tradition history see Klyne Snodgrass, *The Parable of the Wicked Tenants* (Tübingen: Mohr [Siebeck], 1983) 41–71; Jan Lambrecht, *Out of the Treasure* (Louvain Theological and Pastoral Monographs 10; Louvain: Peeters, 1991) 105–25; and John Dominic Crossan, "The Parable of the Wicked Husbandmen," *JBL* 90 (1971) 451–65. Snodgrass argues that Matthew's version is the earliest account because it is

A FAMILIAR STORY WITH A NEW ENDING (v. 33)

Not only has Matthew reworked a tradition from Mark, but there are also unmistakable echoes of Isaiah 5.[3] Both texts relate the same actions of the vine grower: he plants, digs a winepress, and builds a tower (Isa 5:1-2; Matt 21:33). There is the same narrative buildup to the climactic expectation of enjoyment of the produce and the same disappointment that such does not materialize. The same question is posed by the owner: "What will he do?" (cf. Isa 5:4; Matt 21:40).

But there is a critical difference in the ending of Matthew's parable as compared to that of Isaiah 5. In the latter the vine grower is clearly Yahweh who is disappointed with the yield of sour grapes from his carefully cultivated vine, Israel (Isa 5:7). God announces its fate: "Take away its hedge, give it to grazing, / break through its wall, let it be trampled! / Yes, I will make it a ruin: / it shall not be pruned or hoed, / but overgrown with thorns and briers; / I will command the clouds / not to send

---

more understandable as a story and most easily explains the shape of Mark's and Luke's accounts (Mark 12:1-12; Luke 20:9-19). He finds no reason to doubt that the parable originated with Jesus. Crossan believes that the parallel in *Gos.Thom.* §65 represents an independent tradition that is more original than the Synoptic versions. The version in *Gos.Thom.* is more authentically parabolic in form; in the Synoptic Gospels it has become an allegory. Lambrecht and most others, however, hold that the version in *Gos. Thom.* is a late mixed form with elements and details taken from the Synoptic Gospels. Johannes C. DeMoor ("The Targumic Background of Mark 12:1-12: The Parable of the Wicked Tenants," *JSJ* 29 [1998] 63–80) argues for a Jewish origin of the parable on the basis of parallels in Targumic literature for each of its details. While the Targums date later than the New Testament, DeMoor advances that the metaphors employed in Targumic exegesis would have been familiar to a pre-70 C.E. audience.

Some scholars see the quotation of Psalm 118 (vv. 42-43) as secondarily appended to the parable. Snodgrass (*Wicked Tenants,* 63–65, 97, 113–18) makes the case that the two are intimately connected by a word-play between בֵּן, "son," and אֶבֶן, "stone," in the original Aramaic form of the parable. Moreover, rabbinic parables often end with a Scripture citation. David Flusser (*Die rabbinischen Gleichnisse und der Gleichniserzähler Jesus* 1. Teil: *Das Wesen der Gleichnisse.* [Bern: Peter Lang, 1981] 20, 63, 119–20) argues similarly: interpretations of parables are not later additions but belong to the original accounts by Jesus.

[3] Similar references to Israel as a vineyard planted by God are found in Jer 2:21; Hos 10:1.

rain upon it" (Isa 5:5-6). Matthew, however, does not simply repeat the familiar story. He offers a new version in which not the vineyard but the tenants are destroyed. The vineyard remains and is entrusted to others.

The parable is also a familiar story from the world of Jesus. It reflects well the situation of unrest that existed in Galilee at the time of Jesus and continued to intensify up to the first Jewish revolt against Rome (66–70 B.C.E.). The economic situation for many was quite precarious. Famine, lack of rain, overpopulation, and heavy taxes could put a struggling farmer over the brink. In Palestine of Jesus' day it is estimated that somewhere between one-half and two-thirds of a farmer's income went to taxes that included Roman tribute, payment to Herod and the procurators, and land rent to the large landowners. Land remained all important. A peasant would go to any length to retain or regain its ownership. The murderous hostility of the laborers toward an absentee landlord is a true-to-life detail for first-century Palestine.[4] But there are a number of elements in the parable that are not realistic that carry an allegorical meaning.

PROPITIOUS TIME FOR BEARING FRUIT

After the introductory verse that sets the stage (v. 33), the action begins with the notation that vintage time was near (v. 34). This strikes an eschatological note, as *kairos*, "time," propitious time, not chronological *(chronos)* time (recurring again at v. 41), is paired with harvest imagery, a frequent metaphor for the end time (13:30, 39; 24:33; 25:26). In addition, Matthew uses *engizō*, "to draw near," not only for the coming of God's reign (3:2; 4:17; 10:7) but also for the approach of the end time (24:33). Moreover, the language of v. 40 has overtones of expectation of the parousia. At v. 40 the landowner (*oikodespotēs*, v. 33) has become "lord" (*kyrios*, translated "owner" in the *NAB*), and the phrase *hotan elthē*, "when he comes," is the same phrase used of the Son of Humanity coming in glory at 25:31.

---

[4] Douglas Oakman, *Jesus and the Economic Questions of His Day* (SBEC 8; Lewiston/Queenston/Lampeter: Mellen, 1986) 57–72; C. H. Dodd, *The Parables of the Kingdom* (New York: Scribner, 1961) 94; Snodgrass, *Wicked Tenants*, 31–40.

Matthew sounds his message on the importance of bearing fruit with an initial twofold use of *karpos* in v. 34 (*ho kairos tōn karpōn*, "vintage time," and *karpous autou*, "his produce"), which recurs at v. 41 ("the produce") and at the climax at v. 43 ("fruit"). Not only Matthew, but a number of other New Testament writers use "fruit" as a metaphor for repentance, conversion, and actions that manifest such conversion.[5] John the Baptist warns the Pharisees and Sadducees who came for his baptism to "produce good fruit" as evidence of their repentance (3:8). He further warns that every tree that does not bear good fruit will be cut down and thrown into the fire (3:10), a message that is repeated in Jesus' preaching (7:15-20).

SENDING SERVANTS (vv. 34-39)

The landowner's repeated sending of the servants to obtain his produce evokes God's[6] repeated sending of prophets to Israel. Matthew's change from Mark's repeated sending of single servants, to two group sendings (vv. 35-36) may be an intentional allusion to the Former (Joshua through Kings) and Latter (Isaiah through Malachi) Prophets.[7] The prophets were often called "servants" of God (Jer 7:25; 25:4; Amos 3:7; Zech 1:6) and their fates match those described in the parable. Jeremiah was beaten (Jer 20:2); Uriah was killed with a sword (Jer 26:20-23); Zechariah was stoned to death (2 Chr 24:21).[8]

Both narratively and on the level of the allegory of salvation history the statement in v. 37 at first seems illogical. If the tenants have killed all of the previous servants/prophets, why

---

[5] John R. Donahue, *The Gospel in Parable* (Minneapolis: Fortress, 1988) 90.

[6] *Oikodespotēs*, "landowner," may also be a cipher for God at 13:27; 20:1, 11.

[7] Donald Senior, *Matthew* (ANTC; Nashville: Abingdon, 1998) 239.

[8] See Warren Carter and John Paul Heil, *Matthew's Parables* (CBQMS 30; Washington, D.C.: CBA, 1998) 161; John Drury, *The Parables in the Gospels* (New York: Crossroads, 1985) 96–97. Snodgrass (*Wicked Tenants,* 79) points out that while in the Hebrew Scriptures there are related the murders of only two prophets (2 Chr 24:20-21; Jer 26:20), the killing of prophets is a frequent New Testament theme: Matt 23:31-32; Luke 13:34; Acts 7:52; Heb 11:36-38; 1 Thess 2:15.

would they not do the same to the son? Moreover, why would
the tenants expect to acquire the vineyard if they kill the son?
Some scholars assert that the tenants' expectation of ownership by killing the son may not be so far-fetched as it first
seems. There were cases in which an inheritance not claimed
within a specified period of time could be considered "owner-
less" and open to the first claimant.[9] The tenants may think the
owner who "left on a journey" (v. 33) has died and that the arrival of the son means he has come to claim his inheritance. If
they kill the heir, they can be the first to lay claim to the "own-
erless" property. Another explanation is based on a rabbinic
law that a person who lacked proper title deeds could sustain
a claim to ownership if he could prove undisputed possession
for three years.[10]

There is also a certain narrative logic to the killing of the
son. The sequence of actions in v. 39 (which Matthew has altered from Mark 12:8) corresponds to the details of Jesus'
crucifixion. He is seized (26:50), taken outside the city limits
(27:31-32),[11] and then killed (27:35). Within Matthew's narrative the parable parallels the dynamics of the gospel plot.
The murderous plans of the tenants in the vineyard match
the intent of the chief priests and Pharisees (21:46; 22:15)
toward Jesus.[12]

[9] Joachim Jeremias, *The Parables of Jesus* (2d rev. ed.; New York: Scribner's,
1972) 74–76.

[10] Snodgrass, *Wicked Tenants*, 38; J.D.M. Derrett, *Law in the New Testament*
(London: Darton, Longman & Todd, 1970) 289–306. William R. Herzog II (*Parables as Subversive Speech* [Louisville: Westminster John Knox, 1994] 101–03)
sketches a possible scenario in which the tenants were originally owners dis-
placed by economic hardship. The owner attained the land through foreclo-
sure on loans to free peasant farmers who were unable to pay off the loans
because of poor harvests.

[11] See also John 19:17; Heb 13:12, which speak of Jesus' crucifixion outside
the city.

[12] B. B. Scott (*Hear Then the Parable* [Minneapolis: Fortress, 1989] 253–54)
proposes an allusion to Gen 37:20 where the brothers of Joseph likewise say,
"Come, let us kill him." For Scott this allusion makes the parable question
whether the kingdom will surely go to the promised heirs. Its frustrated ending challenges whether the kingdom's true heirs will in the end triumph.

WHAT WILL THE OWNER DO? (vv. 40-41)

The question and answer in vv. 40-41 uses a rhetorical technique similar to Matt 21:31.[13] Like Nathan's "You are the man!" in his parable to David (2 Sam 12:7), it functions like a boomerang that turns back on the speaker.[14] When the chief priests and elders give the answer (v. 41), they pronounce their own self-condemnation. But in the narrative, the Son is not yet killed and the future tense verbs in v. 41 show that the possibility is yet open that the Jewish leaders can still change their minds (21:29, 32).[15] They could still be among those "other tenants" to whom the vineyard will be entrusted.

From the vantage point of Matthew's community v. 41 may have been heard as an allusion to the destruction of Jerusalem in 70 C.E., interpreted by the Christian community as a sign of God's judgment accomplished. For the Christian hearers of the parable, v. 41 sharpens the summons to them not to replicate this rejection of God's son and to produce good fruit at the propitious time. Word plays with *kakous kakōs* (literally "wretched people" he will "wretchedly" destroy) and *kairos* . . . *karpos* ("proper times" . . . "fruit") intensify the contrast between evildoers and producers of good.[16] The repetition of *kairos* and *karpos* in this verse makes a frame around the parable with v. 34 and points to the conclusion in v. 43.

REJECTED STONE (v. 42)

Matthew, ever intent to interpret the story of Jesus as fulfillment of the Scriptures, advances the point made in vv. 40-41 with a quotation from Psalm 118. The psalm recalls God's unlikely choice of David as king and messianic prototype. This allusion points toward the leadership of the new Israel as coming from those currently rejected as unimportant. Matthew's

---

[13] See above, chapter 11.

[14] Snodgrass, *Wicked Tenants*, 97.

[15] Carter and Heil, *Matthew's Parables,* 166.

[16] See above, pp. 148–51 on Matthew's frequent use of contrast between evil *(ponēros)* and good *(agathos)*. The word *kakos* in 21:41 belongs to the same semantic range as *ponēros*.

readers likely understood this to mean the followers of the rejected Jesus (see also Acts 4:11 and 1 Pet 2:7 where this psalm is similarly employed).

The query on the lips of Jesus, "have you not read . . . ?" is a question he poses to Pharisees at 12:3, 5; 19:4; and to the chief priests and the scribes at 21:16. It underscores the conflict between Jesus' interpretation of the Scriptures and that of other religious leaders. For Matthew's community the tension is between their community that sees Jesus as authoritative teacher in whom the Scriptures are fulfilled and Jews who do not follow him and who reject his interpretation of the Law and the Prophets.

NEW TENANTS (v. 43)

The concluding verse repeats the point made in v. 41, but now the vineyard explicitly becomes the reign of God which is taken away from the former tenants and given to a people *(ethnos)* that will produce fruit. The identity of this people remains ambiguous. Most times the word appears in the plural *(ethnē)*, often in the phrase "all the nations."[17] In some instances it refers to nations other than Israel, that is, Gentiles; at other times it denotes Israel along with all the others. What remains unclear is whether the saying in v. 43 envisions new Jewish leaders taking the place of the present ones, or whether the reference is to Christians to whom the vineyard will be entrusted. Matthew has articulated Jesus' mission as saving his own people (1:21), especially the "lost sheep of the house of Israel" (10:6; 15:24). Jesus confronts Jewish leaders who do not accept his authority, but with repeated invitations, continuing to leave open the possibility that they will change their initial "no" and do "the father's will" (21:28-32). Even at the end of the biting denunciation of the Pharisees in chapter 23, the

---

[17] The word *ethnos* appears in the singular only at 21:43 and 24:9 (2x); in the plural *(ethnē)* at 4:15; 6:32; 10:5, 18; 12:18, 21; 20:19, 25; 24:7, 14; 25:32; 28:19. See John P. Meier, "Nations or Gentiles in Matthew 28:19?" *CBQ* 39 (1977) 94–102; Daniel J. Harrington, "'Make Disciples of All the Gentiles' (Matthew 28:19)," *CBQ* 37 (1975) 359–69.

final verse seems to envision a time when they will acknowledge Jesus, as he says to them, "I tell you, you will not see me again until you say, 'Blessed is he who comes in the name of the Lord'" (23:39). Matthew's Gospel reflects the growing tensions between his Christian community and Pharisaic Jews, but it is not clear that he sees Israel as excluded definitively from God's plan of salvation. At the conclusion of the gospel when Jesus sends his followers to make disciples of all nations (*panta ta ethnē*, 28:19), it remains unclear whether or not Israel is still among those to whom Jesus' followers are sent.[18]

MOMENT OF REVELATION (vv. 45-46)

In the Sunday Lectionary the parable ends with the saying in v. 43 about the vineyard being entrusted to a people that will produce fruit. On Friday of the Second Week of Lent the concluding verses of the chapter (vv. 45-46) are also read.[19] Here Matthew brings to light that the Jewish leaders understood this parable clearly as a judgment against them. In the progression of Matthew's narrative this parable is the moment of revelation to the Jewish leaders of Jesus' identity as God's son.[20] The readers of the gospel have known since the beginning that Jesus is son of God (2:15; 3:17; 4:3, 6, 21; 11:27), and the disciples have acclaimed him thus (14:33; 16:16). Demons have recognized Jesus as God's son (8:29). Now the Jewish leaders grasp Jesus'

---

[18] Senior, *Matthew*, 243. See further chap. 16.

[19] Verse 44, "The one who falls on this stone will be dashed to pieces and it will crush anyone on whom it falls," is absent from some manuscripts of the gospel and is not included in the Lectionary. Building on the image of the cornerstone from Ps 118 in v. 42 it becomes a stumbling stone that crushes those who oppose it. A similar use of this image is found in Isa 8:14-15; Rom 9:33; 1 Pet 2:8. This eschatological image may have been drawn from Dan 2:34-35, 44-45, where the prophet interprets a dream of King Nebuchadnezzar in which a stone hewn from a mountain, not by human hands, shatters a statue, and itself becomes a mountain that fills the whole earth. See Senior, *Matthew*, 241.

[20] See Jack Dean Kingsbury, "The Parable of the Wicked Husbandmen and the Secret of Jesus' Divine Sonship in Matthew," *JBL* 105 (1986) 643–55; John R. Donahue, "The 'Parable' of the Sheep and the Goats: A Challenge to Christian Ethics," *TS* 47(1986) 3–31; Carter and Heil, *Matthew's Parables*, 167; Lambrecht, *Out of the Treasure*, 121–22.

identity as son of God, but unlike the disciples who respond by following him when they understand the parables (13:51), the chief priests and Pharisees plot his arrest.

In the episode preceding this trio of parables Jesus' opponents were identified as chief priests and elders (21:23). Now in v. 45, Pharisees come into view, pointing forward to 22:15, where they plot to trap Jesus, and to chapter 23, where Jesus excoriates them for their hypocrisy. While this parable and the preceding one leave the door open for the Jewish leaders' change of heart, the remainder of the gospel depicts them as resolutely resisting this invitation from God's son. The issue of Jesus' divine sonship is central to the interrogation of the high priest at Jesus' trial (26:63). Reminiscent of Satan's temptations (4:5-6), both the leaders (27:43) and the passersby (27:40) taunt the crucified Jesus, demanding that he come down from the cross if he is the Son of God. By contrast, the same sight reveals to the centurion that "Truly, this was the Son of God" (27:54).

The final verse separates the crowds from their leaders. Until the arrest of Jesus, the crowds are depicted favorably in Matthew. They follow Jesus (4:25; 8:1; 14:13; 19:2; 20:29; 21:8-9), listen to his teaching (5:1; 11:7; 12:46; 13:2; 15:10; 22:33; 23:1), witness and are objects of his healings and exorcisms (9:1-8, 32-33; 12:22; 14:14; 15:30; 17:14; 19:2; 20:29-34), and are fed by him (14:13-21; 15:32-38). They respond with astonishment (7:28; 9:33; 12:23; 15:31; 22:33),[21] glorifying God (9:8; 15:31), recognize Jesus as a prophet (16:14; 21:11, 26, 46) with authority from God (9:8), although they are depicted as not privy to the same revelation as Jesus' disciples (9:25; 13:34-46). In several instances the response of the crowds is explicitly contrasted with that of the Jewish leaders (15:1, 10; 21:26). In the passion narrative, however, there is a turn in the crowds, as they are depicted as part of the arresting party at Gethsemane (26:47, 55). Then the chief priests and the elders persuade the crowds to ask for Barabbas instead of Jesus (27:20). Pilate washes his hands in their sight, declaring Jesus' innocence (27:24), to

---

[21] A variety of verbs are used to express this: *ekplēsō* (7:28; 22:33), *thaumazō* (9:33; 15:31) and *existēmi* (12:23).

which they reply, "His blood be upon us and upon our children!" (27:25).[22]

At this point of the story, however, the crowds still respond positively and regard Jesus as a prophet. The parable depicts Jesus as another in a long line of messengers from God (vv. 34-36, 46), who, like John the Baptist (3:1-4; 11:9; 14:5; 21:26) summons people to repentance and conversion. Jesus fulfills what has been prophesied in the Scriptures (2:17, 23; 3:3; 4:14; 5:17; 8:17; 12:17; 13:35; 26:56; 27:9). He suffers the same fate as the prophets before him: persecution and rejection by those not willing to turn toward God (5:12; 13:57; 14:5-9; 21:32; 23:29-32).[23] The parable distinguishes him, however, as the son through whom the inheritance is attained. In the narrative the chief priests and Pharisees now understand this, but instead of believing in Jesus, their opposition escalates. Their fear of the crowds temporarily restrains them, but in a tragic turnaround, the crowds come over to their side at the climax of the drama.

PREACHING POSSIBILITIES

There are a number of preaching possibilities that surface in this parable. Like the other parables in Matthew, there is a stress on the importance of bearing "fruit," a theme which becomes even more urgent as the "propitious time" draws near (vv. 34, 41). At the coming of the Lord (v. 40) will the present tenants (if these are understood to be disciples of Jesus) have brought forth good fruit from the vineyard? Will they have replicated the murderous actions of those who rejected the prophets? Or have they welcomed the Son and followed his way? Have they continued to be like him and his predecessors in offering prophetic witness, knowing the likely rejection and persecution that results from such?

Matthew's version of this parable functions both as a challenge to Jesus' opponents and as an allegorical explanation for the execution of Jesus. It is possible that Jesus himself,

---

[22] See Warren Carter, "The Crowds in Matthew's Gospel," *CBQ* 55 (1993) 54–68.

[23] Donahue, *Gospel in Parable*, 91.

foreseeing his own death, told a form of this parable to move his disciples to reflect in advance on how they would react when he would be put to death.[24] In its Matthean form the parable makes clear first of all, that Jesus' death is not evidence that he is rejected by God; to the contrary, it affirms his authority and his identity as prophetic servant and son through whom his people claim their divine inheritance.

A further question arises if the vineyard owner is a cipher for God. The question "What will the owner of the vineyard do?" (v. 40), brings into sharp relief the character of the vine grower. With the owner as a figure for God, the parable causes the hearer to reflect on what kind of person sends messenger after messenger including their own son? Rather than present an image of God as impervious to the suffering of the servants sent, or as viciously punishing wicked ones, the preacher can stress the pathos of God, who so desires to draw all into divine mercy, that God sends messenger after messenger, even the beloved son.[25] God is so longing for a positive response that God sends invitation after invitation. The choice faces the hearer: will you reject God's offer and incur self-condemnation? Or will you recognize God's invitation in the spurned keystone?[26] The eschatological note of the parable brings into relief that there does come a time at which the fruitful response needs to be evident; one cannot continue to spurn the offer indefinitely.

A different line of interpretation is that when the parable is stripped of its allegorical elements it can depict a true-to-life description of a peasant uprising against an oppressive landowner. From this perspective the owner in the parable is not God and the son is not Jesus. Rather, the parable depicts a typical peasant revolt and explores themes of land ownership and inheritance, forcing the hearers to examine their attitudes

---

[24] Dodd, *Parables*, 98; Snodgrass, *Wicked Tenants*, 102.

[25] Although Matthew has omitted the word *agapētos*, "beloved," from his version of this parable (cf. Mark 12:6; Luke 20:13), he has preserved it in the declaration of the heavenly voice at Jesus' baptism (3:17) and at the transfiguration (17:5). See also Matt 12:18.

[26] Donahue, *Gospel in Parable*, 54–55.

toward the use of violence. The parable portrays the futility of violence and demands the formulation of a different response to oppression.[27] This interpretation opens an opportunity for the preacher to explore nonviolent, direct action responses to contemporary situations of exploitation and oppression.[28] In this manner s/he could invite the hearers to stand in the place of "a people that will produce its fruit" (v. 43) who have yet to arrive on the scene and who turn the tide away from murderous schemes.

The traditional allegorical interpretation of this parable identifies the vineyard as Israel,[29] the tenants as Israel's rulers and leaders, the owner as God, the messengers as the prophets, the son as Christ, and the "others" to whom the vineyard has been entrusted as the Gentile church that "supplants" Israel.[30] This last notion is one that should be firmly rejected by Christian preachers. In the gospel narrative, the change of leadership envisioned in the parable is from Jewish leaders who oppose Jesus to Jews who follow him. By Matthew's time the followers of Jesus who understood themselves as the new tenants, were well aware that they were still inexorably joined to their sibling, Pharisaic Judaism, even as the wedge between them grew. It remains ambiguous whether Matthew sees a

---

[27] Herzog, *Subversive Speech*, 98–113, and James D. Hester, "Socio-Rhetorical Criticism and the Parable of the Tenants," *JSNT* 45 (1992) 27–57 take a similar approach. See also Edward H. Horne, "The Parable of the Tenants as Indictment," *JSNT* 71 (1998) 111–16. Malina and Rohrbaugh (*Social Science Commentary*, 255) suggest that if this parable at its earliest stage were not a counter-challenge by Jesus to his Jerusalem enemies, then it may have been a warning to landowners expropriating and exporting the produce of the land.

[28] Crossan, "Wicked Husbandmen," 451–65, takes the message in the opposite direction. He judges the form in *Gos.Thom.* §65 as closest to the original parable and interprets it as one that urges the hearer to recognize the opportunity in a crisis situation and to act resolutely to accomplish their purpose. In its present form in Matthew, the parable does not convey this message.

[29] This image is reinforced in the first reading from Isa 5:1-7 and the Responsorial Psalm for the Twenty-Seventh Sunday of Ordinary Time. Snodgrass, *Wicked Tenants*, 75, distinguishes that the vineyard in the parable does not stand for the nation of Israel, but rather the elect of God.

[30] E.g., Jeremias, *Parables*, 70. He further interprets the parable as vindicating Jesus' offer of the Good News to the poor (p. 76).

possibility for the inclusion of Israel in the plan of God or not. Whichever way the question is resolved, however, it is crucial that Christians interpret Matthew's parable in the context of his times, that is, the historical conflicts experienced by the early Christians in their efforts at self-definition in relation to their Jewish counterparts. Matthew's theology about Israel needs to be read in tandem with other New Testament texts, such as Romans 9–11, where Paul insists that God's promises to Israel are never revoked, and that all Israel will be saved. Moreover, in this post-Holocaust age in which the Church is engaged in serious efforts at interreligious dialogue and rapprochement, "replacement" or "supersessionist" theology should be definitively rejected.

CHAPTER THIRTEEN

Dressed for the Feast
(Matt 22:1-14)

Twenty-Eighth Sunday of Ordinary Time

Thursday of the Twentieth Week of Ordinary Time

[Jesus again in reply spoke to the chief priests and elders of the people
in parables, saying,
  "The kingdom of heaven may be likened to a king
  who gave a wedding feast for his son.
He dispatched his servants
  to summon the invited guests to the feast,
  but they refused to come.
A second time he sent other servants, saying,
  'Tell those invited: "Behold, I have prepared my banquet,
  my calves and fattened cattle are killed,
  and everything is ready; come to the feast."'
Some ignored the invitation and went away,
  one to his farm, another to his business.
The rest laid hold of his servants,
  mistreated them, and killed them.
The king was enraged and sent his troops,
  destroyed those murderers, and burned their city.
Then he said to his servants, 'The feast is ready,
  but those who were invited were not worthy to come.
Go out, therefore, into the main roads
  and invite to the feast whomever you find.'
The servants went out into the streets
  and gathered all they found, bad and good alike,
  and the hall was filled with guests.]

177

But when the king came in to meet the guests
he saw a man there not dressed in a wedding garment.
The king said to him, 'My friend, how is it
that you came in here without a wedding garment?'
But he was reduced to silence.
Then the king said to his attendants, 'Bind his hands and feet,
and cast him into the darkness outside,
where there will be wailing and grinding of teeth.'
Many are invited, but few are chosen."

TRADITION HISTORY

This parable has parallels in Luke 14:15-24,[1] *Gos. Thom.*
§64, and in rabbinic literature.[2] In the *Gospel of Thomas* the story
is simpler, and has four refusals by businessmen and merchants. The form is closer to Luke's while the ending is more
similar to Matthew's. For some scholars the Lukan version
represents the form of the parable closest to that of Jesus; for
others the version of Thomas; still others attempt a hypothetical reconstruction of a Q parable that underlies the various
redactions.[3] It is clear that each version is carefully crafted to
advance each evangelist's particular theological themes.

The differences between the versions of Matthew and Luke
are considerable. Matthew's host is a king rather than a rich
man, and the banquet is a wedding feast for his son. There are
unrealistic details, including the maltreatment of the servants,
the burning of the city, and the expectation of proper attire from

---

[1] On the Lukan version, see Barbara E. Reid, *Parables for Preachers. Year C*
(Collegeville: The Liturgical Press, 2000) 309–18.

[2] Joachim Jeremias (*The Parables of Jesus* [2d rev. ed. New York: Scribner's,
1972] 178–79) cites a rabbinic parable (*j. San.* 6.6) as the source of the gospel
tradition. It is a story of a tax collector who invited poor people to dinner so
the food would not go to waste. The form and function of this story, however,
is much different than the one in the gospel, as shown by B. B. Scott, *Hear Then
the Parable* (Minneapolis: Fortress, 1989) 171–72.

[3] For more detailed treatment of the tradition history of the parable see
Jan Lambrecht, *Out of the Treasure. The Parables in the Gospel of Matthew* (Louvain Theological and Pastoral Monographs 10; Grand Rapids: Eerdmans,
1991) 127–40; Scott, *Hear Then*, 161–68; John Dominic Crossan, *The Dark Interval: Towards a Theology of Story* (Niles: Argus, 1975) 108–19.

a guest who has no time for preparation. Typical of Matthew, he extends the parable to address the ethical demands of discipleship by adding vv. 11-14 about wearing appropriate garments.[4] Matthew's version of the parable is highly allegorized, as it veers away from parabolic form into a sketch of salvation history.

LITERARY CONTEXT

The setting for the Matthean version is entirely different from the other two: it is the third of three parables that Jesus addresses to the religious leaders in Jerusalem, and should be read in tandem with the parable of the two sons (Matt 21:28-32) and that of the wicked tenants (Matt 21:33-46). At the outset of this section, the chief priests and elders have challenged Jesus' authority (21:23-27), to which Jesus responds in parables. In the ensuing narrative Matthew resumes Mark's sequence, as the controversies between Jesus and the religious leaders continue. He debates with the Pharisees on the question of paying taxes to the emperor (22:15-22), with the Sadducees on the question of resurrection (22:23-33), with a scholar of the law regarding the greatest of the commandments (22:34-40), and with the Pharisees on expectations about the Davidic messiah (22:41-46). This controversy cycle ends with Jesus' opponents reduced to silence (22:34, 46), to which the silent guest (v. 12) points.

FEASTING AT GOD'S TABLE

The opening verse of the parable likens God to a king[5] and the reign of God[6] to a wedding feast for God's son.[7] Marriage imagery is evocative of Yahweh's covenant relationship with Israel,[8] and also recalls Matthew 9:15, where Jesus was

---

[4] Some scholars think that vv. 11-14 reflect a separate parable of Jesus that circulated independently from that in vv. 2-10; others (e.g., Lambrecht, *Out of the Treasure,* 134) see these verses as composed entirely by Matthew.

[5] As also Matt 18:23; 25:34, 40; and frequently in the Scriptures.

[6] See above, pp. 41–42 on "the kingdom of heaven."

[7] Jesus is designated God's son at Matt 2:15; 3:17; 11:27; 16:16; 17:5; 20:18.

[8] E.g., Hosea 1–3; Jer 2:2-3; 3:1-10; Ezek 16:8-63.

likened to the bridegroom, whose presence signals the necessity to feast and not fast. Feasting is a metaphor employed frequently in biblical and intertestamental literature for God's providential care and for participation in God's realm, both now and in the end times.[9] Supplying manna for the journeying Israelites (Exodus 16) is paradigmatic of divine care for God's people and feasting is the way in which the covenant is celebrated (Exodus 12; Isa 55:1-3). Isaiah's vision of God's return to Zion (25:6-10), the first reading for this Sunday, is an image for the eschatological banquet that celebrates God's ultimate triumph over evil.[10]

While the theme of eating and banqueting is not as pronounced in Matthew as in Luke, nonetheless, the First Gospel associates food with God's gracious provision. Jesus teaches his disciples to pray, "give us today our daily bread" (6:11) and shows them how to depend on God to be fed (6:25-31; 7:9-11; 14:15-21; 15:32-39). Banqueting is associated with discipleship, as Jesus eats at the home of Matthew the toll collector immediately after he responds to the invitation to follow Jesus (9:9-10).

However, meals in the gospel also signal conflict and division. To break bread with someone indicates commonality with them. And so Jesus' eating with toll collectors and sinners is a cause of contention with other religious leaders (9:10-11; 11:18-19), as is the plucking of grain on the Sabbath (12:1-8) and the lack of observance of ritual requirements surrounding eating (15:1-20).

REPEATED INVITATIONS (vv. 3-4)

The repeated sending out of the servants is reminiscent of the previous parable (21:33-46), where the multiple envoys are evocative of the many prophets sent to Israel who suffered rejection and maltreatment. The detail of the double invitation (v. 4) reflects the custom known from Esther 5:8; 6:14, which is

---

[9] See Warren Carter, *Matthew and the Margins* (Maryknoll: Orbis, 2000) 434.
[10] See also Isa 62:1-5; *2 Apoc. Bar.* 29:3-8; *1 Enoch* 62:14; Matt 15:32-39; Rev 19:1-6.

also found in ancient papyri.[11] It served the purpose of allowing the potential guest to ascertain who else is coming and whether all was being done appropriately in arranging the dinner. It would also give the invitees time to determine if they could afford to reciprocate in like manner.[12] From the perspective of the host, the time lapse allows him to determine the amount of food he will need to prepare.[13]

There are also overtones of Lady Wisdom's invitation to her banquet. When she had dressed her meat, mixed her wine, and spread her table, she sent out her maidens and she calls from the heights of the city, "Come, eat of my food, / and drink of the wine I have mixed!" (Prov 9:5). But as with Woman Wisdom, the invitation of the king is refused.

SHAMEFUL REFUSALS (vv. 5-7)

Matthew's version of the parable differs considerably at this point from Luke's. In the latter the host is not a king, but an anonymous member of the urban elite. Luke does not state the occasion for the banquet; it could simply be an effort on the part of the host to ingratiate himself with others of his class. Or he may have been reciprocating for previous banquets which he had attended. In Luke the initially invited guests seemingly accepted the original invitation, and then proceed one by one to offer three different excuses when the moment of the banquet arrives. Matthew speaks of refusal of the invited guests from the first (v. 3) and he condenses the excuses into a brief notation that the invitees ignored the invitation, one going off

[11] Chan-Hie Kim, "The Papyrus Invitation," *JBL* 94 (1975) 391–402. Richard Rohrbaugh ("The Pre-Industrial City in Luke-Acts: Urban Social Relations," in *The Social World of Luke-Acts* [Peabody: Hendrickson, 1991] 141) notes also that a later rabbinic commentary on Lamentations also attests to this (*Lam. R.* 4:2).

[12] For the social and geographical arrangements presumed in this parable see Rohrbaugh, "Pre-Industrial City," 125–49.

[13] Kenneth E. Bailey, *Poet and Peasant; Through Peasant Eyes* (2 vols. in 1; Grand Rapids: Eerdmans, 1984) 94, estimates that for 2–4 guests he would kill a chicken or two, for 5–8 a duck, for 10–15 a kid, for 15–35 a sheep, and for 35–75 a calf.

to his farm and another to his business (v. 5). No excuses are offered. This refusal is an unrealistic detail in Matthew's account. None of the urban elites would have passed up an opportunity to curry favor with a king. The refusals are inexplicable, and the king is made to look foolish in proceeding with his preparations for the banquet in the face of shameful snubs. The allegorical nature of the story is most evident.

The brutal maltreatment and the killing of the servants, followed by the burning of the city (vv. 6-7) take the parable further along the line of allegory. These details are absent from the Lukan version, and allude to the killing of John the Baptist and the prophets, and to the destruction of Jerusalem in 70 C.E.

OUTRAGEOUS INTERSECTIONS (vv. 8-10)

While the first response of the king—retaliation—makes perfect sense in an honor-and-shame system, his second response is shocking. In Jesus' world, as in the world of Matthew, likes eat with likes and social classes are not crossed. Eating together signifies shared values and social position.[14] Only other members of the urban elite would have been invited to the king's banquet.

In contrast to modern cities, where the poorest live in the inner city and the rich live in outlying suburbs, the reverse was true in antiquity. The elite, who made up some 5 to 10 percent of the total population, lived in the center of the city. It was they who controlled the political, economic, and religious systems. Physically and socially they were separated from the non-elite who served their needs. These latter often lived clustered in ethnic and occupational groups. Walls and gates, often with watchmen, ensured control of traffic and communication between sections.

The king sends his servants out into the main roads (*diexodous*), the place where the street cuts through the city boundary and goes out into the open country.[15] Rohrbaugh describes,

---

[14] Bruce J. Malina and Richard L. Rohrbaugh, *Social Science Commentary on the Synoptic Gospels* (Minneapolis: Fortress, 1992) 367.

[15] BDAG, s.v., διέξοδος.

"Most streets were unpaved, narrow, badly crowded and would not have allowed passage of wheeled vehicles. Many would have been choked with refuse and frequented by scavenging dogs, pigs, birds, and other animals. Shallow depressions in the streets allowed some drainage, but also acted as open sewers. Large open spaces were few in most cities and those that did exist were often at intersections of the few paved thoroughfares. Such open squares often served as gathering places for ceremonies or public announcements."[16]

We might envision the servants calling out (*kaleō*) the invitation (v. 9) on the roadway, in stark contrast to the private, genteel manner in which the first rich potential guests had been summoned. The kinds of guests now being sought out are those who live immediately outside the city: outcasts, such as tanners, traders, beggars, and prostitutes. These are people whose services are needed in the city, but who are not permitted to live in it. They are socially vulnerable, having neither the protection of the city walls, nor that of a village network.[17]

Matthew does not highlight the status divisions and the social suicide of the host, as does Luke. He does not list the invitees as "poor and the crippled, the blind and the lame" as does Luke (14:21). Nor does he have the detail that the servants had to compel these later guests to come into the banquet.[18] Matthew instead focuses on the ingathering of the bad and good alike, as he does in the parable of the weeds and the wheat (13:24-30), and that of the dragnet (13:47-50). And like those two parables there is an end-time sorting.

PROPER ATTIRE (vv. 11-14)

This last portion of the parable redounds with typically Matthean language and themes. On a narrative level ejection of the last minute guest who is not properly attired is entirely

---

[16] Rohrbaugh, "Pre-Industrial City," 135.

[17] Rohrbaugh, "Pre-Industrial City," 144–45.

[18] Rather than eager recipients of a generous handout, Luke's parable rightly portrays them as wary outsiders who would not easily cross the social gulf between them and the rich man.

unrealistic. How would this one have been expected to be prepared for such an event? That is precisely the point Matthew wishes to make in his allegory: one must be ever ready for the arrival of the end-time banquet, clothed with good deeds and a life of faithful discipleship.

The metaphor of putting on clothing *(enduō)* as signifying the way of life one embraces is found frequently in the Pauline literature. Paul admonishes the Romans, "put on *(endysasthe)* the Lord Jesus Christ, and make no provision for the desires of the flesh" (13:14). To the Galatians he says, "For all of you who were baptized into Christ have clothed yourselves *(endysasthe)* with Christ" (3:27). The Colossians are exhorted, "Put on *(endysasthe)* then, as God's chosen ones, holy and beloved, heartfelt compassion, kindness, humility, gentleness, and patience" (3:12).[19]

The moment of judgment is presented in the image of the king coming to meet his guests. Spotting the one not properly attired, he addresses him as "friend" *(hetaire)*. The address reflects the custom that only friends eat with friends at banquets. In Matthew's allegory all believers who have made themselves ready for the final banquet will be "friends of God and prophets" (Wis 7:27). But there is a bitter irony here. The improperly dressed guest has not responded fully to the invitation to God's friendship. More is involved than simply showing up; one must be prepared to be a full participant in the banquet. As in the other two instances in Matthew in which a person is addressed as *hetaire*, "friend," it highlights their wrong deeds: the worker who grumbles about his wages (20:13)[20] and Judas at the moment of betrayal (26:50). Matthew's theme of the ethical demands of discipleship is played out once again.[21]

In the final act of the drama the punishment is described in typical Matthean phrases: the unprepared invitee is cast into the outer darkness (8:12; 25:30) where there is wailing and grinding of teeth (8:12; 13:42, 50; 24:51; 25:30). A proverbial saying concludes the parable, but does not entirely capture its meaning. The parable has not focused on the king's choice of selected

[19] See also Eph 4:24; Rev 3:4; 19:8.
[20] See above, chap. 10.
[21] See chap. 5 on 7:21, 24-27; see also 12:46-50; 22:37-39.

ones from among those who have been invited. Rather, the contrast has been between those who had been expected to accept the invitation but refused, with those unexpected invitees who have accepted. The parable is an allegorical sketch of how those Jews who were expected to respond positively to Jesus' invitation to discipleship did not. While the religious leaders might be expected to be the ones who would most readily banquet with Jesus as "friends," they have instead set themselves against him. Instead, those on the fringes accept his invitation and become his table companions during his earthly ministry (11:19), a sign of what is to come at the eschatological banquet (8:11). The emphasis in the parable is not on the small number of the chosen, but on how widely flung is the invitation. The last verses stress that initial acceptance must be followed by full embracing of the life of discipleship.

PREACHING POSSIBILITIES

In this parable two dimensions of God's dealings with us are held in tension: God's utterly gracious and undeserved offer of a place at the eternal banquet and divine judgment when the invitation is not fully acted upon. The preacher would do well to keep both aspects in view. Preaching fire and brimstone alone is usually not the most effective way to turn the hearts of people to God, but Matthew's ending does inject a note of sober realism and keeps disciples from becoming complacent or compromising in their efforts at ethical living.

Beginning, as does the parable, with the astounding generosity of God whose invitation extends to the farthest reaches, the preacher can first invite the congregation into that graced space of awe and delight at being so chosen by God. The first reading from Isaiah offers rich imagery as well, of the abundance and sumptuousness of God's invitation. From this stance of having been offered friendship with God and with all the faithful followers of Jesus at the banquet, the homilist can pose the question: how would friends prepare to celebrate the wedding of the child of their most treasured friend? What "clothing" would be needed? What arrangements would need to be made? What details attended to? What gifts would be given?

In the same way that we would expend every effort for such an earthly celebration, how would we then want to prepare for the end time feast? The preacher would also want to invite the congregation to move from the Liturgy of the Word into the Liturgy of the Eucharist as a foretaste of our response to God's invitation through Jesus for the ongoing feast.

In Matthew's allegorical construction of salvation history, he most likely envisions the repeated rejection of the servants as portraying the refusal of Israel to heed the prophets, John the Baptist, Jesus, and now Christian missionaries. In their polemics with Jews who have not believed in Jesus, Matthew and his community may have interpreted the destruction of Jerusalem (v. 7) as God's judgment on the Jewish leaders for their rejection of Jesus. A pitfall that the preacher will want to avoid is any such implication that feeds anti-Judaism.

While in the final form, the parable stresses more the kind of response that is required of a disciple, in its original form, Jesus' parable was likely a justification for his offer of inclusion in God's realm to marginalized Jews.[22] The preacher may find with this parable an opportunity to address inclusivity. If our eucharistic celebrations are a foretaste of the eschatological banquet, do they resemble the banquet in the parable? Who is missing? What steps must be taken to welcome in those who would not come seeking to cross our boundaries on their own? What gates and walls (metaphorical or real) bar access? To whom? What social risks are there in taking steps toward greater inclusivity? From the perspective of those who have been made poor or have been exploited by dominant others, what is needed to be able to eat together at table? Such efforts at establishing a table in the present at which all sit together as brothers and sisters equally redeemed give a foretaste of the end-time banquet.

While Matthew uses the image of God as king in a number of instances, this is an infelicitous image for contemporary believers. In Jesus' world the reality of kings and client kings, such as Herod was familiar. The well-known cruelness and

---

[22] Jeremias, *Parables*, 67–69, 176–80.

political machinations of earthly kings was set in contrast to God, imaged as king, who was the ultimate power and protector of God's people. In some ways, the image of God as king could have been subversive of the status quo. In contemporary parlance, however, this image feeds the notion that God is male and that divine power is monarchical. What is required of a believer in this model is blind obedience. This is a partial and inadequate image to convey all of who God is.[23] The preacher might instead weave together the parable's image of king with that of Wisdom Woman,[24] whose banquet invitation is set out in such similar terms in Proverbs 9. The two images together could open out a fuller expression of what God is like, and could more effectively reach both male and female believers. All disciples could then be moved to imitate the banqueter as their missionary endeavors mirror that of the banquet host.

[23] See above, pp. 41–42 on "kingdom of heaven."
[24] See pp. 235–36 on Wisdom christology in Matthew.

CHAPTER FOURTEEN

Ready Maidens
(Matt 25:1-13)

Thirty-Second Sunday of Ordinary Time

Friday of the Twenty-first Week of Ordinary Time

Jesus told his disciples this parable:
"The kingdom of heaven will be like ten virgins
who took their lamps and went out to meet the bridegroom.
Five of them were foolish and five were wise.
The foolish ones, when taking their lamps,
brought no oil with them,
but the wise brought flasks of oil with their lamps.
Since the bridegroom was long delayed,
they all became drowsy and fell asleep.
At midnight, there was a cry,
'Behold, the bridegroom! Come out to meet him!'
Then all those virgins got up and trimmed their lamps.
The foolish ones said to the wise,
'Give us some of your oil,
for our lamps are going out.'
But the wise ones replied,
'No, for there may not be enough for us and you.
Go instead to the merchants and buy some for yourselves.'
While they went off to buy it,
the bridegroom came
and those who were ready went into the wedding feast with him.
Then the door was locked.
Afterwards the other virgins came and said,
'Lord, Lord, open the door for us!'

But he said in reply,
  'Amen, I say to you, I do not know you.'
Therefore, stay awake,
  for you know neither the day nor the hour."

LITERARY CONTEXT

This parable is the second of three parables that emphasize vigilance in the face of the delay in the second coming. It is part of the end time discourse, the last of the major blocks of teaching in Matthew (24:1–25:46). This discourse has four major parts.[1] It opens with a prediction of the destruction of the Temple and signs of the beginning of the end-time (24:1-14). Next is a series of sayings about signs and events that point to the coming of the Son of Humanity (24:15-31). The third part has sayings and three parables that highlight the need for preparedness and vigilance for the end-time (24:32–25:30). The final section is the parable of the last judgment (25:31-46). For the first half of the discourse Matthew relies chiefly on Markan material (Mark 13:1-32). The last half weaves together Q material[2] with material unique to Matthew. Phrases and motifs that recur throughout the whole discourse emphasize the coming of the Son of Humanity (24:27, 30, 37, 44; 25:31), delay (24:48; 25:5, 19), watchfulness (24:42; 25:13), unexpectedness of the moment of arrival (24:37, 42-44, 50; 25:10, 29), reward for faithfulness (24:46; 25:21, 23; 25:34), and exclusion of those who fail to be ready (24:51; 25:10, 30, 46).

---

[1] See above, pp. 34–37 for various outlines of the overall structure of Matthew. On the four-part division of the discourse in chaps. 24–25 see Donald Senior, *Matthew* (Nashville: Abingdon, 1998) 265–66. Cf. Jan Lambrecht, *Out of the Treasure. The Parables in the Gospel of Matthew* (Louvain Theological and Pastoral Monographs 10; Grand Rapids: Eerdmans, 1991) 185–86, who delineates three major sections after the introduction (24:3-4a): (1) 24:4b-35 The Phases of the Future, (2) 24:36–25:30 Exhortation to Vigilance, (3) 25:31-46 The Last Judgment. John Paul Heil (in Warren Carter and John Paul Heil, *Matthew's Parables* [CBQMS 30; Washington D.C.: CBA, 1998] 177–78) outlines eight sections, placing 24:42-44 and 24:45-51 as parts four and five, respectively.

[2] Matt 25:10c-12 is Matthew's reworking of Q material that Luke has placed at 13:25.

Scholars are of two minds as to whether this parable comes from the earthly Jesus or whether it is a postpaschal construction.[3] If the former, then the delay of the bridegroom is a problematic element. On the lips of Jesus the delay would not refer to his postponed parousia, but rather, he would be speaking more generally about the delay in the full unfolding of God's new future for humankind.[4] Because of the amount of characteristically Matthean themes and vocabulary and the allegorical elements in the parable, others hold that it is an entirely Matthean construction.[5]

In its present form the context indicates that the bridegroom is Jesus. While many texts of the Hebrew Scriptures use the metaphor of Yahweh as the bridegroom of Israel (Isa 54:5; Jer 31:32; Hos 2:16), Matthew has earlier cast Jesus as the bridegroom in the saying about fasting (9:15).[6] Moreover, the whole focus in this last discourse, particularly from 24:29 onward, is on preparedness for the coming of the Son of Humanity.

There are a number of elements in the story that seem unrealistic or even disturbing.[7] When the maidens go out to meet the bridegroom, where are they waiting? Have they stopped to rest? Do they fall asleep somewhere on the street or at the city gate? Why are the maidens who have extra oil so heartless toward those who have none? Weren't these women friends or related to one another? How does this fit with Jesus' command to love one another? Is it a cruel trick for the wise ones to send the foolish to the merchants, who surely would not be open at midnight? Why are the attendants of the groom female? If they were related to the groom why do they call him "Lord"? And why does he not recognize them? Some scholars answer

---

[3] See further Joachim Jeremias, *The Parables of Jesus* (2d rev. ed. New York: Scribner's, 1972) 171–75; Lambrecht, *Out of the Treasure,* 199–215; Susan Praeder, *The Word in Women's Worlds* (Zacchaeus Studies: New Testament. Wilmington: Glazier, 1988) 88–98.

[4] Lambrecht, *Out of the Treasure,* 211; Jeremias, *Parables,* 171–75.

[5] E.g., Donald Senior, *Matthew* (ANTC; Nashville: Abingdon, 1998) 274.

[6] Other New Testament texts that use this metaphor for Jesus include John 3:29; 2 Cor 11:2; Eph 5:21-33; Rev 21:2, 9; 22:17.

[7] Lambrecht, *Out of the Treasure,* 202–03, lists these.

these questions by asserting that the entire parable is to be understood allegorically. Others find the parable quite realistic in its portrayal of Palestinian wedding customs. The parable is best understood as attaining a certain level of verisimilitude while at the same time having allegorical elements.[8]

PALESTINIAN WEDDING CUSTOMS

Unfortunately we have no source that gives us a complete picture of first-century Palestinian Jewish wedding customs. However, it is possible to glean from various Greek, Jewish, and Roman sources a composite of the customs.[9] Marriage at the time of Jesus was not contracted on the basis of a couple falling in love, but it was an arrangement made by the elders of the two families to enhance their social, political, and economic positions. For this reason it was customary to marry within families and tribes. The ideal marriage partner was a first cousin, specifically a father's brother's daughter or son.[10] The marriage was arranged by the fathers, but the mothers would negotiate the terms. The contract was ratified and signed by the fathers.

The wedding took place in two stages. The betrothal was held at the home of the father of the bride. In this ceremony the bridegroom presented the marriage contract and the bride price to the father of the bride. The bride would remain in her father's house for a year or more until the second step of the ceremony was complete.[11] The latter consisted of the transfer of the bride to the home of her husband, who would reside ei-

[8] Daniel Harrington, *Matthew* (SacPag 1; Collegeville: The Liturgical Press, 1991) 349.

[9] See Susan Praeder, *The Word in Women's Worlds: Four Parables* (Zacchaeus Studies, New Testament; Wilmington: Glazier, 1988) 73-79; John Pilch, *The Cultural World of the Bible. Sunday by Sunday. Cycle A* (Collegeville: The Liturgical Press, 1995)160–62; Harrington, *Matthew,* 36–37, 349.

[10] Pilch, *Cultural World,* 160, notes that while contemporary Western cultures forbid such marriages because of the risk of birth defects, current research suggests that the incidence of such was no higher in those ancient cultures than in present day Western ones. See Leviticus 18 for Jewish laws against marriage within certain degrees of consanguinity.

[11] Matthew's account of the conception and birth of Jesus (1:18-25) depicts Mary's pregnancy occurring in this in-between stage.

ther in or near his father's home. This is the stage at which the parable in 25:1-14 is set. The groom has gone to the home of his bride to complete the negotiations of the marriage contract and to bring his wife home with him. The long delay of the bridegroom is realistic. Final negotiations could become quite involved. Each party would try to attain his own advantage. The father of the bride would be intent on highlighting the worth of his daughter by not letting her go too quickly or for too small a recompense. When all was finally settled, a procession of the wedding party to the house of the groom would signal the commencement of the feasting.

WISE AND FOOLISH VIRGINS

The parable opens with the reign of God[12] likened to the situation in which ten young women take their lamps and go out to meet the bridegroom. Ten is often used as a symbolic number for fullness, or completeness.[13] The women are relatives and friends of the groom. They are not bridesmaids, but rather young women from the groom's household. The bride is never mentioned in this parable. The term *parthenos* refers to a virgin, a young, unmarried woman.[14] It connotes a teenager or preteen, as women were considered of marriageable age at twelve years.[15]

---

[12] See above, pp. 41–42 on "the kingdom of heaven."

[13] E.g., ten commandments (Exod 20:1-17; Deut 5:6-21); ten righteous ones required to save Sodom (Gen 18:32); in Judaism a minion of ten is required for prayer.

[14] This is the same term used of Mary at Matt 1:23. Some commentators also relate the *parthenoi* of this parable to Paul's instructions to unmarried women at 1 Cor 7:25-31. That text, however, has a different focus and function than the parable in Matthew. Paul is speaking about not changing one's marital status in light of the imminent parousia. He prefers the married to stay unmarried given the nearness of the end. He remarks on how unmarried men and women are freer to devote themselves to the "things of the Lord" when they do not have the care of a family to take their attention (vv. 33-34). In Matthew's parable the emphasis is on the preparedness of disciples for the delay in the end times; in Paul's letter he expects an imminent end and his emphasis is on not changing social and marital status.

[15] This presumes similar customs in the time of Jesus as that known from rabbinic times, when the minimum age for marriage for a young man was thirteen; for a young woman, twelve. See Str-B 2.373-75.

The contrast of five foolish *(mōrai)* and five wise *(phronimoi)* is reminiscent of Matthew 7:24-27, where the same terms are used of the builders.[16] This detail sets up the story for a separation of the two, a theme which appears also in the parables of the weeds and the wheat (13:36-43), the dragnet (13:47-50), and the sheep and the goats (25:31-46).[17]

LAMPS TRIMMED AND BURNING

There are two words for lamps or lights in the New Testament. In this parable the word is *lampades,* which usually refers to a torch.[18] This is the word used, for example, in Genesis 15:17, for the flaming torch that passed between the two pieces of the offerings of Abram, and for the lanterns and torches brought by the arresting band of soldiers, chief priests, and Pharisees at John 18:3. The word *lychnos* is generally used to denote a household oil lamp, as in the parable of the woman who lights a lamp to search for her lost coin (Luke 15:8).[19] This distinction is not hard and fast, however. At Acts 20:8 there are many lamps *(lampades)* in the upstairs room where Paul is preaching when the drowsy Eutychus tumbles from the window. That the young women of the parable carried flasks of oil (v. 4) seems to point to oil lamps, rather than torches. Verse 6 is often translated as "trimmed their lamps," but the verb *kosmeō* means more generally "to put in order"[20] and could refer to either kind of light. Either the young women "snuff the lamps, removing the burnt wick, and fill them with oil, so that they may burn brightly again"[21] or they apply more oil to the soaked rags wound around the top of a pole that make a burning torch.[22] There are no extant sources that depict young women

---

[16] See above, chap. 5.

[17] See chaps. 7, 8, and 16, respectively.

[18] See also 1 Macc 6:39; Rev 8:10.

[19] See also Job 18:6. This word is also used of lamps in the temple at 2 Chr 4:20.

[20] BDAG, s.v., κοσμέω.

[21] Jeremias, *Parables,* 175.

[22] A happening witnessed by a traveler to Palestine at the turn of the twentieth century. This wedding procession in which unmarried girls carried

carrying lights in wedding processions other than Christian art and literature that postdate this parable.[23] Whichever kind of lamp is implied is left ambiguous, but the meaning of the symbol is not hard to detect.

At the conclusion of the Sermon on the Mount Jesus tells the disciples that they are the light (*phōs*) of the world. Like a city set on a mountain that cannot be hidden, neither can their light; it is like a lamp (*lychnos*) set on a lampstand to illumine (*lampō*) the whole household (7:14-16).[24] This parable concludes by equating light with good deeds that are visible to others and that lead to praise of God (v. 16). There is also a rabbinic reference in the *Midrash Rabbah* to Numbers 7:19 (*Num. Rab.* 13:15-16) in which the phrase "mixed with oil" is interpreted as study of Torah mingled with good deeds.[25] Understanding the oil as good deeds explains the reason why the five wise young women cannot share theirs with the foolish women.

Alternatively, the lamps and the oil in this parable can be understood more generally as the steps that disciples need to take in order to be ready for the eschatological moment.[26] With echoes of Matthew 7:24-27, where the wise are those who hear and act on Jesus' words, so the wise young women of this parable are those who have faithfully prepared for the end-time by hearing and acting on God's word ("a lamp for my feet" in Ps 119:105) as spoken and lived by Jesus. When the end-time comes those who are righteous will "shine like the sun" (Matt

---

torches and danced is cited in Joachim Jeremias, "*LAMPADES* Mt 25:1.3f .7f.," *ZNW* 56 (1965) 198.

[23] Greek sources portray the mothers of the bride and of the groom carrying torches and one rabbinic source has a man and a woman carrying torches during the transport of the marriage bed. Another rabbinic source tells of the father of the bride lining the route of the wedding procession with golden lamps (Str-B 2.510). Roman sources describe a boy carrying the principal torch along with other torch-bearers. See Praeder, *The Word in Women's Worlds*, 75–76.

[24] See above, chap. 4.

[25] John R. Donahue, *The Gospel in Parable* (Philadelphia: Fortress, 1988) 104; K. Donfried, "The Allegory of the Ten Virgins (Matt 25:1-13) as a Summary of Matthean Theology," *JBL* 93 (1974) 427.

[26] So Donald Senior, *Matthew* (ANTC; Nashville: Abingdon, 1998) 277; similarly, Warren Carter, *Matthew and the Margins* (Maryknoll: Orbis, 1998) 486.

13:43; see also Matt 17:2), while those who are not will be consumed by the fire (Matt 13:42). A similar contrast is also found in Proverbs 13:9, which asserts, "The light of the just shines gaily, / but the lamp of the wicked goes out."[27]

THE MIDNIGHT CRY

A loud cry *(kraugē)* heralds the arrival of the apocalyptic moment (so also Rev 14:18) and the summons is issued to meet the coming one. The same language of meeting *(eis apantēsin)* and being with (v. 10) the Lord (v. 11) finds an echo in Paul's eschatological scenario in 1 Thessalonians 4:17, "Then we who are alive, who are left, will be caught up together with them in the clouds to meet the Lord in the air. Thus we shall always be with the Lord."

The arrival of the bridegroom at midnight signals a moment of divine manifestation. Midnight was the hour at which the angel of God went throughout the land of Egypt, slaying the first born of Pharaoh and the Egyptians, and sparing the Israelites (Exod 11:4; 12:29).[28] It is at midnight that Paul and Silas are freed from the prison in Philippi while singing hymns (Acts 16:25). And midnight is the hour when Paul and his companions sight land and rescue during their perilous sea journey (Acts 27:27). Thus, midnight is an apt moment for prayer in time of trouble (Psalm 119:62) and it is an hour at which one should keep watch for the coming Son of Humanity (Mark 13:35).

READY OR NOT

As in so many of Matthew's parables, the eschatological moment is decisive. There is no further time for preparation, there are no last chances. There are those who are ready (24:44; 25:10) and those who are not. Those who are prepared go into

---

[27] See also Job 18:5-6, which has a saying similar to the second half : "Truly, the light of the wicked is extinguished; no flame brightens his hearth. The light is darkened in his tent; in spite of him, his lamp goes out."

[28] Job (34:20) speaks of how death comes at midnight even to the noble and powerful.

the wedding feast[29] with the bridegroom. "[W]ith him" (v. 10) echoes the promise of Emmanuel, "God is with us" in the person of Jesus that frames the entire Gospel of Matthew, from the annunciation of Jesus' birth (1:23) to his great commission to the disciples (28:20).[30]

The five foolish women arrive after the door is locked. While in the Sermon on the Mount Jesus had assured his disciples that if they knock the door will be opened to them (7:7-8), the setting of that saying is different from 25:10-11. The time now is past when choices can be made; judgment is at hand.[31] The plea of the five who are on the outside begins with the same invocation as at 7:21-23, "Lord, Lord." And the reply is the same: "I never knew you" (7:23).[32]

The concluding verse does not fit well the dynamics of the narrative. In fact, all ten young women fell asleep (v. 5). Staying awake is a frequently used metaphor for watchfulness and vigilance for the end time. It is often accompanied by a motif of the unexpectedness of the hour (Matt 24:42, 43; 1 Thess 4:16-17).[33] The fallibility of disciples is never so visible as in the scene at Gethsemane, where Jesus three times asks them to keep watch, but they repeatedly succumb to sleep (Matt 26:36-46).

PREACHING POSSIBILITIES

This is a good news / bad news parable. For the foolish ones this gospel ends on a very sobering note. They are barred from going into the feast with the bridegroom and the wedding

---

[29] As at Matt 22:1-14 (see above, chap. 13), the wedding feast is a symbol of the eschatological banquet.

[30] Carter, *Matthew and the Margins*, 487.

[31] The metaphor of an "open door" is used by Paul connoting a favorable opportunity for missionary activity (1 Cor 16:9; 2 Cor 2:12). In the book of Revelation there is the promise to the church of Laodicea of an open door which "none may shut" (3:8), a saying which may have had particular meaning if these were Christians facing expulsion from the synagogue. At Rev 4:1 the "open door" signifies the entryway into heaven.

[32] An ironic twist on this motif is that Peter claims not to know Jesus when confronted by the maid in the courtyard (26:74).

[33] On Matt 24:42-51 see below, chap. 22.

party. They have let themselves be lulled into thinking that
there is no hurry; the lamp oil can always be gotten later; or
someone else will take up the slack. The end seems so far off.
For the wise ones this is a parable of great jubilation. They have
been preparing all along and are ready when the bridegroom
comes. They can hardly believe that the time has finally come.

None of the people whom the preacher addresses are
completely foolish, nor completely wise; the two extremes in
the parable are for bringing the point into higher relief. Each
one has some aspect of the foolish virgins within. There is
something I've been wanting to change about my lifestyle;
there is someone ill or imprisoned I've been intending to visit;
someone to whom I owe an apology; something I've been
wanting to seek direction about; something I've intended to
talk over with God. But I think I'll get around to it some other
time. It may be now or never.

Every disciple also has some aspect of the wise ones within.
All the myriad ways in which wise disciples have been illu-
mining the world, lighting one small candle at a time, by the
way they hear and live out the word, coalesce into brilliant
torchlight for the banquet. The arrival of the groom at last is no
surprise, but a joyous relief. The parable invites celebration of
our wisdom, even as our foolishness is still being transformed.

When the gospel is read in juxtaposition with the first
reading from Wisdom 6:12-16, it is reassuring that the effort to
be wise does not depend on human striving alone. In the first
reading Wisdom is waiting to be found; she is readily perceived and found and known by those who love and seek her.
Those who keep vigil for her are actually being sought out by
her as she makes her rounds. In another text, Wisdom sends
out her maidens to invite even those who are simple, and lack
understanding, to forsake foolishness and come to her banquet
(Prov 9:1-6). In a number of texts Matthew portrays Jesus as
Wisdom personified.[34] Those who are seeking him as bridegroom must also eschew foolishness so as to be ready to feast
with him. There is a rich interplay of male and female images

---

[34] See below, chap. 18.

in the first and third readings, which invites disciples of both genders to hear themselves fully addressed. Moreover, this is one of the few parables in which the featured characters are women.[35] The preacher might capitalize on the image of the women as bearers of light for the whole community. A challenge for contemporary Christians is how to dismantle sexism so that the light that women bear is not extinguished. With their readiness for all ministries will they find an open door? How can we configure our eucharistic celebrations so that they are a foretaste of the egalitarian eschatological banquet?

This Sunday is one of those rare instances in which there is a good connection also between the second reading and the gospel. The apocalyptic language and symbols used by Paul in his first letter to the Thessalonians (4:13-18) have a number of echoes in the gospel. Paul, too, is dealing with questions surrounding the delay in the parousia. The passage is addressed to those who are tempted to yield to grief as some of their loved ones have died during the delay. In a slightly different key, but with the same message as Matthew, Paul reassures them of the certitude of Christ's coming and his enduring presence with them. The preacher may follow this direction, centering on the confidence that Christ's promises are sure and that a joyous future awaits.

---

[35] Matthew has only one other that features a female character: the parable of the woman hiding leaven (13:33). See above, pp. 107–12. In addition to that one, Luke tells of a woman searching for a lost coin (15:8-10) and of a widow who persistently pursues justice (18:1-8). See Susan Praeder, *The Word in Women's Worlds. Four Parables*. Zacchaeus Studies: New Testament (Wilmington: Glazier, 1988); Barbara E. Reid, *Parables for Preachers. Year C* (Collegeville: The Liturgical Press, 2000) 177–92, 227–32, 293–308.

CHAPTER FIFTEEN

Investing Talents
(Matt 25:14-30)

Thirty-Third Sunday of Ordinary Time

Saturday of the Twenty-first Week of Ordinary Time

[Jesus told his disciples this parable:
"A man going on a journey
called in his servants and entrusted his possessions to them.
To one he gave five talents; to another, two; to a third, one—
to each according to his ability.
Then he went away.]
Immediately the one who received five talents went and traded with them,
and made another five.
Likewise, the one who received two made another two.
But the man who received one went off and dug a hole in the ground
and buried his master's money.
After a long time
the master of those servants came back
and settled accounts with them.
The one who had received five talents came forward
bringing the additional five.
He said, 'Master, you gave me five talents.
See, I have made five more.'
His master said to him, 'Well done, my good and faithful servant.
Since you were faithful in small matters,
I will give you great responsibilities.
Come, share your master's joy.'
(Then) the one who had received two talents also came forward and said,
'Master, you gave me two talents.
See, I have made two more.'

His master said to him, 'Well done, my good and faithful servant.
Since you were faithful in small matters,
I will give you great responsibilities.
Come, share your master's joy.'
Then the one who had received the one talent came forward and said,
  'Master, I knew you were a demanding person,
  harvesting where you did not plant
  and gathering where you did not scatter;
  so out of fear I went off and buried your talent in the ground.
Here it is back.'
His master said to him in reply, 'You wicked, lazy servant!
So you knew that I harvest where I did not plant
  and gather where I did not scatter?
Should you not then have put my money in the bank
  so that I could have got it back with interest on my return?
Now then! Take the talent from him and give it to the one with ten.
For to everyone who has,
  more will be given and he will grow rich;
  but from the one who has not,
  even what he has will be taken away.
And throw this useless servant into the darkness outside,
  where there will be wailing and grinding of teeth.'"

LITERARY CONTEXT AND TRADITION HISTORY

This parable is the third in the series of three parables[1] in the eschatological discourse (24:1–25:46)[2] that stress the need for faithful activity on the part of disciples while the second coming is delayed. All three speak of the absence, delay, and unexpected return of a master of a household. The parable of the talents is one of Matthew's lengthiest. Its introduction, "It will be as when a man who was going on a journey . . ." (which has been slightly augmented in the Lectionary), is abrupt. The introduction to the previous parable at 25:1 is probably intended to serve double duty, so that the scenario painted in 25:14-30 is also understood to be compared to the realm of God.

---

[1] The first is the parable of the faithful servant (24:45-51, see below, chap. 22); and the second that of the wise and foolish virgins (25:1-13, see above, chap. 14).

[2] See above, p. 190 for an outline of the parts of the eschatological discourse.

The Gospel of Luke has a similar parable (19:11-28) but the relationship between the two versions remains unclear. In Luke's account[3] there seem to be two distinct parables interwoven. In verses 12, 14, 24a, 27 Luke introduces a motif of a journeying and returning king, an aspect that is not part of Matthew's rendition.[4] Some scholars postulate that the two versions represent originally independent parables of Jesus that had superficial similarities. Others advance that Matthew and Luke each redacted differently a parable from Q. Still others decide that the Lukan version was composed entirely by the evangelist.[5] There is also a version of the parable in the Gospel of the Nazoreans, which will be taken up in more detail below.

While the Lukan and Matthean versions share a similar structure, there is little verbal agreement between the two. Moreover, their literary contexts are different, giving each a distinctive focus. The Lukan parable comes immediately after the story of Zacchaeus, the rich toll collector who is exemplary in his hospitality and in his almsgiving (Luke 19:1-10). This context makes the Lukan parable part of the third evangelist's theme of the proper use of money as related to discipleship. In Matthew's Gospel the parable is situated in the eschatological discourse, which colors its interpretation.

USE OF TALENTS

A traditional reading of this parable emphasizes the importance of using all one's God-given gifts to the full. This

---

[3] See Barbara E. Reid, *Parables for Preachers. Year C* (Collegeville: The Liturgical Press, 2000) 319–27.

[4] Some scholars think that a historical incident underlies this motif. Josephus recounts (*Ant.* 17.9, 1-3 §208-222; *J.W.* 2.2,2 §18) how Herod the Great's son Archelaus traveled to Rome to obtain the title of king for Judea, Samaria, and Idumea. A delegation of fifty Palestinians also went to Rome to oppose his kingship, and Archelaus came away with the title of ethnarch, not king (*Ant.* 17.11, 1-2 §299-314; *J.W.* 2.6,1-2 §80-92).

[5] See B. B. Scott, *Hear Then the Parable* (Minneapolis: Fortress, 1989) 217–35; Jan Lambrecht, *Out of the Treasure. The Parables in the Gospel of Matthew* (Louvain Theological and Pastoral Monographs 10; Grand Rapids: Eerdmans, 1991) 217–44; Joachim Jeremias, *The Parables of Jesus* (2d rev. ed. New York: Scribner's, 1972) 58–63.

interpretation is facilitated by the fact that the word for the monetary unit, "talents," conveys more than coinage in English.[6] The Greek word *talanton* denotes a measure of weight varying from 58-80 lbs. (26-36 kg.) and a unit of coinage whose value differed considerably in various times and places, but was always comparatively high. It varied also with the metal involved, which might be gold, silver, or copper. The silver talent of Aegina, for example, was worth about half again as much as the Attic talent of Solon, and more than six times that of a Syrian talent.[7] The word "talent" in Greek does not have any nuance beyond monetary or weight measurements. In the parable it connotes a very large sum of money.[8]

While the amount of money involved in the parable would seem to place us in the world of high finance, the language of the opening verse is clearly evocative of discipleship and reveals the allegorical nature of the story. That the man called *(ekalesen)* his servants and entrusted his possessions to them is reminiscent of how Jesus called *(ekalesen)* the first disciples (4:21) and entrusted his mission to them. Also, there are many instances in Matthew in which the noun *doulos*, "slave," (translated by the *NAB* at v. 14 as "servants") and the verb *douleuein*, "to serve," are used in reference to disciples.[9] To each one the man entrusts a different amount, according to ability. Unlike Luke's account, where the slaves are told to do business *(pragmateuomai)* with the money until the master's return (Luke 19:13), in Matthew's version the man does not give instructions to the slaves. Well-trained disciples will know what to do with what is entrusted to them.[10]

---

[6] In Luke's version the unit of money is *mna,* a small amount of money, about one sixtieth of a talent, which is equivalent to a hundred Attic drachmas, approximately twenty-five dollars (so Joseph A. Fitzmyer, *The Gospel According to Luke* [AB28A; Garden City, N.Y.: Doubleday, 1985] 1235).

[7] BDAG, s.v., τάλαντον.

[8] The only other instance of the use of *talanton* in the New Testament is at Matt 18:24 in the parable of the Unforgiving Servant (see above, chap. 9), where *myriōn talantōn*, "ten thousand talents," is used to connote a huge amount of debt in contrast to *hekaton dēnaria*, "one hundred denarii" (v. 28), a vastly smaller amount.

[9] Matt 6:24; 10:24-25; 20:27; 24:45-51.

[10] Warren Carter, *Matthew and the Margins* (Maryknoll: Orbis, 2000) 489.

That there are three characters is a typical narrative device. The climax builds to the interaction with the third, which breaks the pattern with the first two, and therein provides the drama. The one who received one talent dug a hole and buried the money in the ground, which was thought in antiquity to be a good way to preserve valuables from thieves.[11]

JUDGMENT

In Matthew's literary context the return of the master is understood to be the parousia and the settling of accounts is the ensuing judgment. The first two servants double the money entrusted to them and are approved by the master as "good and faithful servants." They have been faithful in small matters *(oliga)* so now the master says, "I will put you in charge over much." There is a curious word play in this line when contrasted with Matthew 6:30; 8:26; 14:31; 16:8; 17:20, where Jesus admonishes his disciples for their little faith *(oligopistoi)*. Now the slaves are rewarded for being faithful *(pistos)* over little things *(oliga)*. There is a narrative tension, however, because *talanta* are not little things, but a very large amount of money. Verses 21 and 23 are best understood in allegorical terms. The argument is from lesser to greater: faithfulness in the time before the parousia (as imperfect as that is) results in being led into something far greater in the heavenly realm. While the phrase *epi pollōn se katastēsō* in v. 21, says literally, "I will appoint you over much," the verb *kathistēmi* without *epi* can mean "to take someone somewhere."[12] The parable points toward the time in which faithful disciples are taken into the heavenly realm where they will share unreservedly in the master's joy. The emphasis in the contrast is not so much on the amounts of responsibility, but the faithfulness now and what it will lead to then. The eschatological joy (as at Matt 13:44) of the good and faithful servant stands in stark contrast to the frightening end of the wicked, lazy servant.

---

[11] See above, chap. 8, on the parable of buried treasure, which presumes such. Cf. Luke 19:20, where the amount is much smaller and the slave stores it in a handkerchief.

[12] E.g., in Acts 17:15, where Paul is escorted to Athens.

MISJUDGING THE MASTER

For some scholars the fatal flaw of the third servant is not the failure to invest the money well, but that he has misjudged the master. At the moment of judgment he characterizes the master as demanding, reaping benefit even from what he has not sown (v. 24). He is wrongly fearful of the master, thinking him harsh, when actually the master has been extraordinarily generous with the gift and with the opportunity given the slave. His downfall is his unwarranted timidity. In this line of interpretation the parable is an admonition to disciples not to see God as a harsh judge, but as a generous giver who entrusts to us all that we need to prosper.[13]

The problem with this approach is that at the end of the parable the master *is* portrayed as demanding, as he exacts cruel punishment on this fearful servant.[14] An explanation that God will treat us in just the way that we perceive God, does not satisfactorily deal with the eschatological context of the parable. Moreover, how would a fearful person, upon hearing this parable, be moved to change their perception of God as a harsh judge? Would it not only confirm their worst anxieties? With the number of times Matthew repeats the phrase about being thrown into outer darkness where there is wailing and grinding of teeth (8:12; 13:42, 50; 22:13; 24:51), it would seem that his gospel is not intent on allaying the fears of those who have misconceptions about God's generous character. Rather, this gospel, especially in the eschatological discourse, seems at pains to stress the opposite: one cannot simply rely on God's graciousness, but a disciple must be intent on preparing for the moment of judgment when active ethical behavior must be in evidence.

---

[13] John R. Donahue, *The Gospel in Parable* (Minneapolis: Fortress, 1988) 105–08; Lane McGaughey, "The Fear of Yahweh and the Mission of Judaism: A Postexilic Maxim and Its Early Christian Expansion in the Parable of the Talents," *JBL* 94 (1975) 235–45.

[14] Jennifer Glancy, "Slaves and Slavery in the Matthean Parables," *JBL* 119 (2000) 67–90 shows that such cruelty and physical abuse was true to life and usual in literary portrayals of slaves.

A TALE OF TERROR

The above interpretations have recently been challenged by scholars who use insights from social science criticism.[15] Taking the stance of a peasant, and placing our sympathies with the third slave, not with the master, yields a very different story. In contrast to capitalist mores, which view wealth as something that can be increased by hard work or investment, the world of the parable is, rather, one of limited good. In such a culture it is thought that there is only so much wealth; any increase to one person takes away from another. The aim of a peasant was to satisfy the needs of his family, not to amass unlimited wealth. From this perspective, the man who expects his money to be increased is the wicked one, who is unfettered in his greed. The purpose of his journey is to increase his investments and initiate new business schemes. He is building new patron-client relations and is currying favor with imperial overlords.[16] Moreover, he is not observant of the Torah, as is evident in v. 27. Usury was forbidden by Exodus 22:25; Leviticus 25:36-37; Deuteronomy 23:29.[17]

The third servant, then, is not wicked, except in the eyes of those who are greedy acquisitors or those who are co-opted by them, as are the first two servants. The third slave is the one who has acted honorably by blowing the whistle on the wickedness of the master. The estimation of the master as demanding is correct, as is the observation that he acquires money he does not earn (v. 24). He exploits the labor of others

---

[15] E.g., Richard L. Rohrbaugh, "A Peasant Reading of the Parable of the Talents/Pounds: A Text of Terror?" *BTB* 23 (1993) 32–39; Malina and Rohrbaugh, *Social Science Commentary*, 149–50; William R. Herzog II, *The Parables as Subversive Speech* (Louisville: Westminster John Knox, 1994) 150–68.

[16] Herzog, *Subversive Speech*, 157.

[17] Some commentators try to maintain the master as a good person by envisioning the transactions being with non-Jews. The Mishnah attests to more liberal regulations regarding relations with Gentiles (*m. Bab.M.* 5:1-6). Daniel J. Harrington (*The Gospel of Matthew* [SacPag 1; Collegeville: The Liturgical Press, 1991] 353), advances that if *trapezitēs* (v. 27) is a reference to money-changers, then the master may be talking about the interest that they charged for their transactions, not the interest accruing to himself.

who do the planting; and he knows how to manipulate money exchanges to his advantage. Verse 29 may be taken as an interpretive comment, denouncing the injustice visible in such practices whereby the rich continually get richer while the poor keep losing even the little they have.[18] The parable is a warning to the rich to stop exploiting the poor and is one that encourages poor people to take measures that expose such greed for the sin that it is. Verse 30 is a sobering, realistic note of what can happen to those who oppose the rich and powerful.

This line of interpretation has confirmation from a third version of the parable from the Gospel of the Nazoreans, which is known to us only from quotations of it and allusions to it in the Church Fathers. Eusebius preserves and comments on this variation of the parable:

> But since the Gospel [written] in Hebrew characters which has come into our hands enters the threat not against the man who had hid [the talent], but against him who had lived dissolutely— For he [the master] had three servants:
>
> A one who squandered his master's substance with harlots and flute-girls,
>
> B one who multiplied the gain,
>
> C and one who hid the talent
>
> and accordingly . . .
>
> C' one was accepted (with joy),
>
> B' another merely rebuked,
>
> A' and another cast into prison
>
> —I wonder whether in Matthew the threat which is uttered after the word against the man who did nothing may refer not to him, but by epanalepsis to the first who had feasted and drunk with the drunken.[19]

---

[18] Verse 29 is most likely a free-floating proverbial wisdom saying. It is a doublet: variations of it from the Markan tradition appear at Mark 4:25; Matt 13:12; and Luke 8:18. Another form of it has been preserved in Q to which Matt 25:29 and Luke 19:26 give evidence.

[19] Eusebius, *Theophania*, 22, as quoted by Rohrbaugh, "A Peasant Reading," 36.

What is evident from Eusebius's comment is that he cannot understand how the first servant is approved, and so proposes epanalepsis (as outlined with A corresponding to A', etc.) as the means by which to find the one who hid the talent as the accepted one. This evidence would confirm that the more appropriate reading of the parable is one in which the slave who buried the money is the one who acted commendably.

PREACHING POSSIBILITIES

If the preacher follows the line of this last interpretation, the parable challenges presuppositions of a capitalistic mentality which promotes ever-increasing production and consumption. The concept of limited good from the world of Jesus could help move the preaching in the direction of the interconnectedness of all life of the cosmos and the questions of sustainability and the consumption of resources that face us today. The parable can be an entree to speak about what Christian response is called for in the light of such global realities today of rich people and rich nations becoming increasingly more wealthy from the investments of international corporations that make huge profits from exploited and underpaid workers in sweatshops. The parable can pose a challenge to believers to be wary of greed in all its forms.

Approaching the parable from its eschatological context in Matthew the preacher would emphasize, as with the other parables in this last discourse, the need for readiness for the final moment. The homilist should be careful, however, not to preach the parable simply as an exhortation to use one's gifts to the full. This misses the eschatological dimension of the parable, which is essential for its full impact.

The element of active discipleship which entails risky choices is one that the preacher might pursue. Discipleship is not a comfortable holding on to tradition. Rather, it is an active endeavor that involves great investment on the part of the Christian. What has been received must be acted upon, passed on to others, increasing the yield, as it were.

It is possible Matthew's community heard this parable in light of their polemics with those Jews who did not become followers of Jesus. They may have seen the third servant, intent on preserving the one talent precisely as it was given, as a metaphor for post-70 Judaism's attempt to build a "fence" around the Torah (*m.*ʾ*Abot* 1:1). This would stand in contrast to their own investment in the Jesus movement, perceiving themselves as the good and faithful servants of God. The parable would help with the Christian community's attempts at self-definition in relation to the Jews of the synagogue.[20] While this understanding may help to illumine how early Christians and Jews related to one another, in a contemporary Christian context a preacher would need to be very attentive not to preach the parable in such a way as to feed anti-Judaism.

A preacher should also recognize a problematic aspect of the imagery in the parable. Portraying Jesus as a master and disciples as slaves uses a metaphor that was very familiar in the everyday life of ancient Palestine and the Greco-Roman world. While it serves to emphasize the power of Jesus and of God, it can be dangerous when used as a vehicle to reinscribe human hierarchies and to justify domination and exploitation of others. Moreover, it can counter the very message of the parable by encouraging servile fear rather than bold and faithful discipleship.

---

[20] Harrington, *Matthew*, 354–55.

CHAPTER SIXTEEN

Final Judgment
(Matt 25:31-46)

Thirty-Fourth Sunday of Ordinary Time;
Feast of Christ the King

Monday of the First Week of Lent

Jesus said to his disciples:
"When the Son of Man comes in his glory,
and all the angels with him,
he will sit upon his glorious throne,
and all the nations will be assembled before him.
And he will separate them one from another,
as a shepherd separates the sheep from the goats.
He will place the sheep on his right and the goats on his left.
Then the king will say to those on his right,
'Come, you who are blessed by my Father.
Inherit the kingdom prepared for you from the foundation of the world.
For I was hungry and you gave me food,
I was thirsty and you gave me drink,
a stranger and you welcomed me,
naked and you clothed me,
ill and you cared for me,
in prison and you visited me.'
Then the righteous will answer him and say,
'Lord, when did we see you hungry and feed you,
or thirsty and give you drink?
When did we see you a stranger and welcome you,
or naked and clothe you?
When did we see you ill or in prison, and visit you?'

And the king will say to them in reply,
  'Amen, I say to you, whatever you did
    for one of the least brothers of mine, you did for me.'
Then he will say to those on his left,
  'Depart from me, you accursed,
    into the eternal fire prepared for the devil and his angels.
For I was hungry and you gave me no food,
  I was thirsty and you gave me no drink,
  a stranger and you gave me no welcome,
  naked and you gave me no clothing,
  ill and in prison, and you did not care for me.'
Then they will answer and say,
  'Lord, when did we see you hungry or thirsty
  or a stranger or naked or ill or in prison,
  and not minister to your needs?'
He will answer them, 'Amen, I say to you,
  what you did not do for one of these least ones,
  you did not do for me.'
And these will go off to eternal punishment,
  but the righteous to eternal life."

LITERARY CONTEXT AND TRADITION HISTORY

This uniquely Matthean parable[1] is the final one in the Gospel of Matthew and is read on the final Sunday in Ordinary Time. It concludes the eschatological discourse addressed to Jesus' disciples (24:1–25:46) and follows three parables that emphasize the need for preparedness in the face of the delay of the parousia.[2] While in those parables the focus is on the in-

---

[1] As John R. Donahue points out (*The Gospel in Parable* [Philadelphia: Fortress, 1988] 110), the parable is similar in form to the similitudes of Enoch (*1 Enoch* 39–71). There are also similarities to a last will and testament, such as those found in the *Testaments of the Twelve Patriarchs,* of a leader who is about to depart and who instructs his followers. Rudolph Bultmann (*History of the Synoptic Tradition* [rev. ed.; tr. J. Marsh; New York: Harper & Row, 1968] 120–23) classifies Matt 25:31-46 as an "apocalyptic prediction" rather than a parable.

[2] These are (1) Matt 24:42-51, the Parable of the Watchful and Faithful Servants (see below, chap. 22); (2) Matt 25:1-13 the Parable of the Wise and Foolish Virgins (see above, chap. 14), and (3) Matt 25:14-30, the Parable of the Talents (chap. 15). For an outline of the eschatological discourse, see above, p. 190.

between-time, in this last one the eschatological moment has arrived: the Son of Humanity comes in his glory (v. 31). The time for judgment is at hand.

This scene is intimately linked with the final verses in the gospel (28:16-20). There the departing Jesus instructs his followers to make disciples of all nations, *panta ta ethnē* (28:19), a command that the parable of 25:31-46 presumes has been fulfilled. All the nations, *panta ta ethnē* (25:32), having heard the gospel, are assembled now to render account.[3]

There are many typically Matthean words and expressions in this parable, such as *panta ta ethnē* ("all the nations"), *tote* ("then"), *thronou doxēs* ("glorious throne"), *angeloi* ("angels").[4] Some scholars consider the entire parable a Matthean creation.[5] Most think that the evangelist took it over from his special source and redacted it according to his own interests.[6]

The parable has four movements.[7] In the first three verses the Son of Humanity comes in glory with his angels for the final judgment, and proceeds to separate the sheep from the goats (vv. 31-33). The next two sections parallel each other.

---

[3] This stands in contrast to the command Jesus gives his disciples at Matt 10:6 to go only to "the lost sheep of the house of Israel." See also 15:24, where Jesus articulates his own mission in similar terms. The mission that began with the Jews extends at the end of the gospel to all the Gentiles.

[4] The expression *panta ta ethnē* ("all the nations") occurs also at 6:32; 24:14; 28:19; *tote* ("then") occurs ninety times in Matthew, six times in this parable; *epi tou thronou doxēs autou* ("on his glorious throne") also at 19:28; angels are mentioned eighteen other times in Matthew.

[5] E.g., Lamar Cope, "Matthew 25:31-46: 'The Sheep and the Goats' Reinterpreted," *NovT* 11 (1969) 32–44; R. H. Gundry, *Matthew: A Commentary on His Literary and Theological Art* (Grand Rapids: Eerdmans, 1982); Jan Lambrecht, *Out of the Treasure. The Parables in the Gospel of Matthew* (Louvain Theological and Pastoral Monographs 10; Grand Rapids: Eerdmans, 1991) 249–82. Lambrecht remarks, however, that even though the text was probably a Matthean construction it did not come into existence apart from the memory of the earthly Jesus and of the way this Jesus committed himself unconditionally to his destitute brothers and sisters.

[6] E.g., Ulrich Luz, "The Final Judgment (Matt 25:31-46): An Exercise in 'History of Influence' Exegesis," in David R. Bauer and Mark Allan Powell, eds., *Treasures New and Old. Recent Contributions to Matthean Studies* (SBL Symposium Series; Atlanta: Scholars Press, 1996) 271–310.

[7] Warren Carter, *Matthew and the Margins* (Maryknoll: Orbis, 2000) 492.

First the reasons for the righteous inheriting the kingdom are spelled out (vv. 34-40), then, in corresponding terms, the explanation for the expulsion of the accursed (vv. 41-45). In the concluding verse (v. 46) the two groups are led away, each to their respective eternal destinies.

SEPARATING SHEEP FROM GOATS (vv. 31-33)

This is one of five Matthean texts that speak of the eschatological coming of the Son of Humanity.[8] The description of the coming of the Son of Humanity with his angels is brief. There is a fuller depiction of the accompanying cosmic signs at 24:27-31. Overtones of Daniel 7:13-14 are clearly discernible. The focus in 25:31-33 is on the separation of the righteous from the wicked. Previously the angels were said to have the role of gathering the elect (24:31) and separating out the evildoers (13:41, 49). Now the Son of Humanity does the separating.

The image of shepherd is a familiar metaphor for God (Psalm 23) and for religious leaders (Ezekiel 34). It recalls a number of passages in Matthew where the image is applied to Jesus. At the outset of the gospel Herod inquires of the chief priests and scribes of the people where the Messiah was to be born. They reply with a quotation of Scripture that it is from Bethlehem that the one who is to "shepherd my people Israel" will come (Matt 2:6, quoting Mic 5:1; 2 Sam 5:2). In the context of his ministry of proclaiming the Good News and healing, Jesus is said to have compassion on the crowds because they were "like sheep without a shepherd" (Matt 9:36). In the Last Supper scene Jesus predicts that all his disciples will have their faith shaken as he quotes Zechariah 13:7, "I will strike the shepherd / and the sheep of the flock will be dispersed." In several instances Jesus uses this metaphor to instruct his disciples on how to follow him in caring for his people. He sends them to "the lost sheep of the house of Israel" to heal and to proclaim the reign of God (10:6; similarly of his own mission at

---

[8] See Matt 13:41; 16:27; 19:28; 24:30-31. This title is only found on the lips of Jesus and is used in two additional ways: to speak of his earthly ministry and of his passion. See above, pp. 101–02 on "The Son of Humanity."

15:24). They themselves are like "sheep in the midst of wolves" (10:16). When healing a man with a withered hand Jesus counters the objections of his opponents by pointing out that if they would rescue a sheep that fell into a pit on the Sabbath, how much more should a man be rescued (12:11-12)? He tells a parable to his disciples of the importance of going after one lost sheep (18:12-14)[9] as a model of pastoral care.

While previous allusions to Jesus as shepherd have emphasized the gathering in of the flock and tending to all its needs, the parable of the final judgment depicts a separating out by the shepherd.[10] The reason for which a shepherd separates sheep *(ta probata)* from goats *(ta eriphia)* is not self-evident. There is no evidence that in Middle Eastern mentality sheep represented something valuable and good in contrast to goats.[11] Commentators most often give the explanation that in Palestine sheep and goats were herded together, but at night the two were separated, as goats are less hardy and need to be kept warm at night. Sheep, on the other hand, are left in the open air at night. Ulrich Luz, however, argues that this is incorrect and has simply been passed on repeatedly in the commentaries.[12] Another suggestion is that since *eriphos* can mean "he-goat" and *probata* can mean "small cattle," including both sheep and goats, the shepherd separates male from female goats for milking. Alternatively, the clue to the meaning may be found in that *eriphos* also connotes a young kid. In almost all instances where this word appears in the LXX, it refers to a young animal that is slaughtered or sacrificed (as also Luke 15:29). Thus, the shepherd separates the kid destined for slaughter from the rest of the herd. Whatever the explanation, the parable presumes the

---

[9] See below, chap. 21.

[10] See further J. P. Heil, "Ezekiel 34 and the Narrative Strategy of the Shepherd and Sheep Metaphor in Matthew," *CBQ* 55 (1993) 698–708. Heil demonstrates that the shepherd motif in the Gospel does not provide a consistent Matthean narrative strategy.

[11] Kathleen Weber ("The Image of Sheep and Goats in Matthew 25:31-46," *CBQ* 59/4 [1997] 657–78) explores this in great detail and concludes that Matthew's audience would have a basically positive attitude toward goats, which makes the absolute condemnation of them in the parable surprising.

[12] Luz, "Final Judgment," 296.

reader is familiar with the imagery and likens a shepherd's separation of animals to the Son of Humanity's dividing to his right and to his left of those assembled for judgment.

Other Matthean parables and sayings speak of end-time separation and point forward to this parable. Wheat is separated from weeds at harvest (13:24-30); what is edible is sorted from what is inedible out of the dragnet (13:47-50);[13] wheat and chaff are winnowed (3:12); one man in a field is taken and another left (24:40); similarly, only one woman grinding wheat (24:41); five wise virgins enter while five foolish do not (25:1-13).[14] The separating in each case is based on previous behavior and is definitive.

The sheep are placed on the right—the favored side. Because most people were right handed and developed more strength and skill with this hand, the right came to symbolize the side of favor, blessing, and honor. Thus, it is the right hand of God that delivers Israel (Exod 15:6; Pss 20:6; 44:3; 98:1). Blessing is conveyed with the right hand (Gen 48:13-20) and to be seated at the right of the host is the position of highest honor (Ps 110:1).[15] Ecclesiastes gives right and left a moral connotation, "The wise man's understanding turns him to his right; / the fool's understanding turns him to his left" (10:2).[16]

THE KING (v. 34)

The image of Jesus shifts in v. 34 from shepherd to king. From the beginning of the gospel Jesus has been identified as king of the Jews (2:2) and he was so acclaimed as he entered Je-

[13] See above, chaps. 7 and 8.

[14] Weber ("Sheep and Goats," 658) notes that in the case of the sheep and the goats, however, the reason for separating is not improper mixture; the two are customarily herded together in Syria and Palestine, in both ancient and modern times. This practice is distinctive to Syria and Palestine in contrast to Asia, Greece, and Italy, where sheep and goats are herded separately.

[15] John 13:23 implies that the Beloved Disciple is seated at Jesus' right, since he can lean against Jesus' bosom to inquire who it is that would betray Jesus. Those reclining at table would be lying on their left sides, using the right hand to eat.

[16] Joel F. Drinkard, Jr., *ABD*, s.v., "Right, Right Hand."

rusalem (21:5). In other parables, that of the Unforgiving Servant (18:21-35)[17] and that of the Great Feast (22:1-14)[18] the king is a referent for God. Here Jesus is king who divides those who will enter the reign of God from those who will go off to punishment. The Father is still in view in the final judgment, as the king addresses those on his right as "blessed by my Father" (v. 34). Also, the kingdom to be inherited has been prepared "from the foundation of the world" (v. 34), indicating God's intimate involvement with humankind and with the reign Jesus proclaims, from the very start of creation.[19] It is likely, as well, that the passive verb *synachthēsontai*, "will be assembled," in v. 32, is a theological passive, indicating that it is God who does the assembling of the nations for judgment. There is a powerful juxtaposition with the parable of the final judgment coming immediately before the passion narrative. The king who is condemned and crucified (27:11, 29, 37, 42) will come in his glory and it is he who will judge those who judged and condemned him.

It is possible that Matthew also wants to complete his depiction of Jesus as the New Moses with this parable.[20] Just as Moses lay before the Israelites the choice of blessing or curse (Deut 11:26) so Jesus separates those "blessed by my Father" (v. 34) from those "accursed" (v. 41). There is no notion of predestination in the gospel. The kingdom has been prepared for the blessed from the foundation of the world (v. 34), but it always remains a choice whether one responds to the invitation or rejects it. In terms of Matthew's Gospel this invitation comes through Jesus and through those who are sent in his name. For those who accept the invitation, which is visible in their deeds, blessing and inheritance in the realm of God await. For those who reject it, by their deeds or lack of them, they choose eternal fire that has been prepared for the devil and his angels (v. 41).

[17] See above, chap. 9.

[18] See above, chap. 13.

[19] This phrase also echoes Prov 8:22-31 which tells of Wisdom having been created at the foundation of the world.

[20] Luz, "Final Judgment," 298. See further D. Allison, *The New Moses: A Matthean Typology* (Minneapolis: Fortress, 1993).

BASIS FOR REWARD AND PUNISHMENT (vv. 35-45)

The basis for judgment should come as no surprise for the hearer of Matthew's Gospel. Throughout, the Matthean Jesus stresses the necessity of doing righteous deeds. These must be visible before others so that they lead to glorifying God (5:16),[21] not to self-aggrandizement (6:1). The contrast between only saying "Lord, Lord" and doing God's will is highlighted in several parables (7:21-27; 21:28-32).[22] Jesus instructs his disciples and the crowd that they must do all that the scribes and Pharisees teach, but he denounces the latter because they do not put their own teaching into practice (23:3). One who responds to Jesus' invitation cannot simply assent intellectually, but faith must be expressed in righteous deeds and ethical behavior, like a wedding guest properly attired (22:1-14), a servant faithfully performing duties (24:42-51), or a maiden who brings a sufficient supply of oil (25:1-13).[23] Just as in these parables, so too in that of the sheep and goats, the emphasis is on the timing and the rigor of the eschatological judgment.[24] There should be no surprise, then, in this final parable, that the deeds one has performed are the basis for judgment.

A litany of six deeds is repeated four times, deeds which are spoken of repeatedly in the Scriptures and which cover the whole spectrum of ministry to the most vulnerable. The prophet Isaiah, for example, described what God desired in terms of sharing bread with the hungry, sheltering the oppressed and homeless, and clothing the naked (Isa 58:6-7). Job's friends, looking for the cause of his misfortune, examine him on whether he has unjustly kept his kin's goods in pawn, thereby leaving them "stripped naked of their clothing," or whether he has given drink to the thirsty or bread to the hungry, or sent widows away empty-handed or destroyed the resources of orphans (Job 22:6-9). When recounting his righteous deeds, Job includes feeding others and offering lodging to strangers

---

[21] See above, chap. 4.
[22] See above, chaps. 5, 11.
[23] See above, chaps. 13 and 14.
[24] Weber, "Sheep and Goats," 658.

(31:31-32). Ben Sira advises, "Neglect not to visit the sick— / for these things you will be loved" (Sir 7:34-35). Ezekiel lists giving food to the hungry and clothing the naked among the righteous things a virtuous person does (Ezek 18:7, 16).[25]

The one deed in Matthew's list which does not appear in the Jewish enumerations is visiting the imprisoned. Perhaps this became a more urgent need in New Testament times as Christians, particularly missionaries, faced the possibility of imprisonment.[26] In Mark's apocalyptic discourse Jesus warns his disciples of the possibility of being arraigned before kings and governors and being handed over to death (13:9-13). In Acts of the Apostles numerous episodes depict the imprisonment of Christians, especially those who are traveling apostles. The pre-Christian Paul was intent on imprisoning followers of the Way.[27] Ironically, this becomes one of the perils he himself faces for the sake of the gospel (2 Cor 6:5; 11:23). Acts 16:23-40 depicts Paul and Silas' imprisonment in Philippi and their rescue by an angel. In his farewell to the elders at Miletus Paul foresees that imprisonment awaits him (20:23). This prediction is fulfilled at Acts 21:33 and in the remainder of Acts Paul remains a prisoner, all the while still evangelizing. A number of Paul's letters are written from prison.[28] Peter and John are also imprisoned for preaching the gospel (Acts 5:18-25). There is a miraculous rescue, as also at 12:3-11, where Peter is imprisoned by Herod. These episodes are an ironic fulfillment of Peter's protest at the Last Supper that he is ready to go to prison and die with Jesus (Luke 22:33). In these narratives imprisonment is directly related to witnessing to the gospel. In antiquity imprisonment was not a form of punishment nor was it a means of reforming a person to return to society. A person was imprisoned while awaiting trial or sentencing. Lifetime imprisonment was not used; if a person were guilty of a capital offense, they would either be executed or

---

[25] Similarly Tob 1:16-17; 4:16; *2 Enoch* 9:1; 42:8; 63:1.

[26] Luz, "Final Judgment," 299.

[27] Acts 8:3; 9:2, 14, 21; 22:4, 19; 26:10.

[28] Col 4:3, 18; Phil 1:7, 13, 14, 17; Phlm vv. 10, 13; likewise the author of the deutero-Pauline letter 2 Timothy writes as if Paul were in prison (1:16; 2:9).

banished.[29] For itinerant Christian missionaries who were imprisoned in a locale far from their families the Christian community would need to play an important role in their care. The letter to the Hebrews admonishes that Christians should be mindful of prisoners, "as if sharing in their imprisonment" (13:3). Interestingly, this exhortation is coupled with a reminder to exercise hospitality, "for through it some have unknowingly entertained angels" (13:2). This text has a resonance with Matthew 25:37-39, 44 in that the one exercising a deed of charity does not recognize the recipient.[30]

The deeds by which "all the nations" are judged in the parable of the sheep and the goats are not only familiar from Jewish mores, but are manifest in Jesus' own ministry. He has compassion on hungry crowds and feeds them (Matt 14:14-21; 15:32-39). Jesus heals all who come to him who are ill (Matt 4:24; 8:5-13, 14-16; 14:14, 35; 15:21-28). He unmasks systems of injustice that leave the poor naked and he points the way for his disciples to subvert such (5:40).[31] He receives the imprisoned John the Baptist's disciples and affirms John's identity as prophet and forerunner of the messiah (11:1-19). He himself is imprisoned and executed. He gives instruction to his disciples on performing these same deeds. When he sends his disciples on mission he instructs them also to cure the sick (10:1, 8). He both demonstrates and speaks to them about how to care for the most vulnerable as a shepherd who seeks lost sheep (18:12-14). He has instructed them that to be leader is to be slave, just as he has come not to be served but to serve (*diakonēsai*, 20:27-

---

[29] Sometimes those who defaulted on a debt were constrained to forced labor until the debt was paid (as in Matt 18:28-30; Luke 12:58-59). Likewise prisoners of war were held in compounds of work camps sometimes designated "prisons." See further Karel van der Toorn, *ABD*, s.v., "Prison."

[30] See also Heb 10:34; 11:36.

[31] See Walter Wink, *Engaging the Powers* (Minneapolis: Fortress, 1992) 175–93 who interprets Matt 5:40 as an example of a creditor taking a poor debtor to court and demanding their cloak as collateral (as in Deut 24:12, 17). Jesus' advice is to strip naked before a creditor who would participate in such a system that demands the very clothes of the poor. The shock and shame heaped upon the creditor could move him to repentance and open a possible way to justice and reconciliation.

28; 23:11). It should come as no surprise then, that judgment is based on fulfillment or not of such service (the same verb, *diakonēsamen* is used at 25:44).

THE SURPRISE

There is no surprise about the kinds of deeds on which people are judged. What is startling to those who come before the king is *to whom* the deeds were done. Jesus' response is that he is encountered in any one of the "least of my brothers and sisters" (vv. 40, 45). But there is a great exegetical difficulty at this juncture that involves two related questions. Are the "least of the brothers and sisters" (vv. 40, 45) to be understood as Christians? Or as any person in need? Furthermore, who are those being judged? The phrase *panta ta ethnē* (v. 32) can mean either "all the nations" or "all the Gentiles" (i.e., all the nations except Israel). Different combinations of these possibilities yield various interpretations.

In the Gospel of Matthew *ethnē* and *panta ta ethnē* often refer to nations other than Israel.[32] But there are several instances in the gospel where a wider meaning is indicated. In the apocalyptic discourse, as Jesus is describing the end-time woes, he tells his disciples that they will be "hated by all nations *(panta ta ethnē)* because of my name" (Matt 24:9) and he exhorts them to persevere to the end. He then says, "this gospel of the kingdom will be preached throughout the world as a witness to all nations *(panta ta ethnē),* and then the end will come" (24:14). In light of this saying it is highly likely that Matthew intends the parable of the final judgment to be understood as the end to which Jesus referred at 24:14. It envisions the completion of the great commission given the disciples at the conclusion of the gospel by the risen Christ, who sends them to "make disciples of all nations *(panta ta ethnē)"* (28:19).

---

[32] Daniel J. Harrington, *Matthew* (SacPag 1; Collegeville: The Liturgical Press, 1991) 356, understands the references at Matt 4:15; 6:32; 10:5, 18; 12:18, 21; 20:19, 25; 21:43; 24:7, 9, 14; 28:19 as signifying Gentiles. See also Douglas R. A. Hare and Daniel J. Harrington, "Make Disciples of All the Gentiles (Mt. 28:19)," *CBQ* 37 (1975) 359–69.

In these texts "all the nations" is all-encompassing: all, including Israel, Gentiles, and Christians, have heard the gospel and are now judged according to their deeds.[33] The parable fills out the saying from 16:27, where Jesus explains to his disciples in the context of the first passion prediction, that the Son of Humanity "will come with his angels in his Father's glory," and will repay each one according to their conduct.

The identity of "the least of my brothers and sisters," *tōn aldelphōn mou tōn elachistōn* (vv. 40, 45) is also a point of debate: does it refer to any person in need or to Christians? *Adelphos,* "brother" or "sister" is a term that is very frequently used in the New Testament to denote members of the Christian community.[34] In addition, *elachistōn* ("least") is the superlative form of *mikros* ("little"), which appears a number of times in Matthew to refer to members of the community who are vulnerable.[35] In the community discourse Jesus warns leaders of the community not to cause scandal to any of these "little ones" (18:6), not to despise them (18:10), nor to allow them to stray (18:14). In another instance, Jesus declares the "least (*mikroteros,* the comparative form of *mikros*) in the kingdom of heaven" to be greater than John the Baptist (11:11). From the context *mikroteros* refers to followers of Jesus.[36]

One last instance of *mikros* identifies "the least of my brothers and sisters" even more precisely as Christians who are sent out on mission. In a text that has strong resonances

---

[33] Luz, "Final Judgment," 293–94. Similarly, John Paul Heil, *Matthew's Parables* (CBQMS 30; Washington, D.C.: CBA, 1998) 201, who understands that at 24:9, 14; 25:32; 28:19 *panta ta ethnē* signifies "all the nations or peoples including the Jews and excluding no one."

[34] For example, Matt 18:15, 27, 21, 35; 23:8; 28:10.

[35] Alternatively, Luz ("Final Judgment," 302) holds that the meaning of *elachistos* should not be construed from the identification of *hoi mikroi*; rather, in the text "least" stands in contrast to the "great" heavenly king. "This phrase emphasizes in rhetorical fashion the enormous distance between those who are suffering and the heavenly judge; and it effectively highlights the surprising marvel of his identification with them."

[36] Alternatively, Benedict T. Viviano ("The Least in the Kingdom: Matthew 11:11, Its Parallel in Luke 7:28 [Q], and Daniel 4:14," *CBQ* 62 [2000] 41–54) argues that Matt 11:11 is a postpaschal reflection on Jesus and John the Baptist, and that *mikrōteros* refers to Jesus who was exalted Son of God yet come in lowliness.

with the parable of the final judgment, at the conclusion of the missionary discourse, Jesus tells his disciples that whoever gives even a cup of cold water to one of these "little ones" *(mikrōn)* in the name of a disciple, such a one will surely not lose their reward (10:42). There is another resonance between the missionary discourse and the judgment parable. The former includes a promise from Jesus that whoever receives a righteous person will receive the reward of a righteous person *(dikaios)* (10:41). The parable depicts the righteous *(hoi dikaioi,* 25:37, 46) receiving their reward. Read in the context of Matthew's missionary theme, the "little ones" in Matthew 25:40, 45 are those sent out on mission, who are vulnerable and in need of hospitality. They come without money, extra clothing, with no traveling bag, no sandals, and no walking stick for defense from wild animals or robbers (10:9-10). They have only the power given them by Jesus to heal the sick and to proclaim the reign of God (10:1, 7-8). They are dependent on whoever will show them hospitality (10:11-13). They are liable to face imprisonment for their proclamation of the gospel. Paul lists these very hardships as what is the lot of an apostle: "To this very hour we go hungry and thirsty, we are poorly clad and roughly treated, we wander about homeless and we toil, working with our own hands" (1 Cor 4:11-12). And his "thorn in the flesh" was likely sickness that he endured in the course of his ministry (2 Cor 12:7-9).

In this line of interpretation, final judgment is based on reception of Christian missionaries who embody the presence of Jesus, who himself was sent on mission by God and embodies the divine presence.[37] It is not suffering people in general with whom Jesus identifies, but with those who have been sent on mission, "Whoever receives you receives me, and whoever receives me receives the one who sent me" (10:40). The basis for judgment, then, is acceptance or not of Jesus and the One who sent him, as he is encountered in his followers who proclaim the gospel. The motif of unawareness is a literary motif which

---

[37] Donald Senior, *Matthew* (ANTC; Nashville: Abingdon, 1998) 283. Similarly, Donahue, *Gospel in Parable,* 120–23.

serves a christological purpose[38] and concretizes a theme that frames the whole of the gospel: God-with-us. In a postresurrection setting, the parable shows to disciples who thought that because Jesus had died they could no longer meet him, that he yet abides in their midst. They do not have to wait until Jesus comes again on his glorious throne (v. 31) to encounter him; he is Emmanuel, always with them (1:23; 28:20).

An alternative line of interpretation is that *panta ta ethnē* (v. 32) refers to Gentiles only and that with the parable of the sheep and the goats Matthew envisions a separate judgment of the Gentiles.[39] This is possible in light of texts such as Ezekiel 39; Joel 3; 1 Enoch 91:14; Psalms of Solomon 17:29; 4 Ezra 13:33-49, which depict separate judgments for Jews and Gentiles. That Paul thinks of separate judgments for Jews and Gentiles may also be inferred from texts such as Romans 2:9-10; 1 Corinthians 6:2-3. In 2 Baruch 72:4-6 the basis on which Gentiles will be judged is their treatment of Israel. This may well be the notion that provides the background for the Matthean parable of judgment.[40] Accordingly, the preceding parables of the faithful servant, the wise maidens, and the use of talents (24:43–25:30), depict the basis on which Christians will be judged (alert readiness for the returning Son of Humanity while doing good in anticipation of that day), while the parable of the sheep and goats depicts the judgment of the Gentiles.

Narratively, however, the parable of the sheep and goats would seem better understood as a climax to the discourse on readiness, all of which is directed toward Christian disciples.[41] The links with the missionary discourse also confirm this ap-

---

[38] Luz, "Final Judgment," 300–01.

[39] Harrington, *Matthew*, 356–60. Senior (*Matthew*, 284) suggests that in addition to Gentiles non-Christian Jews may also be envisioned. Judgment of the latter, he suggests, may be implicit in the conclusion of chapter 23 where their "house" is left desolate until they are willing to receive the Messiah sent to them (23:38-39).

[40] Senior, *Matthew*, 284; Harrington, *Matthew*, 356–60.

[41] As Weber ("Sheep and Goats," 677) observes, "On the level of story, the eschatological judge addresses all nations, but on the level of discourse he quickly returns to addressing the readers of Matthew's Gospel, who are in fact the only ones listening."

proach. The parable envisions the time after the gospel has been proclaimed to all the nations. It does not address a situation of nonbelievers doing good unawares or out of humanitarian reasons. Nor does this parable address the question of what happens to those Jews who have not accepted the gospel. This situation has been previously addressed in the warnings Jesus directs to the Jewish leaders at 21:43; 23:34–24:2. The narrative invites the hearers of the parable to locate themselves with *panta ta ethnē* and to see how their own deeds will be judged. If they have betrayed or hated one another, let false prophets lead them astray, done evil, and let their love grow cold (24:10-12), there is yet time to meet Jesus again in the believing community, in the brothers and sisters who embody Jesus and his mission.[42] Like goats who are basically good but who also have some shortcomings,[43] Matthew's community is to hear in the parable a warning against laxity and a strong exhortation to radical righteousness.[44]

ETERNAL LIFE FOR THE RIGHTEOUS (v. 46)

The parable concludes with a typically Matthean ring. Reward and punishment is a frequent motif in Matthew's parables as is its eternal dimension. Eternal life was what the rich young man sought (19:16), and what Jesus promised his disciples who had given up houses, brothers, sisters, father or mother, children or lands for the sake of his name (19:29). Eternal fire is what is to be avoided by eschewing all causes of sin (18:8; similarly 13:50). The theme of righteousness pervades this gospel. At the outset of the narrative Jesus fulfills all righteousness *(dikaiosynē)* by allowing himself to be baptized by

[42] Luz, "Final Judgment," 305.

[43] Weber, "Sheep and Goats," 657–78, shows that there is no evidence that in the Mediterranean world goats were valued less than sheep, so that their expulsion at the end of the parable is unexpected. In the Greco-Roman world there is abundant evidence that goats were regarded as symbols of eager and promiscuous sexuality. If Matthew's community is aware of such from the Hellenistic world, then the goats in the parable signify good animals who have certain blemishes (p. 673).

[44] Weber, "Sheep and Goats," 673–75.

John (3:15) and at the conclusion Pilate declares him righteous, *dikiaos* (27:19). Jesus pronounces blessed all who hunger and thirst for righteousness, promising that they will be satisfied (5:6). Blessed, too, are those who are persecuted for the sake of righteousness (5:10). Jesus tells his disciples that their righteousness must surpass that of the scribes and Pharisees in order to enter into the reign of God (5:20). Indeed, disciples need worry about nothing but seeking God's reign and righteousness (6:33). Their righteous deeds are not performed for others to see (6:1). Hypocrites who appear righteous but who are filled with wickedness inside are like white-washed sepulchers and are destined for woe (23:28).[45] At the end of the age when the wicked are separated from the righteous (13:49), the righteous shine like the sun in the reign of God (13:43).

PREACHING POSSIBILITIES

Classic works of art and literature like Michelangelo's Sistine Chapel and Dante's *Inferno* reflect an enduring fascination with the final judgment. Angels and devils, fire and clouds, anguish and joy are painted in vivid contrast. Apocalyptic sects as well capitalize on fiery images of damnation and glorious depictions of salvation. Yet what stands out most vividly in Matthew's parable of the final judgment is not otherworldly visions of eternal glory or unrelenting damnation, but the face of the hungry, thirsty, foreign, naked, sick, and incarcerated Jesus. Four times comes the same list of six characteristics. At every turn he is there and unavoidable. Risen to life again, he is still to be encountered in human flesh. A preacher can hardly avoid speaking of how a believer's relationship to Jesus cannot be disconnected from their relationships to real persons.[46] As Matthew so often repeats, faith is very tangible and visible in concrete deeds.

This parable is often understood in a universalist sense, where "the least of the brothers and sisters" is taken to be any

---

[45] See also 1:19; 10:41; 20:4; 23:38; 27:4, 24 where the adjective *dikaios* occurs in uniquely Matthean material. See also 9:13; 11:19; 12:37; 13:17; 21:32; 23:35.

[46] Luz, "Final Judgment," 306.

person in need, and all people are being judged at the end time on the basis of their treatment of anyone who is suffering.[47] While there is a value in such an inclusive direction it is probable that this was not Matthew's perspective. From his missionary stance the end-time judgment comes only after the gospel has been proclaimed to all the nations and the separating will take place on the basis of openness to encountering Jesus. Matthew's audience is Christian and he is concerned with evangelization, not with humanitarianism. That being said, in this day of interfaith exchange, the parable may be read as saying that the judgment of non-Christians is based on how they treat vulnerable Christian missionaries, not whether they accept the gospel message as such.[48] Their compassion and deeds of mercy are visible before God, a worthy witness that they act from Jesus' love command, although they do not articulate fidelity to him as their motive. For Christians the parable proposes an ethics of faithful witness where the Christian, like Jesus himself in the proclamation of the Good News, becomes the locus for the disclosure of God's will for all peoples.[49] Along with the preceding three parables, this one alerts the Christian not to be caught off guard for the end-time. It is a clarion to rouse from any laxity and to be constantly vigilant in the doing of righteous deeds.

Another aspect that a preacher can attend to is where the hearer stands in the story. The narrative dynamics invite the hearer to be one among the assembly being judged. Rather than a message of consolation or vindication for those who have been hungry and thirsty, homeless, strangers, ill, or imprisoned,[50] this parable focuses on one's response to those who willingly accept such for the sake of the gospel. There are two prongs to this: judgment is based on the willingness of the disciple to suffer these hardships for the sake of spreading the

---

[47] See David Buttrick, *Speaking Parables* (Louisville: Westminster John Knox, 2000) 124–29.

[48] Senior, *Matthew,* 285.

[49] Donahue, *Gospel in Parable,* 124.

[50] It is the beatitudes (Matt 5:3-12) that offer comfort to the suffering and the persecuted.

gospel, as well as on one's receptivity to those who most fully embody the presence of the suffering Christ in their apostolic endeavors.[51] Vitally important is that the preacher underscore that suffering is not embraced for its own sake. It is not suffering that makes Christ present, but Christ lives visibly in the believer who willingly accepts hardships for the sake of the mission.

This parable may open the way for a Christian community to examine their outreach programs and make fresh commitments about initiating new endeavors, revitalizing old ones, or collaborating with others in existing ones. In a congregation where such efforts are faltering, the preacher may take the opportunity to challenge the faithful to greater engagement in evangelization and social justice. Abstract exhortation is less effective than concrete invitations to participate in specific programs and organized service to those in need. In a community in which such efforts are well developed, the parable can serve as encouragement to continue in their endeavors, as they become ever more conscious of the face of Jesus in each person they serve.

There is a serious note that cannot be overlooked with this parable: judgment is real and it is final. For those who have been faithfully engaged in the deeds listed, it is not a time to be feared, but a welcome relief as they are embraced into eternal life in God's realm with the righteous.

One final caution about this parable is that there is always a danger with apocalyptic scenarios and their dualism that a hearer can falsely rest on self-assurance that they belong with the saved and the others who they perceive as enemies or opponents are the damned. They let out a cheer that the goats get their just deserts while they smugly line up for the right hand of the king. This kind of approach with such rigid demarcations between good and evil does not allow one to face the mix within each person and each community. There is righteousness and wickedness within each one; there are sheep and goats within each community. What the gospel offers is a mes-

---

[51] Heil, *Matthew's Parables*, 207–08.

sage of hope as the risen Christ returns again and again, waiting to be encountered in the stranger, the needy one, the ill or imprisoned brother or sister. The gospel has not yet been preached to all the nations; the time is still at hand to respond again and again to Christ's invitation.

CHAPTER SEVENTEEN

Wisdom Justified
(Matt 11:16-19)

Friday of the Second Week of Advent

Jesus said to the crowds,
"What comparison can I use to describe this breed?
  They are like children squatting in the town squares,
      calling to their playmates:
'We piped you a tune, but you did not dance!
  We sang you a dirge but you did not wail!'
In other words, John appeared neither eating nor drinking, and people say,
  'He is mad.'
The Son of Man appeared eating and drinking and they say,
  'This one is a glutton and drunkard,
  a lover of tax collectors and those outside the law!'
Yet time will prove where wisdom lies."

LITERARY CONTEXT

This short parable is found in a section (11:2–16:12)[1] that focuses on the diverse responses to Jesus. In the preceding portion (4:12–11:1) the spotlight was on Jesus' ministry of teaching and healing. As the narrative progresses the crowds and disciples react favorably, even though not fully understanding, and the religious authorities become increasingly

---

[1] Following the schema of Donald Senior, *Matthew* (ANTC; Nashville: Abingdon, 1998) 123.

hostile. This parable comes from Q and its parallel in Luke 7:31-35 is close in wording and function.[2]

This section opens with the disciples of the imprisoned John the Baptist coming to Jesus with the question of whether he is the one who is to come or whether they should look for another (v. 3). Matthew says that what John heard about was "the works *(erga)* of Christ" (v. 2). This frames the unit which concludes with a saying about the *erga*, "deeds" or "works" of Wisdom (v. 19). Jesus replies to the query about his identity as "the one who is to come" by instructing John's disciples to report to him what they have seen and heard: how those who were blind now see, those who had been lame walk, those with leprosy are cleansed, those who were deaf now hear, dead people have been raised, and those made poor have had the Good News proclaimed to them (v. 5). Against the background of Isaiah 35:5-6 it should be evident that Jesus is, indeed, the one issuing in the messianic era. Jesus' concluding word, "blessed is the one who takes no offense at me" (v. 6) points ahead to the parable, which contrasts the desired response with the petulant refusal of the children in the marketplace. It furthers the recurring theme of the divided responses to Jesus' deeds.

The next segment (vv. 7-15) focuses on the identity of John the Baptist. Three times Jesus poses to the crowd the question, "What did you go out to see?" (vv. 7, 8, 9). If they have objections to John's unbending asceticism or are offended by his rugged dress, Jesus tells the crowds they are looking for the wrong thing in the wrong places. Those seeking a prophet will not only find one, but the very prophet of whom Malachi (3:23) spoke, the messenger who prepares the way for the coming one (v. 10). While there is differentiation in their roles, both John and Jesus are presented as powerful prophets of God. And both suffer the same divided response to their ministry, as does every messenger of God.

---

[2] For a detailed analysis of the differences in the two versions and a reconstruction of the text from Q see Wendy J. Cotter, "The Parable of the Children in the Market-Place, Q(Lk) 7:31-35: An Examination of the Parable's Image and Significance," *NovT* 29/4 (1987) 289–304.

CHILDREN IN THE MARKETPLACE

The parable opens with a simile (v. 16) followed by an explanation (vv. 17-19a) and ends with a concluding saying (v. 19b). Like many parables, the introductory verse sets up a comparison with the verb *homoioō*, "to liken, compare" (v. 16a) and the adjective *homoios* "like" (v. 16b).[3] The people of "this generation," *genea*, are compared to children sitting in the marketplace calling to one another.[4] The word *genea*, "generation," usually carries a pejorative sense in Matthew. Disciples who are unable to cast out a demon are a "faithless and perverse generation" (17:17). Those that seek signs are an "evil generation" that will be condemned (12:39-42; 16:4). "This generation" will be charged with all the righteous blood of the murdered prophets (23:36). Against this backdrop, the parable prepares the hearer for a negative evaluation of "this generation."

The parable likens "this generation" to a group of children who stubbornly refuse to play with another group. No matter what the one group offers, whether pretending at wedding, or at funeral, the others refuse to participate. The next verses relate this metaphor to the negative reception of the invitations issued by John and Jesus. "This generation" responded neither to John's "dirge" nor to Jesus' "flute."

The children seated in the marketplace introduces an image connected with court proceedings.[5] As the center of public life, the *agora*, "marketplace," was the locale for commercial, social, religious, and civic interchange. One might expect children in the *agora* to be running and chasing after one another in their play, not sitting while voicing their complaint about their unresponsive potential playmates. The verb *kathēmai*, "sit," is frequently associated with judgment, as in Matthew 27:19, where Pilate sits on the *bēma*, "bench," when

---

[3] So also Matt 7:24, 26; 11:16; 13:24, 31, 33, 44, 45, 47, 52; 18:23; 20:1; 22:2; 25:1; Mark 4:30; Luke 6:47-49; 12:36; 13:18-21.

[4] Whereas Luke (7:32) implies two groups calling out to one another, Matt 11:16 implies that there is only one group speaking "to others," *tois heterois*. This difference in detail does not significantly change the meaning.

[5] Cotter, "Children," 298–302.

Jesus is brought before him.[6] That the *agora* was used for court proceedings is evident from Acts 16:19, where Paul and Silas were dragged there to be judged by the magistrates. In addition the verb *prosphoneō*, "to call out," connotes formal address, such as would take place in a court context.[7] The court image, then, presented in the opening line of the parable, introduces a note of judgment. It makes clear that John and Jesus' invitation is not merely a game in which children can participate or not as they will. Rather, it points toward the serious consequences that incur for those who refuse their call. The final verse, using another term from the legal world, *dikaioō*, "to justify, vindicate," completes the court proceedings with the handing down of the verdict.

CALLING AND BANQUETING (vv. 18-19a)

The auditory images of voices calling, flutes playing, dirges being sung (v. 17) shifts to a culinary theme (vv. 18-19a). Both themes are associated with Woman Wisdom's invitation to life and they point forward to the final verse (19b). Just as Wisdom sent out servant girls, calling from the highest places in the town (Prov 9:3), so John called out his invitation in the desert (3:3) and Jesus called out his message for anyone with ears to hear (13:9; 11:15). Wisdom's invitation, like that of Yahweh (Isa 25:6; 55:1; Ps 23:5) is cast in terms of eating her bread and drinking her wine (Prov 9:5). In like manner, banqueting with Jesus is associated with response to his invitation to discipleship.[8]

But just as Wisdom is rejected by the foolish (Sir 15:7-8) so John is dismissed as having a demon (as is Jesus in Matt 12:24) and Jesus is accused of being a glutton and a drunkard. This charge alludes to Deuteronomy 21:20, where the phrase refers to a rebellious son. The final verse shows that this perception is false: Jesus is Wisdom incarnate who is vindicated by her works. The additional slur that he is a friend of toll collectors

---

[6] For other examples see BDAG, s.v., κάθημαι and Cotter, "Children," 299–301.

[7] See Luke 23:20; Acts 21:40; 22:2.

[8] Matt 8:11; 9:11; 14:13-21; 15:27, 32-39; 22:1-14; 25:10; 26:17-29.

and sinners was a charge that was made earlier by the Pharisees when Jesus dined at the home of Matthew (9:11-13). Matthew presents Jesus' table companionship with toll collectors and sinners as part of his missionary strategy to bring all into right relation.[9]

WISDOM VINDICATED (v. 19b)

It is in the final verse of the parable that there is the most significant divergence between Matthew and Luke. Most scholars hold that Luke has the more original wording: "but Wisdom is vindicated by *all her children*" (7:35; emphasis added). In Luke's version the Divine is portrayed as Woman Wisdom, whose justification is made evident by her children, preeminently John and Jesus. Matthew, however, makes Jesus Wisdom personified, not simply a child of Wisdom.[10] Just as Lady Wis-

---

[9] See also Matt 21:31-32, where Jesus asserts that tax collectors and prostitutes are entering the reign of God ahead of the chief priests and elders who oppose him.

[10] Not only in this passage, but in a number of others, Matthew explicitly portrays Jesus as Wisdom personified. It is a theme that first appears in Matt 8:18-22 where the homelessness of the Human One recalls the rejection of Wisdom and her resultant homelessness on earth (Prov. 1:20; Sir. 24:7). The whole of Matthew 11 shows the deeds of Christ (11:2) clearly identified with the deeds of Wisdom (11:19). The final section of chapter 11 (vv. 25-30) completes the identification of Jesus with Wisdom. In a thanksgiving prayer from Q and the peculiarly Matthean invitation to rest (vv. 28-30), Jesus, like Wisdom, is shown to be the sage who teaches apocalyptic mysteries, interprets Torah, and calls disciples. The invitation to come for instruction and to submit to Wisdom's yoke echoes Sir 51:13-20. The linking of Wisdom's yoke and the promise of rest are similar to Sir 6:18-37. In subsequent chapters Jesus is not only identified with Wisdom, but he is also teacher of Wisdom (12:1-8, 9-14; 13:1-53), interpreter of the Torah, revealer of eschatological mysteries, and possessor of Wisdom (12:41-42). The theme is rounded out in Matt 13:54-58, where Wisdom and mighty deeds go hand in hand with one more query about Jesus' identity (13:54). The final portrayal of the Matthean Jesus as Wisdom is found in 23:34-36, 37-39, where Matthew places Wisdom's words on the lips of Jesus and shows them actualized in the present in him. See further Jack M. Suggs, *Wisdom, Christology and Law in Matthew's Gospel* (Cambridge, Mass.: Harvard University Press, 1970); Fred W. Burnett, *The Testament of Jesus-Sophia: A Redaction-Critical Study of the Eschatological Discourse in Matthew*

dom spoke in the streets and marketplaces (Prov 1:20-21) and found herself rejected (Sir 15:7-8; Wis 10:3; Bar 3:12), so does Jesus who now personifies her. The image of Jesus piping a tune evokes that of Woman Wisdom the hymnist (1QPsa 18:12). The rejection of Jesus as prophet is akin to that of Woman Wisdom, a prophet whose words of reproof are ignored (Prov 1:23-25). Jesus' eating and drinking recalls Wisdom, who spreads her banquet and invites, "Come, eat of my food, / and drink of the wine I have mixed" (Prov 9:5). That Jesus' works, *erga* (11:2, 19) identify his relation to God is akin to Wisdom Woman's participation in God's works, *erga* at creation (Prov 8:22-31). The language of righteousness (*edikaiōthē*, "vindicated,") used of Jesus in Matthew 11:19 is evocative of Lady Wisdom, who walks in the way of righteousness, *dikaiosynē* (Prov 8:20) and who speaks with all righteousness (*dikaiosynē*, Prov 8:8).[11]

The parable functions as a vehicle for reflection on the mixed reception experienced by Jesus and his forerunner, John, and for subsequent followers who encounter the same. One of the functions of the parable is christological. It confirms that Jesus is the Coming One who ushers in the messianic age. The complex of episodes to which the parable belongs raises questions such as: What have you seen? What are you looking for? Where are you looking? How will you respond? These challenge predetermined attitudes and expectations that can keep some from perceiving correctly the One who is the Wisdom

---

(Lanham, Md.: University Press of America, 1981); Celia Deutsch, *Hidden Wisdom and the Easy Yoke: Wisdom, Torah and Discipleship in Matthew 11.25-30* (JSOTSup 18; Sheffield, JSOT Press, 1987); *Lady Wisdom, Jesus, and the Sages* (Valley Forge, Penn.: Trinity Press International, 1996). Marshall Johnson, "Reflections on a Wisdom Approach to Matthew's Christology," *CBQ* 36 (1974) 44–64; Frances Taylor Gench, *Wisdom in the Christology of Matthew* (Lanham, Md.: University Press of America, 1997); John S. Kloppenborg, "Wisdom Christology in Q," *LavalThéolPhil* 34 (1978) 129–47; R. S. Sugirtharajah, "Wisdom, Q, and a Proposal for a Christology," *ExpTim* 102 (1990) 42–46; R. A. Piper, *Wisdom in the Q-tradition* (SNTSMS 61; Cambridge: Cambridge University Press, 1989); Elaine M. Wainwright, *Shall We Look For Another? A Feminist Rereading of the Matthean Jesus* (The Bible & Liberation Series; Maryknoll: Orbis, 1998) 67–83.

[11] See above, pp. 225–26 on the theme of righteousness in Matthew.

personified. With the verses that follow (11:20-24) Matthew is at pains to show that the consequences of blindness or petulance are not neutral: judgment will ensue (v. 24) and repentance is expected from all who have seen Jesus' mighty deeds.

PREACHING POSSIBILITIES

The portrayal of Jesus as another in the long line of Sophia's prophets who announce justice, right order, and well-being for all God's creatures, especially those most marginalized, can give hope to all those who today continue to proclaim and work for justice. The preacher can emphasize how the divine presence and power to free is experienced in the midst of the struggles against oppression as Jesus, depicted as Sophia Incarnate, accompanies disciples and leads them through the suffering to victory. When preachers, teachers, and evangelists experience opposition and rejection the parable can give courage and hope, recognizing that all God's prophets have always experienced such, but Jesus has already conquered the forces of death itself.

The parable has both a sorrowful edge to it, yet a note of triumph. While there seems little hope in the gospel that "this generation" will respond positively to the invitation offered by God's prophets, John and Jesus, the invitation continues to be put forth. The preacher can be a vehicle for the ongoing invitation to right relation with God, personified as Wisdom, who will ultimately be vindicated. He or she can invite the congregation to examine false expectations or perceptions that need to be let go in order to heed Jesus' call, and banquet with him. The preacher can also invite disciples into the role of calling out to new "children in the marketplace" the Good News through ministries of evangelization.

For "this generation" today, the parable can offer new possibilities of embracing Jesus not only as Wisdom's prophet, but as Divine Sophia herself Incarnate, inviting us to see all her children, female and male, made in her image, redeemed by her, and continuing her mission. In the church today Wisdom's female children continue to experience the frustration of having been schooled in her Word and in her ways, and yet find inequity and rejection. With the Wisdom christology of this parable the preacher can articulate how the Christ integrates divine femaleness with human maleness, thus overcoming gender dualism. Such reflection can work toward dislodging sexism and enabling the formation of communities of equal disciples, thus creating a new reality by which Wisdom may be justified.

CHAPTER EIGHTEEN

Blind Guides
(Matt 15:1-2, 10-14)

Tuesday of the Eighteenth Week of Ordinary Time
(second option)

The scribes from Jerusalem approached Jesus with the question:
"Why do your disciples act contrary to the tradition of our ancestors?
They do not wash their hands, for example, before eating a meal."
    Jesus summoned the crowd and said to them,
      "Give ear and try to understand.
It is not what goes into a man's mouth that makes him impure;
    it is what comes out of his mouth."
His disciples approached and said,
    "Do you realize the Pharisees were scandalized
    when they heard your pronouncement?"
"Every planting not put down by my heavenly Father will be uprooted,"
    he replied.
"Let them go their way; they are blind leaders of the blind.
    If one blind man leads another, both will end in a pit."

LITERARY CONTEXT

These parabolic sayings are part of the gospel's third narrative block (11:2–16:20) which focuses on Jesus' identity as authoritative agent of God.[1] Within chapter 15 there are four

---

[1] Warren Carter, *Jesus and the Margins* (Maryknoll: Orbis, 2000) 314.

sections. The first (vv. 1-20) depicts a confrontation between Jesus and the Jewish leaders. This is followed by Jesus' encounter with the Canaanite woman (15:21-28), a summary statement about Jesus' healings (15:29-31) and the feeding of the four thousand (15:31-39).

The Lectionary gives a portion of the dispute between Jesus and the religious leaders. Matthew has taken the bulk of this material from Mark and follows the basic contours of Mark's structure (7:1-23), but he also makes substantial changes. Whereas Mark concentrates on the question of cultic purity, Matthew focuses on the traditions of the elders. Matthew reverses the order of Mark so that the issue of *korban* (verses not included in this Lectionary selection) precedes that of hand washing. Matthew drops Mark's radical comment that Jesus "declared all foods clean" (7:19) and he tones down Mark's sweeping critique of Jewish practices (7:13). In contrast to Mark's mostly Gentile community, Matthew's predominantly Jewish Christian community probably still observed many of the Jewish practices and did not find these incompatible with Jesus' teaching. But Matthew does heighten the censure of the Pharisees by adding vv. 12-15.[2]

There is a succession of audiences in Matthew 15. First is a direct confrontation between Jesus and the scribes and Pharisees (vv. 1-9), followed by a declaration Jesus addresses to the crowd (vv. 10-11), concluding with a discussion between Jesus and his disciples (vv. 12-20). A portion of each of these sections is included in the Lectionary selection. What is not immediately evident in this selection is that Matthew regards this as a parable. At verse 15 Peter asks Jesus to "explain this parable *(tēn parabolēn)* to us." From the ensuing explanation "the parable" refers to the enigmatic saying in v. 11 about defilement. As at 13:13-15, parables are not self-evident and they need explanation. The disciples, while having some understanding, are in need of further instruction.

---

[2] Donald Senior, *Matthew* (ANTC; Nashville: Abingdon, 1998) 175–76; Daniel J. Harrington, *Matthew* (SacPag1; Collegeville: The Liturgical Press, 1991) 231–34.

TRADITION OF THE ELDERS (vv. 1-2)

The chapter opens with a confrontation between Jesus and other Jewish religious authorities. Pharisees[3] and scribes[4] are used by Matthew throughout the gospel as a foil for Jesus.[5] The issue at stake is oral tradition and authoritative interpretation. The "tradition of the elders" refers to customs and regulations that developed in interpretation of the Law in order to apply it to everyday life. Josephus says that this consisted of "certain regulations handed down by former generations and not recorded in the Law of Moses" (*Ant.* 13.297). In Jesus' day these traditions were passed down orally. From around the year 200 C.E. these were codified in written collections beginning with the Mishnah. Pharisees of Jesus' day considered the oral traditions authoritative, whereas Sadducees and the Qumran community did not.[6] The debate depicted in the gospel is an intra-Jewish conflict that would have been alive in Jesus' day as well as in Matthew's.

The specific example cited in v. 2 is the tradition of handwashing. This custom is not a matter of hygiene, but concerns the social systems by which boundaries of belonging are

[3] Curiously the Lectionary omits the reference to Pharisees at v. 1, but in light of their mention in v. 12 it is important to note that they are in view from the start.

[4] The two appear together at 5:20; 12:38; 16:21 and 7 times in chapter 23, where they are excoriated as hypocrites. In Matthew's Gospel Pharisees are always portrayed negatively: 3:7; 5:20; 9:11, 14, 34; 12:2, 14, 24, 38; 19:3; 22:15, 34, 41, with the Sadducees at 16:1, 6, 11, 12; and with the chief priests at 21:45; 27:62. Scribes, likewise are opposed to Jesus and appear at 2:4; 5:20; 7:29; 8:19; 9:3; 12:38; 17:10. They are linked with the chief priests at 16:21; 20:18; 21:15 and with the elders at 26:57; 27:41. One positive remark about scribes is found at 13:52.

[5] Whether there were Pharisees in Galilee in the time of Jesus is a matter of debate. Seán Freyne (*Galilee from Alexander the Great to Hadrian 323 B.C.E. to 135 C.E.* [University of Notre Dame Center for the Study of Judaism and Christianity in Antiquity 5; Wilmington, Del., and Notre Dame, Ind.: Glazier and University of Notre Dame Press, 1980] 305–43) argues for the presence of some Pharisees in Galilee. Other scholars, e.g., Jacob Neusner (*From Politics to Piety. The Emergence of Pharisaic Judaism* [Englewood Cliffs: Prentice Hall, 1973] 72) interpret such references to Pharisees and scribes in the Gospels as a narrative convention for opponents to Jesus.

[6] Josephus, *Ant.* 13.297-98; 1QH 4:14-15.

defined. Purity and cleanness have to do with what is in its proper place; impurity and uncleanness deals with what is out of place. Purity distinctions are drawn for times, places, persons, things, meals, and "others" (who can pollute by contact).[7]

The custom of ritual washing has its roots in the mandate in Exodus 30:19; 40:12 that priests wash their hands and feet before coming and entering into the tent of meeting. By the second century B.C.E. a number of Jews had voluntarily assumed the priestly practices of washing their hands before morning prayer and before eating. Some wanted to impose these and other such observances on all Jews. For Pharisees this oral interpretation of the Law was as binding as the written Law. The practice of hand-washing, then (despite Mark 7:3) was not universally observed by Jews, but rather was one that was "above and beyond the call of duty."[8] This tradition was largely defined, maintained, and observed by urban elites. Full observance was nearly impossible for peasant farmers, fishermen, and itinerants such as Jesus, due to scarcity of water for ritual ablutions and to contact with dead fish and other pollutants.[9]

WHAT COMES OUT (vv. 10-11)

In the intervening verses that are omitted from the Lectionary (vv. 3-9) Jesus turns first to another controversial issue, *korban*, concerning the practice of declaring something dedicated to God. He uses this as an example of how a distorted adherence to the tradition of the elders can actually cause one to neglect commandments in the Torah.[10] He then returns to the issue of ritual purity in vv. 10-11, but the focus shifts from a manner of eating that may or may not be polluting to the ques-

[7] Bruce J. Malina and Richard L. Rohrbaugh, *Social Science Commentary on the Synoptic Gospels* (Minneapolis: Fortress, 1992) 222–24; Jerome H. Neyrey, "The Idea of Purity in Mark's Gospel," *Semeia* 35 (1986) 91–128.

[8] Harrington, *Matthew,* 232.

[9] Malina and Rohrbaugh, *Social Science Commentary,* 221; John J. Pilch, *The Cultural World of Jesus. Sunday by Sunday, Cycle B* (Collegeville: The Liturgical Press, 1996) 130.

[10] Harrington, *Matthew,* 232.

tion of what foods are defiling. There is also a shift in audience as Jesus now addresses his remarks to the crowd. In Matthew the crowd is primarily positive toward Jesus, although they do not have the faith or understanding of disciples.[11]

The saying in v. 11 relativizes cultic purity in favor of moral purity. The meaning is further elaborated in vv. 17-20 (omitted from the Lectionary selection): purity of heart is fundamental; from this all authentic ritual practice flows. The theme of what is in the heart was introduced in vv. 7-9, where Jesus quotes Isa 29:13 to the Pharisees:

> "This people honors me with their lips,
> but their hearts are far from me;
> in vain do they worship me,
> teaching as doctrines human precepts."

It is reprised in vv. 17-20, where Jesus asserts that what defiles is not what goes into the stomach but what comes from the heart. "Heart" is used very often in both Testaments in a figurative sense as the source of all emotions, passions, and intellectual life. It is the seat of one's will and the center of one's relationship with God. It is the heart that speaks to God (Ps 27:8) and receives God's word (Deut 30:14). God gives hearts understanding (1 Kgs 3:9) and inspires hearts to action (Neh 2:12).[12] What proceeds from the heart, then, is indicative of one's relationship with God.[13]

BLIND GUIDES (vv. 12-14)

The third and final part of the pericope is a discussion between Jesus and his disciples. The disciples report to Jesus the opposition of the Pharisees to Jesus' words, which provides the opportunity for him now to give further instruction to them.

[11] Warren Carter, "The Crowds in Matthew's Gospel," *CBQ* 55 (1993) 54–67.

[12] See further Thomas P. McCreesh, "Heart," *Collegeville Pastoral Dictionary of Biblical Theology* (ed. Carroll Stuhlmueller; Collegeville: The Liturgical Press, 1996) 422–24.

[13] See Matt 5:8, 28; 6:21; 9:4; 11:29; 12:34; 13:15, 19; 15:8, 19; 18:35; 22:37.

Using first a metaphor found in Isa 60:21,[14] where Yahweh calls Israel "the bud of my planting," Jesus counters that the Pharisees are not the ones planted by his heavenly Father.[15] The implication is that Jesus is. As with weeds among wheat (13:24-30, 36-43) and dragnets that snare all kinds of fish (13:47-50) the Pharisees are to be left alone until a later "uprooting." The verb *ekrizōthēsetai,* "will be uprooted" (v. 13)[16] is likely a theological passive, indicating that the action will be done by God.

The final image (v. 14) is that Jesus' opponents are blind guides who lead the unperceiving into perdition. This Q saying also appears in the Gospel of Luke (6:39), where it is dubbed a parable. In the Third Gospel it is located in the Sermon on the Plain, among a number of loosely connected sayings directed to the disciples about proper ways to guide, correct, and teach one another. The saying has many well known variations in ancient literature. Sextus Empiricus, a second century C.E. skeptic, says that an amateur cannot teach an amateur any more than the blind can lead the blind (Against the Professors 1.31).[17] Horace, the first-century B.C.E. poet and satirist, writes to Scaeva, a patron: "I have still much to learn, but listen to me anyway, even if I appear to be a blind man giving directions" (*Epistles* 1.17.4). In the Gospel of Matthew two accounts of the healing of two blind men frame the discipleship discourses (9:27-31; 20:30-34). Moving from blindness to sight serves as a metaphor for coming to faith in Jesus and is a sign of the inbreaking of the reign of God (11:5; 12:22; 15:30, 31; 21:14). In contrast to Jesus, who leads the blind to sight, the Pharisees are excoriated not only at 15:14 but five times in chapter 23 as blind guides and blind fools. The end result is that both they

---

[14] As noted by Carter (*Matthew and the Margins,* 593 n. 9) the image of Israel planted by Yahweh occurs frequently in the OT: Pss 1:3; 80:15; 92:13; 2 Sam 7:10; Isa 5:1-10; 60:21; Jer 32:41; Ezek 17:22-24; 19:10, 13.

[15] Harrington (*Matthew,* 230) notes that the Qumran community also applied this image to itself (1QS 8:5; 11:8; CD 1:7). See also *Jub* 1:16; 7:34; 21:24; *1 Enoch* 10:16; 84:6; 93:2; Psalms of Solomon 14:3.

[16] Similarly Jer 1:10; 12:17; 18:7.

[17] This and the following example come from Frederick W. Danker, *Jesus and the New Age. A Commentary on St. Luke's Gospel* (rev. ed.; Philadelphia: Fortress, 1988) 153–55.

and their followers will "fall into a pit," a classic metaphor for disaster and judgment.[18]

PREACHING POSSIBILITIES

The preacher should be alert to the differences between Matthew's version of this parable and Mark's. While the latter makes sweeping statements about abrogating Jewish food laws (Mark 7:15), Matthew does not. His community remains true to their Jewish heritage, but claims Jesus as authoritative interpreter of the Law. Matthew is not setting aside Jewish ritual practices; rather he makes the central question one of moral purity. Purity of heart must be at the core of all religious practices.[19]

It is important for the preacher to understand the conflict depicted in the gospel in its historical context: that of the struggle of Matthew's primarily Jewish Christian community to define itself in relation to non-Christian Jews. Matthew is giving us a glimpse of a Jewish family quarrel, in which he uses Pharisees and scribes to caricature those opposed to Jesus' way of observing Torah. A preacher needs to be attentive to the potential for fueling anti-Semitism if the text is misread as a battle between Judaism and Christianity.

For Christians today this parable can serve equally well as a warning against observance of tradition for its own sake, or the performance of ritual that is devoid of the heart. A religious custom that was good in its origin but that has deteriorated into a showy external observance must give way to what will allow encounter with God that moves the heart. The preacher, like Jesus, and like other prophets before him (e.g., Isa 1:11-17; Jer 7:21-26; Amos 5:21-27), may need to call the community to examine observances that are merely external or ceremonial. The interior life with God and its external manifestation are to be in harmony.

The parable also can be an exhortation to those in leadership to take necessary steps to foster their own clear sight.

---

[18] Carter, *Matthew and the Margins*, 319. See Ps 7:15; Prov 26:27; Isa 24:18; Jer 48:44; *T. Reu.* 2:9.

[19] Senior, *Matthew*, 179; Harrington, *Matthew*, 233–34.

Christian teachers and leaders continually pray and study so as to see the way clearly so they can guide those who follow them. At the same time the image that God is the one who plants and uproots (v. 13) keeps leaders from falling into a pit of overreliance on their own abilities. A disciple's eyes are continually fixed on Jesus and on his authoritative word that steers disciples along the way.

CHAPTER NINETEEN

Straying Sheep
(Matt 18:1-5, 10, 12-14)

Tuesday of the Nineteenth Week of Ordinary Time (18:12-14)

Tuesday of the Second Week of Advent

The disciples came up to Jesus with the question,
"Who is of greatest importance in the kingdom of God?"
He called a little child over and stood him in their midst and said:
"I assure you,
    unless you change and become like little children,
    you will not enter the kingdom of God.
"Whoever makes himself lowly, becoming like this child,
    is of greatest importance in that heavenly reign.
"Whoever welcomes one such child for my sake welcomes me.
"See that you never despise one of these little ones.
    I assure you their angels in heaven
    constantly behold my heavenly Father's face.
"What is your thought on this:
A man owns a hundred sheep and one of them wanders away;
will he not leave the ninety-nine out on the hills
and go in search of the stray?
If he succeeds in finding it, believe me he is happier
about this one than about the ninety-nine that did not wander away.
Just so, it is no part of your heavenly Father's plan
    that a single one of these little ones shall ever come to grief."

LITERARY CONTEXT

This parable of the straying sheep (vv. 12-14) is located in Matthew's fourth major discourse, on life in the Christian community. The first section (18:1-14), of which this parable is part, focuses on the need for humility and on pastoral care, particularly for the most vulnerable in the community. The second (18:15-20) gives a procedure for reconciling offenses when members sin against one another within the Christian community. The third part (18:21-35) relays Jesus' teaching on unlimited forgiveness from the heart, concretized in the parable of the unforgiving servant.[1]

There are three extant forms of the parable of the lost sheep. The apocryphal *Gospel of Thomas* §107 reads, "Jesus said: 'The kingdom is like a shepherd who had a hundred sheep. One of them, the largest, went astray. He left the ninety-nine and sought the one until he found it.' After he had gone to this trouble, he said to the sheep, 'I love you more than the ninety-nine.'"[2] Most scholars regard this as later than the Q version redacted by Matthew and Luke.[3] The parable in *Gospel of Thomas* adds two details which focus on the great value of the sheep: the size of the lost sheep and the love of the shepherd for this sheep that exceeds that for the others. In the Synoptic versions the focus is more on the effort in the search and the subsequent joy in finding.

Luke's version (15:4-7) is perhaps the best known, as it stands at the head of the trio of lost-and-found parables in Luke 15. It is linked with two other parables, the lost coin (15:8-10) and the lost sons (15:11-32), both unique to Luke. Shifting the

---

[1] See above, chapter 9. Varying divisions for the fourth discourse are proposed by different scholars. William G. Thompson (*Matthew's Advice to a Divided Community: Mt. 17,22–18,35* [AnBib 44; Rome: Biblical Institute 1970]), followed by Warren Carter and John Paul Heil (*Matthew's Parables* [CBQMS 30; Washington, D.C.: Catholic Biblical Association, 1998] 96), delineates seven units from 17:22–18:35. Others begin with 18:1 and divide the chapter into two, three, four, or six parts (see Thompson, *Advice*, 2–4 for a summary of various outlines). Donald Senior (*Matthew* [ANTC; Nashville: Abingdon, 1998] 204–05) advances a tripartite division.

[2] Marvin Meyer, *The Gospel of Thomas* (HarperSanFrancisco, 1992) 63.

[3] Based on differences in style, Thompson (*Advice*, 168–74) concludes that Matthew's version is more primitive than Luke's. See also Jan Lambrecht, *Out of the Treasure* (Louvain Theological and Pastoral Monographs 10; Louvain: Peeters, 1992) 37–52, for analysis of the tradition history of the parable.

image from shepherd, to woman, to father, all three portray the costly love of God, who is willing to go to any length to seek out the lost and draw them back into the divine embrace. In the narrative of the Third Gospel these parables are aimed at the Pharisees and scribes who complain that Jesus is welcoming toll collectors and sinners and eating with them.[4] While Christians often hear these parables from the stance of the lost one who is drawn back to God, the gospel setting aims them at the religious leaders who criticize Jesus' inclusive table sharing. The parables function to justify Jesus' practice and to offer one more invitation to the Jewish religious leaders. When Christian leaders take these parables to heart, they function as a warning not to imitate the Pharisees and scribes, but to emulate Jesus' practice of seeking out the lost.

In Matthew's Gospel the parable is directed to the disciples (v. 1), not to the Jewish religious leaders. It is not aimed at those who are vulnerable or lost, but to those who are Christian leaders. The first verses in chapter 18 are addressed to those who have some degree of power, privilege, and status, as they are enjoined to humble themselves and to welcome the most vulnerable ones (vv. 1-5). Next are warnings to them not to put a stumbling block in the path of these "little ones," *mikrōn* (vv. 6-9, not included in the Lectionary selection). Immediately preceding the parable is an admonition not to despise any of these "little ones" (v. 10).[5] The parable concludes with a statement that the will of the heavenly Father is that none of these "little ones" be lost (v. 14). Concern for the "little ones" frames the parable and makes pastoral care of such the focus.[6]

---

[4] See Barbara E. Reid, *Parables for Preachers. Year C* (Collegeville: The Liturgical Press, 2000) 177–91.

[5] Some manuscripts add a verse 11, "For the Son of Man has come to save what was lost," which echoes Matt 9:13 and Luke 19:10, and is probably a later addition.

[6] Who these "little ones" are is not precisely spelled out. They may have been new converts or those whose faith is not yet strong. In several episodes Matthew's Jesus addresses the disciples as "people of little faith," *oligopistoi* (6:30; 8:26; 14:31; 16:8; 17:20). In the one other occurrence of *mikrōn* at Matt 10:42 it refers to Christian missionaries. At the last judgment scene punishment or reward is meted out according to one's treatment of "the least," *elachistōn* (25:40, 45). See above, chap. 16.

JOYFUL FINDING

In addition to their differing literary contexts, there are a number of other variances between the Matthean and Lukan versions of the parable. Both begin with a question, meant to hook the hearer. In Luke, Jesus clearly wants his hearers to identify with the shepherd as he asks, "What man among you having a hundred sheep . . . ?" (Luke 15:4). In Matthew's opening verse Jesus also poses a question to the hearers, his disciples, but more in a manner of telling them a story about which they are to make a judgment.[7]

There are actually two questions posed in v. 12. The second is framed in such a way that the expected answer is affirmative. If a sheep goes astray *(planēthē),*[8] a shepherd will most certainly go in search of it. Sheep were valuable commodities; no matter what the size of the flock none is expendable. The point of the story is not about abandoning or putting at risk the other ninety-nine. A flock of one hundred ordinarily would be tended by more than one shepherd.[9] The original hearers would have understood that the others would also be cared for. What the story presumes is that a sheep is so precious that it would be unthinkable to let one wander away without attempting to retrieve it.

The metaphor "shepherd" is a familiar one for God (Pss 23; 100; Isa 40:11) and for religious leaders. It is possible that Jesus' parable is told with Ezekiel 34 in mind. There the religious leaders, the "shepherds of Israel," are excoriated for looking after their own interests, and not those of the "sheep." They have not pastured the sheep but have fed off their milk, worn their wool, and slaughtered their fatlings (v. 3); worse yet, they

---

[7] The same phrase introduces the parable of the two sons at 21:28. This is similar to the technique used by the prophet Nathan with king David (2 Sam 12:1-15), and Jesus with Simon (Luke 7:40-44).

[8] Matthew uses this verb in his eschatological discourse to warn the disciples not to be led astray by false prophets and messiahs (24:4, 5, 11, 24). This verb is used of moral lapse in Jas 5:19-20. In Luke's version the shepherd loses *(apolesas)* the sheep.

[9] Kenneth E. Bailey, *Poet and Peasant: A Literary-Cultural Approach to the Parables in Luke* (Grand Rapids: Eerdmans, 1976) 149.

have not strengthened the weak or tended to the sick or injured. Not only have they not sought out the strayed, but they have lorded it over them harshly and brutally (v. 4). Therefore God promises to serve as shepherd who will seek the lost and bring back the strayed, rescuing them from all their distress (Ezek 34:8-12). Using the same metaphor, Jesus spoke of his own compassion for the people who were "like sheep without a shepherd" when he feeds the multitude with the loaves and fishes (Matt 9:36). When he sends out his disciples on mission he instructs them to seek out the "lost sheep of the house of Israel" (10:6). He uses this same phrase to describe his own mission in his retort to the Canaanite woman who beseeches him to heal her daughter (15:24). Using this familiar metaphor Jesus instructs his own disciples that if any of the Christian community stray, they are to make every effort to bring them back. No one is expendable; each one is of utmost value to the shepherd. Recalling the episode in which Jesus heals a man with a withered hand, the hearer knows "how much more valuable a person is than a sheep" (12:12).[10]

In Matthew's version the outcome of the search is not assured. *If* the shepherd finds the sheep then he rejoices greatly over it (v. 13). In Luke, by contrast, there is no question of whether the sheep will be found. Rather, *when* the shepherd finds it, he hoists it onto his shoulders with great joy and calls together his friends and neighbors to share his joy (Luke 15:5-6). Matthew downplays somewhat the great effort expended by the shepherd. Luke's shepherd does not cease looking until the sheep is found, and no matter how much rocky, dry terrain[11] and how many nooks and crannies he has investigated, he beams with joy at the prospect of hauling a sixty- or seventy-pound beast on his shoulders. Matthew's parable also lacks the communal dimension of the partying over the found sheep.

---

[10] In that episode the emphasis is on the timing. Jesus observes that his opponents would pull out a sheep who has fallen into a pit on the Sabbath. Arguing from the lesser to the greater, he justifies the timing of his healing of the man's hand.

[11] Luke's sheep are in the desert, *en tē erēmō* (v. 4), whereas Matthew's are on the hillside, *epi ta orē* (v. 12).

In his parable the focus remains entirely on the shepherd and his joy. A similar note is struck as in the parable of the found treasure (13:44): the joy of finding far outweighs whatever the cost of seeking.

Finally, Matthew's parable concludes differently from Luke's. The third evangelist continues to keep the celebrative joy at the center and elevates it to eschatological joy, as he rounds off the parable, "I tell you, in just the same way there will be more joy in heaven over one sinner who repents than over ninety-nine righteous people who have no need of repentance" (15:7). Typical of Luke, he inserts a favorite theme, repentance, *metanoia*, which does not really match the contours of the parable. The sheep does not "turn," or "change its mind,"[12] rather the shepherd seeks it, finds it, and carries it home. Matthew, by contrast, keeps the focus on the urgent task of a shepherd to follow God's will in not losing any of the "little ones."

The theme of God's will is a recurring one in Matthew. It is first sounded in the prayer that Jesus teaches his disciples, "your will be done" (6:10) as he himself prays fervently in Gethsemane (26:39, 42, 44). The parables of the two builders (7:21-27) and of the two sons (21:28-32)[13] emphasize doing the will of God. Jesus tells the crowds that whoever does the will of God is kin to him (12:50). While in these other passages it is not entirely clear what it is that constitutes doing the will of God, here it is explicitly the act of seeking out those who have strayed and rejoicing if these efforts are successful.

---

[12] BDAG, s.v., μετάνοια. *Metanoia* is a particular favorite of Luke and is often inserted by him into his source. He alters Mark's conclusion of the call of Levi, so that Jesus declares as his mission, "I have not come to call the righteous to repentance but sinners" (Luke 5:32). Warnings about repentance appear in other passages unique to Luke: 13:3, 5; 16:30. In Luke 17:3-4, unlike the corresponding sayings in Matt 18:15, 21-22, repentance is a condition for forgiveness of one's brother or sister. Finally, the concluding instruction of the Lukan Jesus to his disciples as he is about to ascend, is to proclaim "repentance and forgiveness of sins" (Luke 24:47). Repentance is a particular theme of the Third Evangelist, which he inserts into the tradition, especially wherever forgiveness appears.

[13] See above, chapters 5 and 11.

PREACHING POSSIBILITIES

One of the temptations of the preacher may be to extrapolate from the familiar text of Luke, when presented with the less vivid parable of Matthew. It is preferable to attend to the specific details of Matthew and his particular theological emphases and not to conflate the two. What is most pronounced in Matthew is the intense concern for the "little ones" and the grave responsibility of Christian leaders not to let such persons wander away—they must go to great lengths to bring the lost home. There is none whom we can afford to be without; as long as any are missing the sheepfold is not complete. This parable can be a source of encouragement for all Christians, but especially leaders, to engage in ministries of welcome, of hospitality, of evangelization, of seeking to reconcile disaffected believers, and of reaching out to those among the baptized who are lapsed in their practice of the faith.

While the major focus of the parable invites disciples to imitate the shepherd, it is also possible for the preacher to invite the hearers to situate themselves with the sheep, whom God will never let stray without seeking until found. God's will is for the life and well-being of God's people, each of whom is precious and indispensable. Upon being brought back home the one who strayed finds that the intimate joy with God exceeds what might have been had they never ventured away.

The metaphor of God as shepherd is a rich one. Unlike "heavenly Father"[14] it allows for either a female or male image, since it was common for girls and women, as well as men and boys to be engaged in shepherding. It also introduces a provocative dimension. Although "shepherd" was a familiar metaphor for God (Pss 23; 100; Isa 40:11), and for religious leaders (Ezekiel 34), real shepherds were disdained. They were thought to be dishonest and thieving, leading their herds onto other people's land and pilfering the produce of the herd.[15] It is something of a shock for respected religious leaders

---

[14] See above, pp. 55–59.

[15] Joachim Jeremias, *Jerusalem in the Time of Jesus* (Philadelphia: Fortress, 1969) 303–05, 310, cites examples from the Mishnah that list herdsmen among the despised trades.

to be asked to think of themselves as lowly shepherds. Yet this is precisely the import of Matthew's emphasis on the "little ones." Christian leaders cannot become swallowed up with their own importance, but must keep uppermost the importance of the "little ones." They need to ask continually, "Who's not here that should be?" and then must strategize with their congregations how to engage in seeking, finding, and rejoicing.

When this parable is the gospel reading on Tuesday of the Second Week of Advent, the first reading, taken from Isaiah 40:1-11 intersects well with the gospel. Both capitalize on the image of God as shepherd. In the first reading God feeds and leads the flock, carrying Israel with tender care back from exile. On Tuesday of the Nineteenth Week of Ordinary Time in Year I the first reading is taken from Deuteronomy 31:1-8, where Moses is about to die. He reminds the Israelites that God will march before them and that Joshua will take his place to lead them into the land of promise. Like the shepherd of the gospel, God does not let the Israelites wander aimlessly. The same vigilance and care is what is asked of Christian disciples, particularly their leaders.

CHAPTER TWENTY

Faithful Servants
(Matt 24:42-51)

Thursday of the Twenty-First Week of Ordinary Time

Jesus said to his disciples:
  "Stay awake therefore!
  You cannot know the day your Lord is coming.
  Be sure of this: if the owner of the house
  knew when the thief was coming,
    he would keep a watchful eye and not allow his house to be broken into.
  You must be prepared in the same way.
  The Son of Man is coming at the time you least expect.
  "Who is the faithful, farsighted servant,
    whom the master has put in charge of his household
    to dispense food at need?
  Happy that servant whom his master discovers at work on his return!
    I assure you, he will put him in charge of all his property.
  But if the servant is worthless and tells himself,
    'My master is a long time in coming,'
  and begins to beat his fellow servants, to eat and drink with drunkards,
  that man's master will return when he is not ready and least expects him.
  He will punish him severely and settle with him as is done with hypocrites.
    There will be wailing then and grinding of teeth."

LITERARY CONTEXT AND TRADITION HISTORY

This is the first of three parables in the eschatological discourse (24:1–25:46) that emphasize the need for preparedness
on the part of disciples in face of the delay of the parousia.[1] In

---

[1] On the second parable, that of the wise and foolish virgins (25:1-13) see
above, chap. 14. On the third in the triad, the parable of the talents (25:14-30)
see chap. 15. For an outline of the eschatological discourse, see above, p. 190.

all three the same motifs appear: the absence and return of a master, his delay and unexpected return.

The exhortation to watchfulness in the opening verse of the Lectionary selection (v. 42) is taken from Mark (13:35), but the remaining verses come from Q. The short parable about the thief in the night (vv. 43-44) has a parallel in Luke 12:39-40. The parable of the faithful servant (vv. 45-51) has its counterpart at Luke 12:41-46. In Luke's Gospel these are joined with other sayings and short parables loosely linked by catchwords. In Luke they are juxtaposed with material that counsels against greed and emphasizes God's providence. Luke places these parables as part of Jesus' journey to Jerusalem, not in the eschatological discourse, where Matthew has located them.

Scholars debate whether these parables were told by Jesus or whether they are constructions of the early Church.[2] Would Jesus have spoken about his own parousia? Possibly a simpler form of the parable of the faithful servant goes back to the historical Jesus and was first directed to his opponents.[3] With the parable he is warning them that the time of reckoning is approaching, in which their faithfulness or wickedness will be revealed.[4] In its present literary context, however, the parable is directed to disciples. Its function can be understood variously. It may have been heard by the Matthean community as advice to those entrusted with leadership of the community.[5] Alternatively, it can be understood as part of Matthew's polemic

---

[2] Erich Grässer. *Das Problem der Parusieverzögerung in den synoptischen Evangelien und in der Apostelgeschichte* (Berlin: Töpelmann, 1960). For discussion of various positions, see B. B. Scott, *Hear Then the Parable* (Minneapolis: Fortress, 1989) 210; John R. Donahue, *The Gospel in Parable* (Philadelphia: Fortress, 1988) 99; Jan Lambrecht, *Out of the Treasure* (Louvain Theological and Pastoral Monographs 10; Louvain: Peeters, 1992) 183–98.

[3] So Joachim Jeremias, *The Parables of Jesus* (2d rev. ed.; New York: Scribner's, 1972) 166.

[4] Donahue, *Gospel in Parable*, 98.

[5] It may be the case with other parables as well, e.g., the Lost Sheep (Matt 18:10-14), that a parable originally aimed at Jesus' opponents has been transformed into a teaching for disciples.

against the Jews of the synagogue, that is, the parable helps to bolster his community's identity as faithful servants in contradistinction to those who do not join with them.[6]

WATCHFUL PREPARATION (vv. 42-44)

The first verse in the Lectionary pericope (v. 42) is a hinge verse that interprets both the sayings that precede and the parables that follow. Wakeful attention is needed, whether at work during the day, as the pairs of men in a field and women grinding corn (vv. 40-41), or whether at rest during the night. This exhortation to vigilance for the coming of the Son of Humanity extends from 24:36–25:30.[7] Not knowing the day or the hour is a motif that frames the parabolic saying about the thief in the night (vv. 42, 44). This motif has already been sounded twice (vv. 36, 39), and is repeated in the next two parables (24:50; 25:13). The plea to stay awake *grēgoreite* (v. 42) resounds again in the scene at Gethsemane (26:38, 40, 41), as Jesus enjoins his disciples to keep vigil with him, but they are unable.

In the first parabolic saying (vv. 43-44) it is a master who is watchful; in the second (vv. 45-51) it is servants who need to be vigilant. The meaning is clear: just as a householder would be especially prepared if he knew the time of a break-in, so must disciples be prepared for the coming of the Son of Humanity. The theme of the unexpected burglar is a popular one in New Testament texts that deal with the parousia, e.g., 1 Thessalonians 5:2-4; 2 Peter 3:10; Revelation 3:3; 16:15.

FAITHFUL SERVANTS (vv. 45-51)

The image shifts to servants of the master, in particular the one put in charge over the household. The parable is directed especially to leaders in the community, who are the servants of the rest, and responsible for their well-being. Like so many of the gospel parables, this one begins with a technique

---

[6] Daniel J. Harrington, "Polemical Parables in Matthew 24–25," *USQR* 44 (1991) 287–98.

[7] Lambrecht, *Out of the Treasure*, 189.

that immediately involves the hearer. Two possible scenarios are given in response to a pointed question: will the servant be reliable[8] and prudent[9] or wicked and abusive? The desired choice is obvious.[10]

Whereas in the previous verses the emphasis is on watchfulness for the coming of the master, here the vigilance is over the day-to-day tasks that must be fulfilled in the in-between time, particularly the distribution of food. This detail takes on particular significance in light of other New Testament texts that reveal difficulties in the early Church over food and eating. In 1 Corinthians 11:17-22 Paul deals with problems that have arisen at eucharistic gatherings at Corinth due to differing social status, a problem that may have also been in the purview of the Lukan and Matthean communities as they reflected on the parable of the great banquet (Matt 22:1-14; Luke 14:15-24). There were difficulties over Jewish and Gentile Christians eating together (Gal 2:11-14). A problem arose in the Jerusalem community involving the widows of the Hellenists who were being overlooked in the serving (Acts 6:1-6). The Twelve resolve it by appointing seven who will tend to ministering at table (*diakonein trapezais*, Acts 6:2).[11]

---

[8] Frequent in Matthew is the use of the noun "faith," *pistis* (Matt 8:10; 9:2, 22, 29; 15:28; 17:20; 21:21; 23:23) and the verb *pisteuein*, "to believe" (Matt 8:13; 9:28; 18:6; 21:22, 25, 32; 24:23, 26), as well as the motif "of little faith," *oligopistos* (Matt 6:30; 8:26; 14:31; 16:8; 17:20). Here, however, the adjective *pistos* connotes "reliable" or "faithful" more than "believing." Other texts that mention this as an important characteristic of a Christian leader are 1 Cor 4:1-2, 17; Col 1:7; Eph 6:21; Titus 1:9. See Donahue, *Gospel in Parable*, 99; Harrington, *Matthew*, 343.

[9] The term *phronimos*, "wise" or "prudent," is the same used to describe the one who built a house on rock (7:24) and the virgins who brought sufficient oil (25:1-10). When Jesus sends the disciples on mission, it is with the admonition to be "shrewd *(phronimoi)* as serpents and simple as doves" (10:16).

[10] Other scholars think that two different servants are being contrasted in the parable, rather than two choices facing the one servant.

[11] It is not clear from the text whether the problem was that the widows were not receiving what was their due or whether they were not being given their turn to exercise table ministry. The phrase in v. 1, *en tē diakonią*, translated in the *NAB* "in the daily distribution," literally means "in the serving." The noun *diakonia* and the verb *diakonein* have many different ministerial connotations, including table ministry (Acts 6:2), ministry of the word (Acts 6:4), financial ministry (Luke 8:3; Acts 11:29; 12:25), apostolic ministry (Acts

Food and eating can also be a metaphor for teaching and learning (1 Cor 3:2; John 6:25-33) and spiritual nourishment (Heb 5:12-14).[12] Consequently, the parable in vv. 45-51 may have been heard by the leaders in Matthew's community as an exhortation to exercise their ministry well, particularly in teaching and in sensitive areas of conflict centering around eucharistic celebrations.

The opposite choice is painted in vivid contrast. The wicked servant sees the delay of the master as an opportunity to exploit his situation and to take advantage of his temporary power. He begins to use his power abusively, to indulge himself in excessive food and drink.[13] There is an ironic twist as he who had been entrusted with the distribution of food to his fellow servants[14] instead gorges himself on the provisions.

The unexpected return of the master cuts short the servant's reverie. The consequences are dire for betraying the master's confidence and misusing his authority. What is translated in the *NAB* as "punish severely," *dichotomēsei*, literally means "to cut in two." It refers to the dismemberment of a condemned person.[15] In the context of the parable, it is an ironically fitting punishment for the double life that the steward is leading. Using some of his favorite language, Matthew concludes, saying the servant will be assigned a place *(meros)* with the hypocrites[16] where there will

---

1:17, 25), etc. See further Elisabeth Schüssler Fiorenza, *In Memory of Her* (New York: Crossroad, 1984) 165–66.

[12] Donahue, *Gospel in Parable*, 100.

[13] In 1 Cor 6:10 Paul warns that drunkards will not inherit the kingdom. Drunkenness was one of the abuses at the eucharistic gatherings that Paul addressed (1 Cor 11:21). The qualifications for overseers and ministers given in 1 Tim 3:3, 8 and Titus 1:7 warn that the person must not be a drunkard. Note that one of the slurs aimed at Jesus in Matt 11:19 is that he is "a glutton and a drunkard."

[14] Matthew's version of the parable emphasizes the equality of the servant who is put in charge with the others by using the term *syndouloi*, "fellow servants." In Luke 12:45 they are *paidas*, "menservants" and *paidiskas*, "maidservants."

[15] BDAG, s.v., διχοτομέω.

[16] Matthew uses *hypocritēs* six times in chap. 23 and twice elsewhere (15:7; 22:18) to excoriate the scribes and the Pharisees. At 6:2, 5, 16; 7:5 he warns his disciples not to act like such. Mark only uses the term once (7:6) and Luke three times (6:42; 12:56; 13:15).

be wailing and grinding of teeth.[17] The word for place, *meros,* can mean a portion of property (Luke 15:12; Acts 5:2), but it can also carry connotations of "share" in eternal inheritance, as in John 13:8, where Jesus tells Peter he will have no "part" in him if Jesus does not wash him. In the context of Matthew's eschatological discourse, this second meaning, with a connotation of a lasting assigned "place" is implied.

Because of the harshness of "dichotomizing" the servant and the seeming disjuncture with then assigning him a place with the hypocrites, some scholars have thought *dichotomēsei* to be a mistranslation of an Aramaic phrase, לֵהּ יְפַלֵּג (*yĕpallēg lēh*), "he will distribute to him [blows]," meaning to "punish with many blows."[18] Jennifer Glancy, however, has shown that such torture and execution of slaves was ubiquitous in the ancient Mediterranean world.[19] Another solution is that it refers to such a person being "cut off" from the community. A text from Qumran (1QS 2,16-17) is thought to provide a parallel. It records a curse against a hypocrite who enters the covenant but walks in his own ways, "God will single him out for evil so he will be cut off from the midst of all the sons of light . . . he will give his allotted portion in the midst of those accursed forever . . ."[20] Other scholars read the Qumran text as speaking of eschatological destruction, not simply excommunication from the community,[21] and this may be Matthew's intended meaning as well. Whichever the sense, the conclusion to the parable paints a cataclysmic end for those who are not reliable servants. Those who are found exercising their commission

---

[17] Matt 8:12; 13:42, 50; 22:13; 25:30.

[18] Jeremias, *Parables,* 57.

[19] Jennifer Glancy, "Slaves and Slavery in the Matthean Parables," *JBL* 119/1 (2000) 67–90.

[20] Otto Betz, "The Dichotomized Servant–Mt 24:51," *RevQum* 5 (1964) 43–58; Eduard Schweizer, *The Good News According to Matthew* (Atlanta: John Knox, 1975) 463. Donahue, *Gospel in Parable,* 100, notes that similar language of exclusion is found at Qumran and that Matt 18:17 and 1 Cor 6:7-13 attest to exclusionary practices in the early Christian communities.

[21] Kathleen Weber, "Is There a Qumran Parallel to Matthew 24,51 // Luke 12,46?" *RevQum* 16 (1995) 657–63.

faithfully are pronounced blessed[22] and are given even more responsibility. Those who abuse the charge entrusted to them will suffer severe punishment.

PREACHING POSSIBILITIES

For most Christians two millennia of waiting for the parousia have dulled the sense of urgency in watching for it. These parables startle the hearer out of any complacency or any false sense of security with the status quo. The preacher may find that a better approach than bullying the congregation into faithfulness with the frightening image of the last verse, would be to focus on the blessedness that awaits those who are prepared to meet Christ at the end. The last verse makes it very clear, however, that being faithful is not just a nice option; the opposite has deadly consequences.

Rather than speak about a vague watching for an abstract future return of Christ, the preacher might elaborate on the vigilance needed to perceive Christ's very palpable presence when we meet him unexpectedly at every turn in the present. It is our present manner of responding to such encounters that prepares disciples for Christ's eschatological coming. For those who are entrusted with leadership, part of their task is to keep before the community the notion that no "fellow servant" is beyond their purview. Being put in charge of all the property (v. 47) can be seen as a metaphor for the concern of Christians to work toward responsible distribution of food and other resources throughout the entire globe.

One problematic aspect of the parables in this gospel selection is their use of the metaphor of a master-slave relationship. While neither Jesus nor any of the writers of the New Testament challenged the institution of slavery, but rather accepted it as the prevailing social structure of their day, for modern Christians it is abhorrent. Nonetheless, metaphors that cast

---

[22] In addition to the beatitudes (Matt 5:3-11), see also 11:6; 13:16, where those who respond positively to Jesus' words and deeds are pronounced "blessed," as is Peter when he proclaims Jesus as Messiah (16:17). At the final judgment those who inherit the kingdom are blessed (25:34).

God and Jesus as "master" and disciples as "servants" or "slaves" still abound. There is a particular danger that the use of such language reinforces systems of oppression in our day, giving them theological legitimation. Holding up the ideal of faithful servanthood to people who are caught in the underside of systems of domination only serves to justify human bondage as the will of God. It keeps dominated peoples from recognizing the injustice of their situation and mobilizing to confront it.[23] A particular challenge for the preacher will be to find a way in which to make the gospel message understandable in a contemporary context without relying on imagery and language of masters and slaves.

[23] See Elisabeth Schüssler Fiorenza, "'Waiting at Table': A Critical Feminist Theological Reflection on Diakonia," *Concilium 198. Diakonia: Church for the Others* (ed. N. Breinacher and N. Mette; Edinburgh: T. & T. Clark, 1988) 84–94.

Conclusion

The Gospel of Matthew is the one that in some ways has had the most influence of any on the life of the Church, having been the one most commented on and most preached from the earliest Christian centuries. The uniquely Matthean parables of the final judgment, the workers in the vineyard, the unforgiving servant, the wise and foolish maidens, the pearl of great price, the weeds among the wheat, all have a unique hold on the imagination of Christians. With his conclusions that always stress the ethics of discipleship, Matthew continues to engage us powerfully with the words of Jesus the Teacher. In our treatment of the Matthean parables our aim has been not to give an exhaustive summary or analysis of all the work that has been done on these. Rather, our intent has been to sketch some of the new directions in parables research and Matthean studies so as to aid the preacher in her or his understanding of the text. Our hope has been that this exploration of new possibilities of meaning will spark the creativity of preachers as they break open the word for other believers. We have suggested ways in which the homilist may direct the parables, but ultimately the difficult task of discerning which is the word their congregation needs at this time and place rests with the preacher. While many points are possible and valid in parable interpretation, the effective homilist will do well to develop only one on any given occasion. Each time that a parable appears in the Lectionary, the task of wrestling with the text begins again. There are no "one size fits all" interpretations.

In the Gospel of Matthew the term "parable" applies to many varied kinds of figurative speech. Some parables are vivid stories, others are wisdom sayings, still others are extended similes. Their functions are varied. At times they comfort; at other times they instruct and exhort; at still others they challenge. They are directed to both Jesus' disciples and to his opponents. They invite adversaries to a change of heart and they instruct disciples on how to live so that their deeds match what they believe and profess. Originally directed at a people in transition, as they forged a new identity in relation to their Jewish heritage, Matthew's parables continue to help communities of believers in changing times to emulate the wise scribe who draws from the storehouse both the new and the old.

Bibliography

Albright, William F. and C. S. Mann. *Matthew*. AB26; Garden City: Doubleday, 1971.

Allison, Dale. *The New Moses: A Matthean Typology*. Minneapolis: Fortress, 1993.

Anderson, Janice C. and Stephen D. Moore, eds. *New Approaches in Biblical Studies*. Minneapolis: Fortress, 1992.

Aune, David E. ed. *The Gospel of Matthew in Current Study*. Grand Rapids: Eerdmans, 2001.

Bacon, Benjamin W. *Studies in Matthew*. London: Constable, 1930.

Bacq, Philippe and Odile Ribadeau Dumas, "Reading a Parable: The Good Wheat and the Tares (Mt 13)" *LumVit* 39 (1984) 181–94.

Bailey, Kenneth E. *Poet and Peasant and Through Peasant Eyes*. Combined ed. Grand Rapids: Eerdmans, 1984.

Barr, James. "*ʾAbba* and the Familiarity of Jesus' Speech," *Theology* 91 (1988) 173–79.

_____. "*ʾAbba* Isn't Daddy," *JTS* 39 (1988) 28–47.

Barré, Michael L. "The Workers in the Vineyard," *TBT* 24 (1986) 173–80.

Batey, Richard A. "Jesus and the Theatre," *NTS* 30 (1984) 564–65.

Bauer, David R. and Mark Allan Powell, eds. *Treasures New and Old. Recent Contributions to Matthean Studies*. SBL Symposium Series 1; Atlanta: Scholars Press, 1996.

Bergant, Dianne. *Preaching the New Lectionary*. 3 vols. Collegeville: The Liturgical Press, 1999, 2000, 2001.

Betz, Otto. "The Dichotomized Servant–Mt 24:51," *RevQum* 5 (1964) 43–58.

Blomberg, Craig. *Interpreting the Parables*. Downers Grove, Ill.: Inter-Varsity Press, 1990.

Boff, Clodovis and Jorge Pixley. *The Bible, the Church, and the Poor*. Theology and Liberation Series. Maryknoll, N.Y.: Orbis, 1989.

Bonneau, Normand. *The Sunday Lectionary: Ritual Word, Paschal Shape*. Collegeville: The Liturgical Press, 1998.

Borges, Jorge Luis. *Ficciones*. New York: Grove, 1962.

265

Boucher, Madeleine. *The Parables*. NTM 7. Wilmington: Glazier, 1981.

Bowker, J. W. "Mystery and Parable: Mark 4:1-20," *JTS* 25 (1974) 300–17.

Brown, Raymond E., J. A. Fitzmyer, and R. E. Murphy. *The New Jerome Biblical Commentary*. Englewood Cliffs, N. J.: Prentice Hall, 1990.

Brown, Raymond E. and John P. Meier, *Antioch and Rome: New Testament Cradles of Catholic Christianity*. New York/Ramsey: Paulist, 1983.

Bultmann, Rudolph K. *The History of the Synoptic Tradition*. rev. ed. tr. J. Marsh. New York: Harper & Row, 1968.

Burghardt, Walter J. *Preaching the Just Word*. New Haven: Yale University Press, 1996.

Burnett, Fred W. *The Testament of Jesus-Sophia: a Redactional-Critical Study of the Eschatological Discourse in Matthew*. Washington D.C.: University Press of America, 1981.

Butler, B. C. *The Originality of St. Matthew: A Critique of the Two-Document Hypothesis*. Cambridge: Cambridge University, 1951.

Buttrick, David. *Speaking Parables*. Louisville: Westminster John Knox, 2000.

Cadoux, Arthur T. *The Parables of Jesus, Their Art and Use*. London: James Clarke, 1931.

Carter, Warren. *Matthew and the Margins. A Sociopolitical and Religious Reading*. The Bible and Liberation Series; Maryknoll: Orbis, 2000.

_____. "The Crowds in Matthew's Gospel," *CBQ* 55 (1993) 54–67.

Carter, Warren and John Paul Heil, *Matthew's Parables*. CBQMS 30; Washington, D.C.: CBA, 1998.

Christ, Felix. *Jesus Sophia: Die Sophia-Christologie bei den Synoptikern*. ATANT 57; Zürich: Zwingli, 1970.

Collins, John N. *Diakonia: Re-Interpreting the Ancient Resources*. New York: Oxford University Press, 1990.

Collins, Raymond F. *Preaching the Epistles*. New York: Paulist, 1996.

Cope, Lamar. "Matthew xxv 31-46. 'The Sheep and the Goats' Reinterpreted," *NovT* 11 (1969) 32–44.

Cotter, Wendy J., "The Parable of the Children in the Market-Place, Q(Lk) 7:31-35: An Examination of the Parable's Image and Significance," *NovT* 29/4 (1987) 289–304.

Court, J. M. "Right and Left: the Implications for Matthew 25.31-46," *NTS* 31 (1985) 223–33.

Crossan, John Dominic. *Cliffs of Fall. Paradox and Polyvalence in the Parables of Jesus*. New York: Seabury, 1980.

_____. *The Dark Interval: Towards a Theology of Story*. Niles, Ill.: Argus Communications, 1975.

_____. *Finding is the First Act. Trove Folktales and Jesus' Treasure Parable*. Philadelphia: Fortress, 1979.

_____. *The Historical Jesus*. HarperSanFrancisco, 1991.

_____. *In Parables: The Challenge of the Historical Jesus*. New York: Harper & Row, 1973.

_____."The Seed Parables of Jesus," *JBL* 92 (1973) 244–66.

_____. "The Parable of the Wicked Husbandmen," *JBL* 90 (1971) 451–65.

Culbertson, Philip L. *A Word Fitly Spoken. Context, Transmission, and Adoption of the Parables of Jesus*. Albany: State University of New York Press, 1995.

Dalman, Gustaf. *Die Worte Jesu. Mit Berücksichtigung des nachkanonischen jüdischen Schrifttums und der aramäischen Sprache erötert*. 2d ed. Darmstadt: Wissenschaftliche Buchgesellschaft, 1965.

D'Angelo, Mary Rose "ʾABBA and 'Father': Imperial Theology and the Jesus Traditions," *JBL* 111/4 (1992) 611–30.

_____. "(Re)Presentations of Women in the Gospel of Matthew and Luke-Acts," *Women & Christian Origins*. Ed. R. S. Kraemer and M. R. D'Angelo. New York: Oxford University Press, 1999, 171–95.

Danker, Frederick W., ed. *A Greek-English Lexicon of the New Testament and Other Early Christian Literature*. 3d rev. ed. based on 2d ed. by Walter Bauer, W. F. Arndt, F. W. Gingrich, and F. W. Danker. Chicago: University of Chicago Press, 2000.

Danker, Frederick W. *Jesus and the New Age. A Commentary on St. Luke's Gospel*. rev. ed. Philadelphia: Fortress, 1988.

Daube, David. *The New Testament and Rabbinic Judaism*. New York: Arno Press, 1973.

Davies, W. D. and Dale C. Allison Jr., *The Gospel According to Saint Matthew*. ICC; 3 vols. Edinburgh: T. & T. Clark, 1988, 1991, 1997.

de Mello, Anthony. *The Song of the Bird*. Garden City, N.Y.: Doubleday, 1984.

DeMoor, Johannes C. "The Targumic Background of Mark 12:1-12: The Parable of the Wicked Tenants," *JSJ* 29 (1998) 63–80.

Derrett, J. Duncan M. *Law in the New Testament*. London: Darton, Longman & Todd, 1970.

_____. "Law in the New Testament: The Treasure in the Field (Mt. XIII,44)," *ZNW* 54 (1963) 31–42.

Deutsch, Celia. *Hidden Wisdom and the Easy Yoke: Wisdom, Torah and Discipleship in Matthew 11:25-30*. Sheffield: JSOT, 1987.

_____. *Lady Wisdom, Jesus, and the Sages* (Valley Forge, Penn.: Trinity Press International, 1996.

Dodd, C. H. *The Parables of the Kingdom*. rev. ed. London: Collins, 1961.

Donahue, John R. *The Gospel in Parable. Metaphor, Narrative, and Theology in the Synoptic Gospels*. Philadelphia: Fortress, 1988.

_____. "Tax Collectors and Sinners: An Attempt at Identification," *CBQ* 33 (1971) 39–61.

_____. "The 'Parable' of the Sheep and the Goats: A Challenge to Christian Ethics," *TS* 47 (1986) 3–31.

Donfried, Karl. "The Allegory of the Ten Virgins (Matt 25:1-13) as a Summary of Matthean Theology," *JBL* 93 (1974) 415–28.

Doty, W. G. "An Interpretation: Parable of the Weeds and Wheat," *Int* 25 (1971) 185–93.

Duling, Dennis C. "Matthew 18:15-17: Conflict, Confrontation, and Conflict Resolution in a 'Fictive Kin' Association," *BTB* 29 (1999) 4–22.

Edwards, Richard. *A Theology of Q. Eschatology, Prophecy and Wisdom*. Philadelphia: Fortress, 1976.

_____. *Matthew's Narrative Portrait of Disciples*. Harrisburg: Trinity Press International, 1997.

Elliott, John H. "Matthew 20:1-15: A Parable of Invidious Comparison and Evil Eye Accusation," *BTB* 22 (1992) 52–65.

Evans, Craig A. "A Note on the Function of Isaiah 6:9-10 in Mark 4," *RB* 99 (1981) 234–35.

Ellis, Peter F. *Matthew: His Mind and His Message*. Collegeville: The Liturgical Press, 1974.

Farmer, William R. *The Synoptic Problem. A Critical Analysis*. Dillsboro: Western North Carolina Press, 1976.

Fitzmyer, Joseph A. *Essays on the Semitic Background of the New Testament*. Sources for Biblical Study 5. Atlanta: Scholars Press, 1974.

_____. *To Advance the Gospel: New Testament Studies*. 2d ed. The Biblical Resource Series. Grand Rapids: Eerdmans, 1998.

_____. *A Wandering Aramean: Collected Aramaic Essays*. Missoula, Mont.: Scholars Press, 1979.

Flusser, David. *Die rabbinischen Gleichnisse und der Gleichniserzähler Jesus* 1. Teil: *Das Wesen der Gleichnisse*. Bern: Peter Lang, 1981.

Foley, Edward. *Preaching Basics. A Model and A Method*. Chicago: Liturgy Training Publications, 1998.

Frank, Tenney, ed. *An Economic Survey of Ancient Rome*. Baltimore: Johns Hopkins Press, 1938.

Freedman, David Noel, ed. *The Anchor Bible Dictionary*. 6 vols. New York: Doubleday, 1992.

Freyne, Seán. *Galilee from Alexander the Great to Hadrian 323 B.C.E. to 135 C.E.* University of Notre Dame Center for the Study of Judaism and Christianity in Antiquity 5; Wilmington, Del., and Notre Dame, Ind.: Glazier and University of Notre Dame Press, 1980.

Fuller, Reginald H. *Preaching the Lectionary*. Collegeville: The Liturgical Press, 1984.

_____. "Son of Man," *Harper's Bible Dictionary*. Ed. Paul J. Achtemeier. San Francisco: Harper & Row, 1985, 1981.

Funk, Robert W. "Beyond Criticism in Quest of Literacy: The Parable of the Leaven," *Int* 25 (1971) 149–70.

_____. *Language, Hermeneutic, and Word of God. The Problem of Language in the New Testament and Contemporary Theology*. New York: Harper & Row, 1966.

_____. "The Looking Glass Tree is for the Birds," *Int* 27 (1973) 3–9.

_____. *Parables and Presence. Forms of the New Testament Tradition*. Philadelphia: Fortress, 1982.

Gardner, Jane F. *Women in Roman Law and Society*. Bloomington/Indianapolis: Indiana University, 1986.

Gaster, Theodore. *Myth, Legend and Custom in the Old Testament*. New York: Harper and Row, 1969.

Gench, Frances Taylor. *Wisdom in the Christology of Matthew* (Lanham/New York/Oxford: University Press of America, 1997.

Gerhardsson, Birger. "The Parable of the Sower and its Interpretation," *NTS* 14 (1968) 165–93.

Gillingham, M. J. "The Parables as Attitude Change," *ExpTim* 109 (1998) 297–300.

Glancy, Jennifer. "Slaves and Slavery in the Matthean Parables," *JBL* 119 (2000) 67–90.

Goulder, Michael. *Midrash and Lection in Matthew*. London: SPCK, 1974.

Gowler, David B. *What Are They Saying about the Parables?* New York: Paulist, 2000.

Grässer, Erich. *Das Problem der Parusieverzögerung in den synoptischen Evangelien und in der Apostelgeschichte*. Berlin: Töpelmann, 1960.

Gundry, Robert H. *Matthew. A Commentary on His Literary and Theological Art*. Grand Rapids: Eerdmans, 1992.

Hare, Douglas R. A. "How Jewish Is the Gospel of Matthew?" *CBQ* 62/2 (2000) 264–77.

_____. *The Son of Man Tradition*. Minneapolis: Fortress, 1990.

_____. *The Theme of Jewish Persecution of Christians in the Gospel According to St. Matthew*. SNTSMS 6; Cambridge: Cambridge University, 1967.

Hare, Douglas R. A. and Daniel J. Harrington, "Make Disciples of All the Gentiles (Mt. 28:19)," *CBQ* 37 (1975) 359–69.

Harrington, Daniel J. *Matthew*. SacPag1; Collegeville: The Liturgical Press, 1991.

_____. "'Make Disciples of All the Gentiles' (Matthew 28:19)," *CBQ* 37 (1975) 359–69.

_____. "Polemical Parables in Matthew 24–25," *USQR* 44 (1991) 287–98.

Hedrick, Charles W. *Parables as Poetic Fictions*. Peabody: Hendrickson, 1994.

Heil, John P. "Ezekiel 34 and the Narrative Strategy of the Shepherd and Sheep Metaphor in Matthew," *CBQ* 55 (1993) 698–708.

Hendrickx, Herman. *The Parables of Jesus*. rev. ed. San Francisco: Harper & Row, 1986.

Hester, James D. "Socio-Rhetorical Criticism and the Parable of the Tenants," *JSNT* 45 (1992) 27–57.

Herzog, William R., II. *Parables as Subversive Speech. Jesus as Pedagogue of the Oppressed*. Louisville: Westminster/John Knox, 1994.

Hoppe, Leslie J. *A Retreat With Matthew*. Cincinnati: St. Anthony Messenger Press, 2000.

Horne, Edward H. "The Parable of the Tenants as Indictment," *JSNT* 71 (1998) 111–16.

Hummel, Reinhart. *Die Auseinandersetzung zwischen Kirche und Judentum im Matthäusevangelium*. München: Kaiser Verlag, 1963.

Hylen, Susan E. "Forgiveness and Life in Community," *Int* 54 (2000) 146–57.

Jeremias, J. *Jerusalem in the Time of Jesus. An Investigation into Economic and Social Conditions During the New Testament Period*. Philadelphia: Fortress, 1969.

_____. *The Parables of Jesus*. 2d rev. ed. New York: Scribner's, 1972.

_____. *Rediscovering the Parables*. New York: Scribner's, 1966.

_____. "*LAMPADES* Mt 25:1.3f .7f.," *ZNW* 56 (1965) 196–201.

Jocz, J. *The Jewish People and Jesus Christ*. London: SPCK, 1949.

Johnson, Elizabeth. *She Who Is. The Mystery of God in Feminist Theological Discourse*. New York: Crossroad, 1992.

Johnson, Marshall. "Reflections on a Wisdom Approach to Matthew's Christology," *CBQ* 36 (1974) 44–64.

Jülicher, A. *Die Gleichnisreden Jesu*. 2 vols. Tübingen: Mohr [Siebeck] 1888, 1899.

Kerr, A. J. "Matthew 13:25: Sowing *zizania* among another's wheat: realistic or artificial?" *JTS* ns. 48/1 (1997) 106–09.

Kim, Chan-Hie. "The Papyrus Invitation," *JBL* 94 (1975) 391–402.

Kingsbury, Jack Dean. "The Parable of the Wicked Husbandmen and the Secret of Jesus' Divine Sonship in Matthew," *JBL* 105 (1986) 643–55.

Kloppenborg, John S. "Wisdom Christology in Q," *LTP* 34 (1978) 129–47.

Koester, Helmut. "Recovering the Original Meaning of Matthew's Parables," *Bible Review* 9/3 (1993) 11, 52.

Kraemer, R. S. and M. R. D'Angelo, ed. *Women & Christian Origins*. New York: Oxford University Press, 1999.

Krentz, Edgar. *The Historical-Critical Method*. Guides to Biblical Scholarship. Philadelphia: Fortress, 1975.

LaVerdiere, Eugene. "Teaching in Parables," *Emmanuel* 94 (1988) 438–45, 453.

Lambrecht, Jan. *Out of the Treasure*. Louvain Theological and Pastoral Monographs 10; Louvain: Peeters, 1992.

Levine, Amy-Jill. *The Social and Ethnic Dimensions of Matthean Salvation History*. SBEC 14; Lewiston/Queenstown/Lampeter: Mellen, 1988.

Linnemann, Eta. *Jesus of the Parables. Introduction and Exposition*. New York: Harper & Row, 1966.

Long, Thomas C. *Matthew*. WBC; Louisville: Westminster/John Knox, 1997.

Luz, Ulrich. "The Final Judgment (Matt 25:31-46): An Exercise in 'History of Influence' Exegesis," in David R. Bauer and Mark Allan Powell, eds., *Treasures New and Old. Recent Contributions to Matthean Studies*. SBL Symposium Series; Atlanta: Scholars Press, 1996, 271–310.

MacMullen, Ramsey. *Roman Social Relations 50 B.C. to A.D. 284*. New Haven: Yale University Press, 1974.

Maddox, R. "Who are the 'Sheep' and the 'Goats'? A Study of the Purpose and Meaning of Matthew xxv:31–46," *AusBR* 18 (1965) 19–28.

Malina, Bruce J. *The New Testament World. Insights from Cultural Anthropology*. rev. ed. Louisville: Westminster/John Knox, 1993.

Malina, Bruce J. and Jerome H. Neyrey, "First-Century Personality: Dyadic, Not Individual," *The Social World of Luke-Acts: Models for Interpretation*. Ed. J. H. Neyrey. Peabody, Mass.: Hendrickson, 1991, 67–96.

Malina, Bruce J. and Richard L. Rohrbaugh. *Social-Science Commentary on the Synoptic Gospels*. Minneapolis: Fortress, 1992.

McArthur, H. K. "The Parable of the Mustard Seed," *CBQ* 33 (1971) 198–210.

McCreesh, Thomas P. "Heart," *The Collegeville Pastoral Dictionary of Biblical Theology*. Ed. C. Stuhlmueller. Collegeville: The Liturgical Press, 1996, 422–24.

McFague, Sallie. *Models of God. Theology for an Ecological, Nuclear Age.* Philadelphia: Fortress, 1987.

McGaughy, L. "The Fear of Yahweh and the Mission of Judaism: A Postexilic Maxim and Its Early Christian Expansion in the Parable of the Talents," *JBL* 94 (1975) 235–45.

McNeile, A. H. *The Gospel According to St. Matthew.* London: Macmillan, 1952.

Meier, John P. *A Marginal Jew. Rethinking the Historical Jesus.* ABRL. 2 vols. Garden City, N.Y.: Doubleday, 1991, 1994.

_____. *Matthew.* NTM 3; Wilmington: Glazier, 1980.

_____. *The Vision of Matthew.* New York: Paulist, 1979.

_____. "Nations or Gentiles in Matthew 28:19?" *CBQ* 39 (1977) 94–102.

Mesters, Carlos. *Defenseless Flower. A New Reading of the Bible.* Maryknoll, N.Y.: Orbis, 1989.

Metzger, Bruce. *A Textual Commentary on the Greek New Testament.* 3d ed. New York: United Bible Societies, 1971.

Meyer, Marvin. *The Gospel of Thomas. The Hidden Sayings of Jesus.* San Francisco: Harper, 1992.

Michaels, J. Ramsey. "Apostolic Hardships and Righteous Gentiles. A Study of Matthew 25:31-46," *JBL* 84 (1965) 27–37.

_____. "The Parable of the Regretful Son," *HTR* 61 (1968) 15–26.

Myers, Ched. *Binding the Strong Man.* Maryknoll: Orbis, 1988.

Nauck, W. "Salt as a Metaphor in Instructions for Discipleship," *Studia Theologica* 6 (1952) 164–78.

Neusner, Jacob. *Judaism in the Beginning of Christianity.* Philadelphia: Fortress, 1984.

_____. *From Politics to Piety. The Emergence of Pharisaic Judaism.* Englewood Cliffs: Prentice Hall, 1973.

Newsom, Carol A. and Sharon H. Ringe, eds., *The Women's Bible Commentary.* rev. ed. Louisville: Westminster/John Knox, 1998.

Neyrey, Jerome H., ed. *The Social World of Luke-Acts. Models for Interpretation.* Peabody, Mass.: Hendrickson, 1991.

Nowell, Irene. *Sing a New Song. The Psalms in the Sunday Lectionary.* Collegeville: The Liturgical Press, 1993.

Oakman, Douglas. E. *Jesus and the Economic Question of His Day.* SBEC 8. Lewiston/Queenston: Edwin Mellen, 1986.

Oesterley, W.O.E. *The Gospel Parables in the Light of their Jewish Background.* New York: Macmillan, 1936.

Osiek, C. "Literal Meaning and Allegory," *TBT* 29/5 (1991) 261–66.

_____. *What Are They Saying About the Social Setting of the New Testament?* 2d ed. New York: Paulist, 1992.

Overman, J. Andrew. *Matthew's Gospel and Formative Judaism: The Social World of the Matthean Community.* Minneapolis: Fortress, 1990.

Parker, A. *Painfully Clear. The Parables of Jesus.* Biblical Seminar 37. Sheffield: Sheffield Academic Press, 1996.

Patte, D. *What Is Structural Exegesis?* Guides to Biblical Scholarship. Philadelphia: Fortress, 1976.

Pazdan, Mary Margaret. "Hermeneutics and Proclaiming the Sunday Readings," *In the Company of Preachers.* Ed. R. Siegfried and E. Ruane. Collegeville: The Liturgical Press, 1993. Pp. 26–37.

Perelmuter, Hayim G. *Siblings. Rabbinic Judaism and Early Christianity at their Beginnings.* New York: Paulist, 1989.

Pilch, John J. *The Cultural Dictionary of the Bible.* Collegeville: The Liturgical Press, 1999.

_____. *The Cultural World of Jesus. Sunday by Sunday, Cycle A.* Collegeville: The Liturgical Press, 1995.

_____. *The Cultural World of Jesus. Sunday by Sunday, Cycle B.* Collegeville: The Liturgical Press, 1996.

_____. *The Cultural World of Jesus. Sunday by Sunday, Cycle C.* Collegeville: The Liturgical Press, 1997.

Piper, R. A. *Wisdom in the Q-tradition* (SNTSMS 61; Cambridge: Cambridge University Press, 1989.

Porter, Lawrence B. "Salt of the Earth," *Homiletic and Pastoral Review* 95 (July 1995) 51–58.

Powell, Mark Allan. *What is Narrative Criticism?* Guides to Biblical Scholarship. Philadelphia: Fortress, 1990.

_____. *God With Us: A Pastoral Theology of Matthew's Gospel.* Minneapolis: Fortress, 1995.

Praeder, Susan M. *The Word in Women's Worlds: Four Parables.* Zacchaeus Studies, New Testament. Wilmington: Glazier, 1988.

Race, Marianne and Laurie Brink. *In This Place. Reflections on the Land of the Gospels for the Liturgical Cycles.* Collegeville: The Liturgical Press, 1998.

Ramoroson, L. "'Parole-semence' ou 'Peuple-semence' dans la parabole du Semeur?" *ScEs* 40 (1988) 91–101.

Ramshaw, Gail. *God Beyond Gender. Feminist Christian God-Language.* Minneapolis: Fortress, 1995.

Reid, Barbara E. *Choosing the Better Part? Women in the Gospel of Luke.* Collegeville: The Liturgical Press, 1996.

_____. "Once Upon a Time . . . Parable and Allegory in the Gospels," *TBT* 29/5 (1991) 267–72.

_____. *Parables for Preachers. Year B.* Collegeville: The Liturgical Press, 1999.

_____. *Parables for Preachers. Year C.* Collegeville: The Liturgical Press, 2000.

_____. "Preaching Justice Parabolically," *Emmanuel* 102/6 (1996) 342–47.

Rhoads, David. "Social Criticism: Crossing Boundaries," *Mark & Method. New Approaches in Biblical Studies.* Ed. J. C. Anderson and S. D. Moore. Minneapolis: Fortress, 1992. Pp. 135–61.

Ringe, Sharon H. *Jesus, Liberation, and the Biblical Jubilee. Images for Ethics and Christology.* OBT 19. Philadelphia: Fortress, 1985, 54–60.

Robinson, J.A.T. "Elijah, John and Jesus: An Essay in Detection," *NTS* 4 (1957–58) 263–81.

Rohrbaugh, Richard L. "A Peasant Reading of the Parable of the Talents/Pounds: A Text of Terror?" *BTB* 23 (1993) 32–39.

_____. "The Pre-Industrial City in Luke-Acts: Urban Social Relations," *The Social World of Luke-Acts. Models for Interpretation.* Ed. J. H. Neyrey. Peabody: Hendrickson, 1991. 125–50.

Rowland, Christopher and Mark Corner. *Liberating Exegesis. The Challenge of Liberation Theology to Biblical Studies.* Louisville: Westminster/John Knox, 1989.

Ruether, Rosemary Radford. *Gaia and God. An EcoFeminist Theology of Earth Healing.* San Francisco: Harper, 1992.

_____, ed. *Religion and Sexism. Images of Woman in the Jewish and Christian Traditions.* New York: Simon & Schuster, 1974.

_____. *Sexism and God-Talk. Toward a Feminist Theology.* Boston: Beacon, 1983.

Safrai, S. and M. Stern, ed. *The Jewish People in the First Century. Historical Geography, Political History, Social, Cultural and Religious Life and Institutions.* 2 vols. Assen/Amsterdam: Van Gorcum, 1976.

Saldarini, Anthony J. *Pharisees, Scribes and Sadducees in Palestinian Society: A Sociological Approach.* Wilmington: Glazier, 1988.

_____. *Matthew's Christian-Jewish Community.* CSHJ; Chicago: University of Chicago Press, 1994.

Sanders, E. P. *Jesus and Judaism.* 2d ed. Philadelphia: Fortress, 1985.

_____. "Sin, Sinners," *The Anchor Bible Dictionary.* Ed. D. N. Freedman. New York: Doubleday, 1997. 6.31–47.

Schneiders, Sandra. "God is More Than Two Men and a Bird," *U. S. Catholic* (May 1990) 20–27.

_____. *Women and the Word. The Gender of God in the New Testament and the Spirituality of Women.* New York: Paulist, 1986.

Schottroff, Luise. *Let the Oppressed Go Free. Feminist Perspectives on the New Testament.* Gender and the Biblical Tradition. tr. A. S. Kidder. Louisville: Westminster/John Knox, 1991.

Schottroff, Luise and W. Stegemann. *Jesus and the Hope of the Poor*. tr. M. J. O'Connell. Maryknoll: Orbis, 1986.

Schüssler Fiorenza, Elisabeth. *In Memory of Her. A Feminist Theological Reconstruction of Christian Origins*. New York: Crossroad, 1983.

_____. *Jesus: Miriam's Child, Sophia's Prophet. Critical Issues in Feminist Christology*. New York: Continuum, 1994.

_____. *Rhetoric and Ethic. The Politics of Biblical Studies*. Minneapolis: Fortress, 1999.

_____, ed., *Searching the Scriptures. A Feminist Commentary*. 2 vols. New York: Crossroad, 1993, 1994.

_____. *Sharing Her Word. Feminist Biblical Interpretation*. Boston: Beacon, 1998.

_____. "'Waiting at Table': A Critical Feminist Theological Reflection on Diakonia," *Diakonia: Church for the Others*. Ed. N. Greinacher and N. Mette. Concilium 198. Edinburgh: T. & T. Clark, 1988, 84–94.

Schweizer, Eduard. *The Good News According to Matthew*. Atlanta: John Knox, 1975.

Scott, Bernard Brandon. *Hear Then the Parable. A Commentary on the Parables of Jesus*. Minneapolis: Fortress, 1989.

_____. "The King's Accounting: Matthew 18:23-34," *JBL* 104 (1985) 442.

_____. "Lost Junk, Found Treasure," *TBT* 26 (1988) 31–34.

Segal, Alan F. *Rebecca's Children. Judaism and Christianity in the Roman World*. Cambridge: Harvard University Press, 1987.

Senior, Donald. *Matthew*. ANTC; Nashville: Abingdon, 1998.

_____. *What Are They Saying about Matthew?* Rev. ed. New York/Mahwah: Paulist, 1996.

_____. "Between Two Worlds: Gentile and Jewish Christians in Matthew's Gospel," *CBQ* 61/1 (1999) 1–23.

Shillington, V. George, ed. *Jesus and His Parables. Interpreting the Parables of Jesus Today*. Edinburgh: T. & T. Clark, 1997.

Siegfried, R. and E. Ruane, ed. *In the Company of Preachers*. Collegeville: The Liturgical Press, 1993.

Sim, D. C. *The Gospel of Matthew and Christian Judaism: The History and Social Setting of the Matthean Community*. Studies of the New Testament and Its World; Edinburgh: T. & T. Clark, 1998.

Snodgrass, Klyne. *The Parable of the Wicked Tenants*. Tübingen: Mohr [Siebeck] 1983.

Stanton, Graham N. *A Gospel for a New People. Studies in Matthew*. Edinburgh: T. & T. Clark, 1992.

_____. "The Origin and Purpose of Matthew's Gospel: Matthean Scholarship from 1945 to 1980," *Aufstieg und Niedergang der Römis-*

chen Welt. Eds. H. Temporini and W. Haase; II (Principat), 25.3; Berlin/New York: Water de Gruyter, 1985. Pp. 1910–21.

Stegemann, Wolfgang. *The Gospel and the Poor*. Philadelphia: Fortress, 1984.

Stock, Augustine. *The Method and Message of Matthew*. Collegeville: The Liturgical Press, 1994.

_____. "Jesus, Hypocrites, and Herodians," *BTB* 16 (1986) 3–7.

Strack, H. and P. Billerbeck, *Kommentar zum Neuen Testament aus Talmud und Midrasch*. 6 vols. Munich: Beck, 1922–61.

Strecker, Georg. *Der Weg der Gerechtigkeit: Untersuchung zur Theologie des Mattäus*. Rev. ed.; Göttingen: Vandenhoeck & Ruprecht, 1966.

Stuhlmueller, Carroll, ed. *The Collegeville Pastoral Dictionary of Biblical Theology*. Collegeville: The Liturgical Press, 1996.

Suggs, M. Jack. *Wisdom, Christology, and Law in Matthew's Gospel*. Cambridge: Harvard University Press, 1970.

Sugirtharajah, R. S. "Wisdom, Q, and a Proposal for a Christology," *ExpTim* 102 (1990) 42–46.

Thompson, William. *Matthew's Advice to a Divided Community. Mt. 17,22–18,35*. AnBib 44; Rome: Biblical Institute Press, 1970.

Tolbert, Mary Ann. *Perspectives on the Parables. An Approach to Multiple Interpretations*. Philadelphia: Fortress, 1979.

Trible, Phyllis. "God the Father," *TToday* 37 (1980) 118.

Tripp, David H. "*Zizania* (Matthew 13:25): Realistic if Also Figurative," *JTS* 50 (1999) 628.

Untener, Kenneth E. *Preaching Better*. New York: Paulist, 1999.

van Merrienboer, Edward J. "Preaching the Social Gospel," *In the Company of Preachers*. Ed. R. Siegfried and E. Ruane. Collegeville: The Liturgical Press, 1993, 76–90.

Via, Dan O. *The Parables: Their Literary and Existential Dimension*. Philadelphia: Fortress, 1967.

_____. "Parable and Example Story: A Literary-Structuralist Approach," *Semeia* 1(1974) 105–33.

Viviano, Benedict T. "Matthew," *NJBC*, ed. Raymond E. Brown, Joseph A. Fitzmyer, Roland E. Murphy. Englewood Cliffs, N. J.: Prentice Hall, 1990. Pp. 630–74.

_____. "The Least in the Kingdom: Matthew 11:11, Its Parallel in Luke 7:28 [Q], and Daniel 4:14," *CBQ* 62 (2000) 41–54.

Wainwright, Elaine M. *Towards a Feminist Critical Reading of the Gospel According to Matthew*, BZNW 60; Berlin/New York: de Gruyter, 1991.

_____. *Shall We Look for Another? A Feminist Rereading of the Matthean Jesus*. Maryknoll: Orbis, 1998.

Waller, Elizabeth. "The Parable of the Leaven: A Sectarian Teaching and the Inclusion of Women," *USQR* 35 (1979–80) 99–109.

Weber, Kathleen. "The Image of Sheep and Goats in Matthew 25:31-46," *CBQ* 59/4 (1997) 657–78.

_____. "Is There a Qumran Parallel to Matthew 24,51 // Luke 12,46?" *RevQum* 16 (1995) 657–63.

West, Fritz. *Scripture and Memory: The Ecumenical Hermeneutic of the Three-Year Lectionaries*. Collegeville: The Liturgical Press, 1997.

Wiesel, Elie. *The Gates of the Forest*. tr. F. Frenaye. New York: Holt, Rinehart and Winston, 1966.

Wilder, Amos N. *The Language of the Gospel. Early Christian Rhetoric*. New York: Harper & Row, 1964.

_____. *Jesus' Parables and the War of Myths. Essays on Imagination in the Scripture*. Philadelphia: Fortress, 1982.

Wink, Walter. *Engaging the Powers. Discernment and Resistance in a World of Domination*. Minneapolis: Fortress, 1992.

Witherup, Ronald D. *Matthew. God with Us*. Spiritual Commentaries on the Bible. Hyde Park, N.Y.: New City Press, 2000.

Young, Brad H. *Jesus and His Jewish Parables. Jewish Tradition and Christian Interpretation*. Peabody: Hendrickson, 1988.

_____. *The Parables. Jewish Tradition and Christian Interpretation*. Peabody: Hendrickson, 1998.

Zerwick, Maximillian. *Biblical Greek. Illustrated by Examples*. Scripta Pontificii Instituti Biblici 114. Rome: Biblical Institute, 1963.